# The Arabs, Israelis, and Kissinger

# Books by Edward R. F. Sheehan

**NONFICTION**

*The Arabs, Israelis, and Kissinger*

*Take Along Treasury,*
edited by Leonora Hornblow
and Bennett Cerf (contributor)

*Exploring Psychology,*
edited by Ivan N. McCollom
and Nancy Lloyd Badore (contributor)

**FICTION**

*Kingdom of Illusion*

*The Governor*

**DRAMA**

*Napoleon and Pius:* A Play in Three Acts
(to be published)

EDWARD R. F. SHEEHAN

# The Arabs, Israelis, and Kissinger

*A Secret History of American Diplomacy in the Middle East*

READER'S DIGEST PRESS
*Distributed by*
*Thomas Y. Crowell Company*
*New York   1976*

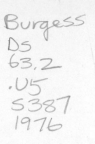
This book was written under the auspices of the Center for International Affairs, Harvard University. Portions of this book have appeared, in somewhat different form, in *Foreign Policy* magazine and in *The New York Times Magazine*.

Copyright © 1976 by Edward R. F. Sheehan

Manufactured in the United States of America

LIBRARY OF CONGRESS CATALOGING IN PUBLICATION DATA

Sheehan, Edward R     F
  The Arabs, Israelis, and Kissinger.

  Includes bibliographical references and index.
  1. United States—Foreign relations—Near East.
2. Near East—Foreign relations—United States.
3. Kissinger, Henry Alfred. 4. Jewish-Arab relations, 1967–1973. 5. Jewish-Arab relations—1973–
I. Title.
DS63.2.U5S387    327.73'056    76-21811

ISBN 0-88349-100-1

10 9 8 7 6 5 4 3 2 1

Excerpts on pages 23–25 from THE ROAD TO RAMADAN, by Mohamed Heikal, copyright © 1975 by Times Newspapers Limited and Mohamed Heikal. First published 1975 by William Collins Sons and Co. Ltd., London. Reprinted by permission of Quadrangle/The New York Times Book Company.

Excerpts on pages 137–38 from KISSINGER, by Bernard Kalb and Marvin Kalb, copyright © 1974 by Bernard Kalb and Marvin Kalb. Reprinted by permission of Little, Brown and Co.

Maps in Appendix Nine © 1975 by The New York Times Company. Reprinted by permission.

A. M. D. G.

This book is dedicated
*in general*
To those officers of the United States Foreign Service
who for thirty years have struggled—often vainly,
always valiantly—to advance the American interest
in the Middle East
*and in particular*
To a gentleman who embodies
the noblest traditions of that Service.

# Contents

Author's Preface, ix

Prologue. Miss Berger's Birthday Party, 1

Chapter 1. Watershed and Bloodshed, 11

Chapter 2. Time for a Shock, 15

Chapter 3. Strike with Your Sword . . . and Draw Honey, 30

Chapter 4. An Arab Policy, 40

Chapter 5. "The Communists and the Jews!" 62

Chapter 6. Saladin and the Crusader, 78

Chapter 7. Kisses and Mangoes, 98

Chapter 8. Farewell, Miss Israel, 113

Chapter 9. Of Promises and Doom, 129

Chapter 10. King of Jerusalem? 136

Chapter 11. Masada, 151

Chapter 12. The Spirit of 76, 164

Chapter 13. Cornucopia, 179

Chapter 14. Futurology, 201

Appendixes, 219

Acknowledgments and Sources, 266

Index, 275

# Author's Preface

*Newsweek* magazine, in a lengthy article in March 1976 devoted to those portions of this book already published, described Henry Kissinger's negotiations in the Middle East as "one of the most extraordinary diplomatic sagas of modern times." I agree. If I did not, I should never have written this book.

It was my purpose, when I embarked upon the project in early 1975, to write the most comprehensive—and readable—account of Dr. Kissinger's diplomacy in the Middle East published to our present time. I am a journalist by necessity, a novelist and dramatist by preference; I am not a political scientist, and I have avoided the literary conventions of that calling. My purpose was to compose a narrative which rendered full justice to historical fact but which filled my pages as well with the flesh and blood of real characters—Dr. Kissinger, Anwar Sadat, Golda Meir, King Faisal, and the other luminaries of the Middle East.

Others must assess the literary merit of my labors, but I am confident they will not complain of this essay's scope. I have endeavored to lead the reader from the beginning of Dr. Kissinger's involvement in the Middle East, through the war of October 1973, through the Geneva conference and the disengagements he negotiated in the Sinai peninsula and the Golan Heights, through his vicissitudes in Washington as well, down to the spring of 1976. The book contains considerable new material from the negotiations with Arabs and Israelis. At the end of the book I have provided (for the historian or whomever) appendixes that contain essential documents on the Middle East—United Nations resolutions, American statements of policy, texts of the agreements Dr. Kissinger negotiated and some of the secret memoranda, maps of the Middle East, and other curiosities.

Controversy erupted around this book from the moment its initial portions appeared in *Foreign Policy* magazine in late February 1976. Dr. Kissinger declared that he was "thunderstruck" to see some of his conversations with foreign chiefs of state in print, and for several weeks a storm raged in the State Department and in the press. I refused, in the beginning, to discuss any of my sources. When the State Department—in a formal press conference—identified itself as one of my sources, I was no longer bound to remain silent about the role of the department in my research.

In April 1975, I wrote a memorandum to Assistant Secretary of State Alfred L. Atherton, Jr., requesting Dr. Kissinger's assistance for my project. I recognized that I could not fulfill my purpose unless I had access to Dr. Kissinger and to other primary sources in America and the Middle East. Dr. Kissinger approved my request and authorized Assistant Secretary Atherton to brief me. The exact nature of the Secretary's authorization was never communicated to me. During the course of my research, I conversed with Dr. Kissinger on several occasions with others present, and I had a private interview with him in late 1975. He did not, during any of these conversations, consult any documents. Mr. Atherton and his deputy, Harold Saunders, briefed me—over several months, on at least 20 separate occasions—on the basis of the secret record. I was not shown secret documents, but I took copious and exact notes as the material of conversations was read out to me. It was my understanding, except when specific items were forbidden, that I was at liberty to use the material communicated to me—and not merely as "background."

When the material was published, Dr. Kissinger reacted vigorously. Only several weeks earlier, he had denounced a committee of the United States Congress for "leaking" intelligence documents, and the appearance of my article soon afterward seemed to suggest a "double standard." Some publications described Dr. Kissinger's reaction to my article as a "charade," but I have no reason to doubt the authenticity of his emotions.

After the controversy began, Assistant Secretary Atherton informed me that, in providing me with information based upon secret records, he had relied on his own judgment. The State Department announced that he had exceeded the Secretary's instructions, and Mr. Atherton and Mr. Saunders were reprimanded. I released a statement to the press that I wished to share in the responsibility. No newspaper or magazine of consequence published that part of my statement. Mr. Atherton became a martyr in the press, and the Secretary was blamed. Happily both Mr. Atherton and Mr. Saunders retained their posts, nor do their careers appear to have been damaged.

Such was the essence of the affair. I must add a few remarks. The controversy, though unforeseen, attested to the authenticity of the conversations I cited from the negotiations. But it would be erroneous to suppose that my article—or this book— depended on any single source. The State Department, as important as it was, represented only one of many scores of sources I consulted in Washington, the United Nations, London, Paris, Cairo, Damascus, Amman, Riyadh, Jerusalem, and other capitals of the Middle East. Some of those other sources, as in Washington, were primary. I have relied as well upon the public record, not to mention my own experience in the Middle East, which began in 1956. (A section of acknowledgments and sources will be found after Appendix Ten.)

Thus this book is not in any fashion an "official" or "authorized" account from any quarter. No *quid pro quo* was asked of me in the State Department or anywhere, and I offered none. I admire Dr. Kissinger, but I fancy he will disagree with much that I have written. My interpretations of what happened are mine alone, and the voice of the narrator belongs—for better or for worse—exclusively to me.

E. R. F. S.
*Center for International Affairs*
*Harvard University*
*May 5, 1976*

*On Reconciling Arabs and Israelis:*

THE MANAGER (jumping up in a rage): Ridiculous? Ridiculous? . . . Yes, sir, you put on the cook's cap and beat eggs. Do you suppose that with all this egg-beating business you are on an ordinary stage? Get that out of your head. You represent the shell of the eggs you are beating! (*Laughter and comments among the Actors.*) Silence! and listen to my explanations, please! "The empty form of reason without the fulness of instinct, which is blind." . . . It's a mixing up of the parts, according to which you who act your own part become the puppet of yourself. Do you understand?

LEADING MAN: I'm hanged if I do.

THE MANAGER: Neither do I. But let's get on with it. It's sure to be a glorious failure anyway.

> Luigi Pirandello,
> *Six Characters in Search of an Author.*
> (English version by Edward Storer)

*On Step-By-Step Diplomacy:*

FIRST PRIEST: But again, is it war or peace?
MESSENGER: Peace, but not the kiss of peace.
A patched-up affair, if you ask my opinion.
And if you ask me, I think the Lord Archbishop
Is not the man to cherish any illusions,
Or yet to diminish the least of his pretensions.
If you ask my opinion, I think that this peace
Is nothing like an end, or like a beginning.

> T. S. Eliot,
> *Murder in the Cathedral.*

*On Henry A. Kissinger:*

He was finely attuned to the subtlest currents of any environment, and produced measures precisely adjusted to the need to prevail.

> Henry A. Kissinger,
> in an essay on the Prince von Bismarck.

# The Arabs, Israelis, and Kissinger

# Miss Berger's Birthday Party

During the third week of August in the summer of 1975, Secretary of State Henry A. Kissinger arrived at Tel Aviv on his twelfth major mission to the Middle East. He came to resume the negotiation, unsuccessful the previous March, for a new interim agreement between Israel and Egypt, and another Israeli withdrawal in the Sinai peninsula. At Ben-Gurion Airport, before a multitude of microphones, surrounded by Israeli and American officials, his personal bodyguards, local policemen, television crews, representatives of the world press, Dr. Kissinger recalled that he had left Israel in March "with a heavy heart, fearing that still another horrible tragedy was in store for the people of Israel and the Middle East. I return today with the same concerns but with renewed hope that a strong desire for peace will prevail over tendencies toward war."

Israeli helicopters forthwith flew the Secretary and his party to Jerusalem and the King David Hotel, that famous stone monolith, once the headquarters of the British mandate, overlooking the mellow, medieval walls of the Arab city. The King

1

David was encircled now by steel barricades, security police, troops with Uzi submachine guns—for mobs of Israelis were manifesting their disenchantment with the Secretary, chanting through loudspeakers, *"Kissinger go home!"* Inside, the hotel had been transformed into a miniature State Department—a warren of stenographers, staff aides, Xerox machines, Telex installations, intercontinental telephones. Most of the hotel had been expropriated to provide shelter for the Secretary and his wife, Nancy, for Undersecretary of State Joseph J. Sisco, for Assistant Secretary and Mrs. Alfred L. (Roy) Atherton, Jr., Deputy Assistant Secretary Harold H. Saunders, Ambassador Robert P. Anderson (the Secretary's spokesman), Winston S. Lord (the State Department's Director of Planning and Coordination), Robert Oakley (of the National Security Council staff), Peter Rodman (the Secretary's amanuensis), David Hume Kennerly (President Ford's personal photographer), a senior official of the Central Intelligence Agency, and Dr. Martin Wolfe, a State Department physician, bearing miracle drugs and blood plasma should an assassin inflict wounds upon the Secretary.

That was improbable, because Kissinger was protected by 35 agents of the United States Secret Service, the Praetorian Guard of presidents and assigned to him as well for this peregrination through Israel and Araby. Now, as the Secretary penetrated the teeming lobby of the King David, the Secret Service was his phalanx, revolvers flapping in holsters on their hips, whilst they chattered to each other on walkie-talkies. The Kissingers mounted to a suite on the sixth floor, overlooking the swimming pool and the Old City. Their rooms were close to Atherton's and Sisco's, which were buttressed by the Secretary's Command Post, a Special Assistant's Office, a "Holding Room" (whatever that was), and a Secret Service Command Post on the same floor; senior staff and secretarial offices on the fifth floor; "Visitor Control" and "package" rooms on the first floor; a press room on the ground floor; and a motor pool in the lobby. Nearly 20 correspondents had accompanied Kissinger on his airplane from Washington—Bernard Gwertzman of *The New York Times*,

Marilyn Berger of *The Washington Post*, Jerrold Schecter of
*Time*, Bruce Van Voorst of *Newsweek*, Richard Valeriani of
N.B.C., Bernard Kalb of C.B.S., representatives of A.B.C.,
A.P., U.P.I., Reuters, *The Chicago Tribune*, *The Los Angeles
Times*, *The Christian Science Monitor*, *et al.*—and now their
numbers were multiplied by other journalists who had reached
Jerusalem on commercial aircraft. The American Ambassador to
Israel, Malcolm Toon, and Mrs. Toon were also in residence at
the King David, supported by nearly 40 American and local
members of the Embassy staff.

Thus 134 persons comprised the Secretary's entourage in that
hotel, not counting servants, Israeli officials, journalists, and
security police—or the legions of police and troops outside.
(Alexandria, Damascus, Taif, and Amman were yet to come, but
more choirs of aides and bodyguards were waiting in those capitals to attend upon the needs of Dr. Kissinger.) The King David
was to function as his base whilst he conducted this latest epi-
sode of "shuttle diplomacy," and indeed as the nerve center of
America's global business during the 13 days he remained in the
Middle East. For weeks the bureaucracy in Washington had
been engaged in preparations, cabling to Tel Aviv and the Arab
capitals a plethora of instructions, transporting to Jerusalem a
cornucopia of communications equipment. Two bulletproof
limousines were part of the precautions; separate Air Force
planes few ahead with them to the various destinations, so that
one limousine would always be on hand whenever the Secretary
might require it. Estimates of the journey's cost ran to several
million dollars.

The lobby of the King David swarmed with Israeli journalists
and officials, eager to convey to the American correspondents
their view of the negotiations. I drank beer with them late the
night of Kissinger's arrival, then retired to my room on the
fourth floor. Throughout the night the demonstrators outside
kept me awake, whilst silent hands slipped Xeroxed sheets beneath my door. In the morning, as I munched on breakfast, I
struggled to digest as well the accumulation of communiqués

from the press room, translations of the Israeli media, instructions from (I supposed) some command post upstairs. For example:

August 21, 1975

### DEPARTURE NOTICE

I.   The Secretary's aircraft will depart Ben-Gurion Airport at 1500 hours on Friday, August 22, 1975.

II.  Members of the party who are traveling to the airport via privately arranged transport must be aboard the aircraft by 1430 hours.

III. Members of the party who have special material they will need to retain until shortly before departure from the hotel should be prepared to carry it with them to the airport.

IV.  Luggage should be packed and left outside hotel rooms by 1000 hours and *must be left unlocked.*

V.   Personnel listed on the attached sheet as assigned to Helicopter no. 2 should assemble in the hotel lobby at 1400 hours. They will proceed to the helipad at the YMCA Soccer Field on foot at 1410 hours and take-off for Ben-Gurion Airport will be at 1420 hours.

VI.  Personnel assigned to Helicopter no. 1 will proceed to the helipad by motorcade which will depart the hotel at 1420 hours. Take-off for Ben-Gurion Airport will be at 1430 hours.

VII. The Visitor Control Room (No. 129) will be open from 0700 hours on Friday, August 22, for exchange of currency.

We were off to Alexandria. Dr. Kissinger had conferred with the Israelis that morning; now he had to present their proposals to President Anwar al-Sadat. My notebook reminds me that I was assigned to Helicopter no. 2:

We left the King David on foot at about 2:20 in the afternoon carrying our hand luggage. We walked around the block to a nearby soccer field and a waiting helicopter of the Israeli air force, the Star of David emblazoned upon its tail, its choppers already chopping, blowing a hot and gusty wind that disheveled one's hair as we boarded the craft. It was warm and noisy inside that helicopter, so deafening we could not speak. The windows were few and I could not see the countryside as we chopped our way to Tel Aviv. Soon I was moist with sweat, and I began to get a headache. I got up, glanced out the window, and glimpsed an orange grove, a kibbutz or two, the parched and rolling hills of Palestine. In about twenty minutes we touched down at Ben-Gurion Airport, where, before we boarded Dr. Kissinger's aircraft, the Secret Service inspected our hand luggage. The airplane was a white Boeing 707B, escutcheoned with an American flag and THE UNITED STATES OF AMERICA in large blue letters, flown by the 89th Military Airlift Wing, Military Airlift Command, of the United States Air Force. It was the symbol of Kissinger's method in the Middle East—shuttle diplomacy.

I mounted the ramp, and found peanuts and candy at my designated seat in the rear section reserved for the press and the Secret Service. A steward in civil dress brings me lemonade from a tap at the rear of the craft, and I sip whilst I scribble these notes. God, it is hot in here. Ah! A commotion! I think Kissinger is coming! I look out the window, and there he is—surrounded by his senior aides, his Praetorian Guard, and sundry hangers-on. Simcha Dinitz (the Israeli Ambassador to Washington) walks excitedly at his side, gesturing with animation. Mrs. Kissinger comes along, her blond hair wind-blown, wearing slacks. She is taller than her husband. The Kissingers wave, walk up the front ramp to their private stateroom. Winston Lord enters through the rear door, strides past me to the front, his attaché case and jacket in his hand, the back of his blue shirt drenched with sweat.

We took off at ten minutes past three, and flew out over the Mediterranean. Presently Ambassador Anderson appeared, to invite the press forward for a briefing by the Secretary. We passed from our section through the compartment reserved for Kissinger's senior aides. Atherton, Saunders, and Oakley were submerged in documents that dealt with the negotiation; Lord was working on the major speech that Kissinger intended to deliver on September 1st to the General Assembly of the United Nations. (He never did, for the negotiation dragged on; Ambassador Daniel Patrick Moynihan read the speech for him.) In his office, Dr. Kissinger sat in white shirtsleeves at an L-shaped table covered with rough green cloth, Undersecretary Sisco at his side. Nearby, in that wood-paneled compartment, reposed a high-backed armchair, a television set, and a telephone console that could connect the Secretary through the Pentagon switchboard to President Ford or to anybody anywhere on earth.

The correspondents huddled round the green table, above the drone of the engines, bombarding Kissinger with questions inspired by rumors in the Israeli press: In exchange for this interim agreement would the United States promise to intervene if Israel were threatened by a "world power"—meaning the Soviet Union? "We're not giving Israel any such assurance," Kissinger replied pleasantly. "No, I'm not carrying a letter from the President to Prime Minister Rabin. The stories of hundreds of F-16s for Israel—we don't have that many—are sheer insanity." Nancy Kissinger is reputed to have said, and not unkindly, "Henry gets up early in the morning, and starts talking. He goes to bed late at night, and he's still talking." He devotes an extravagant measure of his conversation to cultivating luminaries of the press. I marveled at how little he tells them.

Within less than an hour we were above the Egyptian desert. We landed in the desert, at a military airfield far from Alexandria. I was assigned to Helicopter no. 5, flown by the Egyptian air force. There were more windows in that helicopter, and I gazed out now upon desert, now upon a network of canals and groves of mango in the delta of the Nile. Half an hour passed before we glimpsed Alexandria, its long corniche lapped by a turquoise sea, its souks, its slums, its slender minarets and bulbous domes resplendent in the sun of the waning afternoon. We circled over Montaza Palace and its glorious pink bridge, on the lagoon not far from Maamura Guest House, Sadat's Alexandrian residence where Kissinger would confer with him. Kissinger slept that night on the other side of the city, at Ras al Tin Palace, built by Mohammed Ali, the first Khedive of Egypt—a marvel of throne rooms, golden ceilings, marble balconies surrounded by gardens illumined with colored lanterns, a place of pure Egyptian Gothic. I wondered if Dr. Kissinger dreamed a dream about the squalor of Egypt beyond those palace walls.

We remained at Alexandria only overnight; by noon we were once more above the Mediterranean, in quest of Damascus. The

President of Syria was already murmuring against the impend-
ing agreement between Israel and Egypt; Kissinger was resolved to reassure him. We were invited to gather again round
the green table, where the correspondents endeavored to discover what Kissinger had achieved with Anwar Sadat. "We discussed the hills along the coast of Sinai," the Secretary said. "I
know the elevation of every hill. You think I'm kidding?" The
Arab he was about to meet, the cunning Hafez al-Assad, clearly
fascinated him. "I'll tell President Assad my candid opinion,"
Kissinger continued. "It's stupid to tell anybody what he wants
to hear. I genuinely like Assad. He's a romantic. I give him
tutorials on world politics. He tells me stories of Arab leaders,
mounts cavalry charges in conversation—sometimes it takes me
an hour to get him back to business. He's not exactly a man of
minor passions."

Cradled by brown hills and a high escarpment, Damascus
shimmered below us in the sun of that August noon. The cupolas
of the mosques seemed all of silver, and I remembered the
verses of an Irish poet I had cited in my first novel. "While as far
as sight can reach, beneath as clear/And blue a heaven as ever
blest this sphere/Gardens and minarets and glittering domes/
And high-built temples fit to be homes/Of mighty gods."

We remained in Damascus less than seven hours. At sunset
we returned to Tel Aviv, and no sooner were we aloft than Dr.
Kissinger in white shirtsleeves wandered back to the press compartment.

He intimated that his audience with Assad had gone well, but
as he chattered on I wondered. "The more you're nervous with
the Syrians, the worse off you are," he said. "Assad will do
nothing, absolutely nothing, for *my* reasons. For me to want
something is nothing to Assad. It's what *he* wants—that's what
counts. He's very intelligent." Kissinger developed variations of
this theme, then defined the essence of his own diplomacy in the
Arab-Israeli conflict: "Look, you guys, my greatest contribution
is to explain clearly to each party the position of the other."

We landed at Tel Aviv in darkness; when we descended the

Boeing, Ambassador Simcha Dinitz emerged from the darkness
and placed his arm upon Sisco's shoulder. "Joe . . ." he said, and
they strode off, exchanging secrets. Dr. Kissinger faced an evening of negotiation in Tel Aviv before he could return to
Jerusalem and bed. The rest of us boarded Helicopter no. 2 and
flew at once to Jerusalem. The flight consumed at least an hour;
for some reason (security, I fancied) we circled the holy city
again and again and again. I extracted my notebook and began to
scribble.

The helicopter banks for the hundredth time. I am near the window
now. Jerusalem is illumined. I glimpse, I think, the Garden of
Gethsemane. The air in here is suffocating. The choppers chop. My
head throbs. I've been but two days on Kissinger's shuttle; unlike the
correspondents I've no daily dispatches to crank out, and whilst Kissinger is busy I've time for tourism and sea-bathing. And yet, after only
two days, *I'm pooped.* How much of this torment must Kissinger
endure—another week, another fortnight? He's up, they say, at six
each morning, to read cables from the State Department, to dictate
replies, to prepare the day's negotiation. Tomorrow he'll haggle all day
with the Israelis, then return to the King David to prepare more
position papers, read and reply to more messages from Washington,
then dictate a long dispatch to the President on the progress of the
talks. He'll get to bed at three in the morning, if then. He'll rise at
dawn, and fly to Alexandria. Isn't the worst part the long helicopter
rides, the heat, the sweat, the chopping noise, the landing in deserts,
the hot winds? A fortnight of this? He did it for more than a month
during the Syrian negotiations. *Jesus.*

At the King David, beneath my door, I found another batch of
Xeroxed announcements.

Saturday, August 23, 1975

NOTICE

This is to remind you that members of the press traveling with the
Secretary have been invited to a "surprise" birthday party in the Secretary's suite after he returns this evening.

Joe Vogel
USIS

I napped awhile, then near midnight mounted to the sixth floor, flashed my credentials to the Secret Service, and entered Dr. Kissinger's suite. It was nondescript modern, with vases of roses and waiters in white jackets tendering trays of chocolates, petits fours, and (I think) Israeli champagne. Sisco and Ambassador Anderson stood with the correspondents clustered round the Secretary, who was seated against the wall. Nancy Kissinger had remained in Alexandria as Mrs. Sadat's guest, but seated opposite the Secretary was Marilyn Berger, diplomatic correspondent of *The Washington Post* and the star of the occasion, for this was Miss Berger's birthday party.

Dr. Kissinger had evidently just returned from Tel Aviv; Ambassador Dinitz and Foreign Minister Yigal Allon were also present, standing round like the rest of us listening to the Secretary. "Does Golda hate me?" he asked.

"Oh no, Mr. Secretary," Ambassador Dinitz said.

"Will she refuse to see me?"

"Certainly not, Mr. Secretary," the Foreign Minister said.

"I'm very, very fond of her." Memories of Mrs. Meir seemed to flood his mind. He sat in his blue business suit, his tie slightly askew, slumped in an armless chair. He sipped champagne, and looked exhausted.

"Ten years ago," Miss Berger said, "on my twentieth birthday, I saw *Fiddler on the Roof.*"

"Fiddler on the Roof?" a correspondent asked.

"It was so lovely," she continued. "You wouldn't understand. You're not Jewish."

She complained about her hotel in Alexandria and about the Egyptian press. "Did you read that ridiculous editorial this morning in *The Egyptian Gazette?*" she asked.

"No," said Kissinger.

"It compared the Israelis to the French colonialists in Algeria." She neglected to add that it also compared Dr. Kissinger to General de Gaulle.

Kissinger glanced up at Dinitz and Allon. "The Egyptian press treats me better than the Israeli press," he said.

Soon the Foreign Minister remarked on the late hour, and

took his leave. Kissinger remained seated. His eye roamed the room and came to rest on me.

"I put in a good word for you," he said.

"So I've been told," I replied. "Thank you, Mr. Secretary. I shall look forward to seeing him."

"Who's he seeing now?" Miss Berger demanded.

"Assad," said Kissinger.

This evoked more memories; the Secretary reminisced at length about the Syrian president, the most intractable of the Arab leaders and by far his favorite. "It was near the end of the Golan negotiation," he mused. "The talks had broken down. We were writing the communiqué. At the last minute, Assad told me, 'What a pity. We've come so far. . . . '"

I was curious about the seminars on world affairs that Dr. Kissinger had conducted for the benefit of Assad. I asked, "Were they similar to your seminars at Harvard?"

"Less structured," Kissinger said.

I found it fascinating that the American Secretary of State should have a militant Arab president as his pupil. I endeavored to pursue the subject, but this was Miss Berger's birthday party, and she invoked her right to interrupt.

No matter, for Dr. Kissinger ruminated as the spirit moved him. Ambassador Dinitz excused himself, and went home. Some of the correspondents drifted off. I wondered why the Secretary did not go to bed, but he remained there, his arm hanging over the back of his chair . . . talking. The names of great acquaintances tumbled from his tongue. "Golda . . . Assad . . . Sadat . . . Brezhnev . . . Chou En-lai. . . ." Power, he had once observed, is an aphrodisiac. He seemed very tired, and very happy.

# CHAPTER

# 1

# Watershed and Bloodshed

Since the Arab-Israeli war of October 1973, Henry Kissinger devoted more of his time and craft to the consequences of that conflict than to any other problem of American foreign policy. The war was a watershed of our present epoch, for it altered the international balance of power. Hitherto the United States and the Soviet Union had confronted each other in the Middle East from behind protégés who were very unequal in skills and strength. During the Six-Day War of 1967, Israel had crushed the armies of Egypt, Syria, and Jordan, and emerged as the mightiest nation in the Middle East—nourished thereafter by transfusions of American money and guns and a growing mystique of invincibility. Egypt and Syria were sustained by Moscow, but their MIGs and SAM missiles seemed no match for Israel's Phantoms and sophistication in the technology of battle. This was the conventional wisdom until late 1973; the October war shattered it. In the interval since 1967 the Arabs had grown up, learned how the world is run, limited their military objectives for the sake of their political purpose. The Arabs did not

11

win the war in battle, but neither did they endure another
humiliating defeat, and politically they were the victors. The
fourth Arab-Israeli war, in fact, may come to be considered as
one of the major events of Arab history. It may rank in retrospect
with the Arab conquests of the Middle Ages—with the rise of
the Ommayad Caliphate, with the defeat of the Crusaders, with
the birth of Arab and Egyptian nationalism, with the seizure of
the Suez Canal—in political and metaphysical importance. Not
as a triumph of arms, but as a crucial intersection which man-
ifested the end, after five centuries, of the Arab decline.

In bloodshed the Arabs leaped the abyss from backwardness
to modernity, proving to all, including themselves, that they
were not inferior, that with tenacity they could master the mys-
teries of technology. In bloodshed, by destroying perhaps a
fourth of the Israeli air force and hundreds of Israeli tanks, the
Arabs provoked the world to take them seriously. In
bloodshed—and by an oil embargo. The embargo, imposed
whilst the war raged, compounded by a stunning rise in the
price of oil soon afterwards, cost America tens of billions of
dollars and Western Europe an even greater measure of its af-
fluence. Soon Abu Dhabi's per-capita income exceeded $40,000;
Saudi Arabia contemplated accumulating a third of the world's
central bank reserves. The Persian Gulf at large emerged as a
major source of world capital, and the Arabs—in their
collectivity—joined America, Russia, China, Western Europe,
and Japan in the fellowship of global powers.

Dr. Kissinger was amongst the first to recognize this shift of
power. He knew he could not cope with it unless he could
contain the Arab-Israeli conflict. Never has American
diplomacy—or the man who conducts it—become so dra-
matically committed to the solution of a problem. Throughout a
dozen missions to the Middle East, throughout thousands of
hours of negotiations there and in Washington, throughout
300,000 miles or more of flying to and fro, Kissinger summoned
all the power of his prodigious intellect to the fashioning of a
new equation between the greatest of the Semitic peoples, the

better to prevent a new embargo, a worse recession, another war that might overwhelm the world beyond. Now, nearly three years after he began, we must assess his achievements, his failures, and his method—step-by-step diplomacy.

The most crucial of Kissinger's labors occurred during moments of great tension: between October 6, 1973, when war broke out, and late December of that year, when the Geneva conference was convened; during January 1974, when he separated the Israeli and the Egyptian armies and asserted the necessity of his personal intervention to achieve interim solutions; during May 1974, when he separated the Israeli and Syrian armies whilst the Syrians were waging a war of attrition; during March 1975, when his endeavor to negotiate a new agreement in the Sinai collapsed amidst recriminations with the government of Israel; and in August 1975, when he finally achieved that agreement at a high cost to the United States—though much lower, he insisted, than its alternative, another war.

I shall suggest in these pages that, endeavoring to accommodate the shift of power caused by the October war, Dr. Kissinger created a coherent Arab policy for the United States—the first Secretary of State to do so. The policy was based on a quasi-alliance between Washington and Cairo—or more particularly, upon friendship between Kissinger and the president of Egypt, Mohammed Anwar al-Sadat. Kissinger assumed that with Sadat in hand the other Arabs would follow, but today that supposition is cast in doubt.

Kissinger's Arab policy, until late 1975 at least, tenaciously avoided the Palestinian problem, though that problem is crucial to the Arab-Israeli conflict. Kissinger entertained a different conception of priorities. Simultaneously with his endeavor to diminish the Arab-Israeli quarrel, he pursued a parallel policy in the Arab world—promotion of American technology—as a means of entrenching American influence throughout the Arab republics, kingdoms, and sheikhdoms. Obviously all of his undertakings with the Arabs affected his relations with the

Israelis—not to mention American Jews. Relations between the United States and Israel, which began to erode during the October war, have deteriorated to a condition of chronic crisis—dramatized by Kissinger's recurring clashes with Israeli leaders and with Israel's American constituency. Indeed, Dr. Kissinger has even had doubts about his own policy of supplying immense quantities of arms to Israel. We shall have much to say about that. But not before we go back—to the beginning.

# 2

# Time for a Shock

Henry Kissinger seemed indifferent to the Middle East before September 1973, when he became Secretary of State. For the previous four and a half years, as President Nixon's Assistant for National Security Affairs, he had been absorbed by Vietnam, the Soviet Union, détente, China, and Western Europe. Nevertheless, as the President's most powerful adviser on foreign policy, he also involved himself in a number of major decisions concerning the Middle East—particularly as they related to the Russians or the supply of arms to Israel. Peace plans he would not touch; given the prevailing passions of the Arab-Israeli conflict, he felt they would fail. He was skeptical about United Nations Security Council Resolution 242—which called for Israeli withdrawal from Arab territory in return for secure and recognized frontiers—as a functional framework for a settlement.*

Kissinger was equally cynical about the plan for peace an-

---

*Resolution 242, adopted by the Security Council on November 22, 1967, five months after the Six-Day War, is fundamental to any discussion of the Arab-Israeli conflict; the full text will be found in Appendix One.

nounced in 1969 by Secretary of State William P. Rogers, and
about Rogers' initiatives in the Middle East in 1970 and 1971.
During the most important address he delivered as Secretary of
State, Rogers (on December 9, 1969) publicly endorsed substantial Israeli withdrawal from occupied territory in exchange for
contractual peace from the Arabs:

A lasting peace must be sustained by a sense of security on both
sides. To this end, as envisaged in the Security Council resolution,
there should be demilitarized zones and related security arrangements
more reliable than those which existed . . . in the past. . . . We believe
that while recognized political boundaries must be established and
agreed upon by the parties, any changes in the preexisting lines should
not reflect the weight of conquest and should be confined to insubstantial alterations required for mutual security. We do not support expansionism. We believe troops must be withdrawn as the resolution provides. We support Israel's security and the security of the Arab states
as well. . . .

The . . . future status of Jerusalem, because it touches deep emotional, historical, and religious wellsprings, is particularly complicated. We
have made it clear repeatedly . . . that we cannot accept unilateral
actions by any party to decide the final status of the city. . . . We do,
however, support certain principles which we believe would provide
an equitable framework for a . . . settlement. . . . Jerusalem should be a
unified city . . . [taking] into account the interests of . . . the Jewish, Islamic, and Christian communities. And there should be roles for both
Israel and Jordan in the civic, economic, and religious life of the
city. . . .

In the context of peace and agreement on specific security
safeguards, withdrawal of Israeli forces from Egyptian territory would
be required. Such an approach . . . would require [Egypt] to agree to a
binding and specific commitment to peace. It would require withdrawal of Israeli armed forces from [Egyptian] territory to the international border between Israel (or Mandated Palestine) and Egypt which
has been in existence for over a half century. It would also require the
parties themselves to negotiate the practical security arrangements to
safeguard the peace.

We believe that this approach is *balanced* and fair.*

The speech was the product of elaborate staff work inside the State Department, which honestly sought to reconcile the essential needs of both belligerents. (To this day, neither Kissinger nor the two presidents he has served have disavowed its principles.) But Kissinger doubted that the Israelis would swallow near-total withdrawal or that the Arabs were ready to pay the price of total peace. Kissinger was contemptuous of Rogers. He considered him naïve, a neophyte in foreign policy, well-intentioned no doubt but induced by his inexperience to bite off more than he could chew. The "Rogers Plan," Kissenger felt, was a perfect example—it defined a final settlement prematurely, erected the architecture before fashioning the foundation. True, Rogers arranged a cease-fire on the Suez Canal in 1970, but when he proposed an interim agreement between Israel and Egypt to reopen the canal, he got nowhere. The Egyptians would have accepted a partial Israeli retreat into the Sinai, but they demanded an Israeli commitment to withdraw completely later on. The Israelis refused.

Perceptive Arab diplomats recognized early during the Nixon years that real power in the administration reposed with Kissinger, not Rogers; a few urged Kissinger to undertake an active role in seeking a settlement. Dr. Ashraf Ghorbal, then chief of the Egyptian Interests Section in Washington (now ambassador), perhaps despairing of conventional diplomacy, tried his hand at doggerel, which he dispatched to Kissinger on the morrow of his first visit to Peking:

> On one of my recent excavations
> I ran across an old exclamation.
> It was in Amenhotep's tomb,
> The god of medicine of ancient gloom.
> It said, "Come and visit my Nile."
> And you do not have to stand in file.

*The full text of this address, commonly called the "Rogers Plan," will be found in Appendix Two.

For your stomachaches I have a cure
And for your headaches for sure.
How about it, dear Henry,
Shall we make the Middle East a double entry?

To an Arab statesman whose plea, though more prosaic, was essentially similar, Kissinger retorted, "I will never get involved in anything unless I'm sure of success. And if I do get involved, it means I'm going to succeed. I hate failure." The Middle East, he mused to friends, "isn't ready for me."

Dr. Kissinger was convinced that, until the Arabs saw that Soviet guns could not regain their territory, until the Israelis understood that massive American support could not of itself bestow security for the great future, and until both Arabs and Israelis were truly ready to render up important concessions to one another, his own or any American intervention was doomed to be abortive. Time alone could alter the perceptions of the parties; until that happened Kissinger was content to cope with other problems. In fact, he contributed to Nixon's decision that Rogers' endeavors in the Middle East should collapse quietly of exhaustion. That eventually, after he replaced Rogers as Secretary of State, he should adopt the Rogers policy of pursuing peace in the Middle East through interim agreements, is not the least irony of his subsequent diplomacy.

Moreover, though not a Zionist and diffident about his own Jewishness, Dr. Kissinger accepted and helped to promote the conventional strategic wisdom of the first Nixon administration—that in the absence of fruitful negotiations a strong Israel, militarily much superior to her Arab foes, would prevent war and serve as the surest sentinel of American interests in the Middle East. When Kissinger glanced at the map of the Middle East, he did not see Israel, Egypt, Jordan, Syria; he saw the Soviet Union and the United States. He was distressed by the flow of Soviet weapons and military technicians into Egypt, and he had no mind to permit American munitions in Israel to be vanquished by Russian logistics to Cairo. He suspected, with some justification, that the Russians were using

Egypt as a base to pursue an expansionist strategy in the Mediterranean, along the coast of North Africa, in the Red Sea and in the Indian Ocean. Soviet pilots were flying MIGs in operational missions near the Suez Canal. More than that, with their radar and reconnaissance flights out of Egypt, the Russians were monitoring the movements of the American Sixth Fleet, particularly the deployment of submarines with Polaris missiles, and scrutinizing the operations by sea and air of the other NATO powers as well.

Kissinger's fear of an expansionist Soviet strategy in the Mediterranean and points south was well founded, but he appears to have misperceived the Russian role in Egypt itself. President Gamal Abdel Nasser was engaged in a war of attrition with Israel along the Suez Canal. By late 1969, the Israeli air force was roaming at will over Cairo and the Nile delta, as yet not dropping bombs but breaking the sound barrier and intimidating the population. Then, in early January 1970, the Israelis embarked upon "deep-penetration" raids into the delta and the suburbs of the capital. Flying American planes, they bombed industrial installations at Kanka, ten miles northeast of Cairo, and returned in February to bomb Abu Zabal, two miles north of Kanka, killing 80 workers. In January, February, and March they bombed military factories at Helwan, 15 miles south of Cairo, and at Digla, nearby, causing heavy damage and dislocating Egypt's war production. On April 8 they hit a primary school at Bahr al-Baqr, 15 miles west of the canal, killing 30 children.

In late January, Nasser flew secretly to Moscow to appeal for more Russian help. The Kremlin, faced with the debasement of its client before the world, came to Nasser's rescue. After all, Nasser was not demanding an assault on Israel. He was attempting to defend Egyptian territory.

The Soviet response to the deep-penetration raids was the SAM-3—a surface-to-air missile that had never before been deployed outside Eastern Europe—and about 150 Soviet pilots, half of them instructors and advisers, the other half virtually a

Soviet squadron flying the latest MIG-21 fighters, with Egyptian markings, over the Nile delta but not crossing to the eastern side of the canal, where the Israelis sat entrenched. Earlier, the Russians had been standing over the Egyptians telling them when to push the buttons of the SAM-2s, but now the SAM-3s were entirely manned by Russians. At that point the number of Soviet technicians in Egypt surpassed 10,000; in addition to the SAMs, the Russians also provided tanks and 203-mm. howitzers. The Russian pilots and the SAM-3s constrained the Israelis to halt their deep-penetration raids in mid-April and to concentrate their attacks thereafter on the missile sites and other fortifications near the Suez Canal. The Russians' purpose was essentially defensive. They introduced the SAMs to protect the Nile valley from the offensive of Israeli Phantoms.

Thus Nasser accepted Secretary Rogers' cease-fire in the summer of 1970 because Egypt had (to an extent) adjusted the military balance and could undertake negotiations with its heartland secure. Nasser cheated, however, by moving Soviet missiles closer to the canal on the night the cease-fire took effect. This angered Kissinger. A former aide of Kissinger's who worked intimately with him during this period recalls that "Kissinger was already wary of Soviet adventures outside the Middle East. Until 1970, we restrained our supply of arms to Israel. It's true that the Israelis provoked the massive Soviet arms build-up in Egypt, but this has to be measured against Kissinger's perception of Soviet and Arab perfidy. Nasser's cheating was not so great as the Israelis pretended, but for the next two years Kissinger was 100 percent pro-Israeli—and the flow of American arms to Israel proved it." Indeed, Kissinger became very much a "hard-liner" on the Middle East. He grew close to Israeli Ambassador Yitzhak Rabin, and privately for a period he favored Israel's aspiration to retain significant portions of Arab territory.

Nasser died in September 1970. By the end of President Sadat's first year in office, Nixon's arms assistance to Israel exceeded $600 million, vastly more than President Johnson's, including substantial shipments of supersonic Phantoms with the promise of more to come. Some specialists in the State Department (not all of them Arabists) argued that the Israelis' growing superiority enabled them to tighten their grip on conquered territory, encouraged them to resist American rhetoric to make concessions, and exposed the United States itself to the accusation of occupying Arab land by proxy. Kissinger brushed aside this reasoning. He shared Assistant Secretary of State Joseph J. Sisco's argument that the Israelis would never make concessions until they had confidence, and they could not have confidence until they achieved invincibility. To those Arabs who managed to reach him, Kissinger replied, "Don't worry. Be patient. The Phantoms are to deliver Israel when the time comes." In retrospect this reasoning may seem disingenuous, but it corresponded neatly with Kissinger's current notions of the balance of power and comfortably with the requirements of domestic American politics.

In fact, though President Sadat agreed in early 1971 to sign an eventual peace treaty with Israel (theoretically at least meeting one of Kissinger's requirements), it was clear from the beginning that Israel would not produce analogous concessions save as the result of strong American pressure. Rogers and Sisco promised Sadat that they would work seriously for Israeli withdrawals, and they engaged Prime Minister Golda Meir and her cabinet in heated arguments behind closed doors, but they never enjoyed the real support of Nixon or Kissinger. By late summer of 1971, the "Rogers Plan" passed into oblivion; in October, the formulation of Middle East policy was shifted from the State Department to the White House. Henceforth it was Nixon in tandem with Kissinger who made Middle East policy, which was in effect to play for time, to entertain no policy that disturbed the Israeli lobby or endangered the status quo. For 1972 was reserved for the reelection of Richard Nixon. Ambassador Rabin publicly endorsed Nixon.*

*In their biography *Kissinger* (1974), Marvin and Bernard Kalb note that "because of the special Kissinger-Rabin relationship, many Israelis came to regard Kissinger as a 'good friend,' even though Kissinger regards Israel as only a

Sadat, meanwhile, was thrashing about in quest of a new policy. His "Year of Decision" (1971) had ended ignominiously,
and—deprived by them of the offensive arms he needed to
match Israel's—he was going nowhere with the Russians. Rogers
had suggested to Sadat in Cairo that Nixon might be more forthcoming were Sadat to diminish the enormous Soviet presence in
Egypt; in a famous indiscretion, Kissinger had already announced that the American purpose was to "expel" the Russians.
In the spring of 1972, Prince Sultan, the Saudi Minister of Defense, visited Washington, where the hint of a *quid pro quo* was
repeated; he stopped in Cairo en route home and told Sadat.
Such hints no doubt contributed to Sadat's subsequent decision,
but they did not determine it. Provoked primarily by the contradiction of Soviet policy—the Russians' preference for improved relations with the United States versus their inadequate
posture as Egypt's arsenal against Israel—and by internal pressure from his own army, Sadat that summer expelled nearly all
of his 20,000 Soviet technicians.

Kissinger was astounded. "Why has Sadat done me this favor?" he asked his aides. "Why didn't he get in touch with me?
Why didn't he demand of me all kinds of concessions first?" For
in a curious intelligence failure, Kissinger learned of the expulsion from news dispatches. Sadat in desperation had decided
upon a *coup de théâtre,* a colossal thrust to buy more time,
whilst he groped to elude his demon of "no war, no peace."

---

special part of a larger strategic contest with the Soviet Union. When, in
mid-1971, Rogers leaned on Rabin to make 'unilateral concessions' in the
ongoing negotiations about an interim solution to reopen the Suez Canal, even
threatening for a brief time to hold up jet plane deliveries, Kissinger inter-
ceded. Later in the year, when the Rogers-Rabin dispute began to make
headlines in the press and problems for the Republican National Committee,
Kissinger got the President's permission to assure Rabin that plane deliveries
would continue and State Department pressure would stop. That intercession
paved the way for [Golda] Meir to visit the President in early December and
set the stage for Israel's sympathetic view of his candidacy in 1972. Rabin spoke
undiplomatically about his admiration for Nixon and Kissinger and his fear of
McGovern, and he helped swing many traditionally Democratic Jewish votes
into the GOP column."

Whatever his immediate motivations, he must have known that the expulsion would be perceived as another cry for American help, and he as a hapless gambler who in casting away his most potent card supposed he might at last induce Nixon and Kissinger to hasten to his rescue.

They did not. Publicly Nixon all but ignored Sadat's epochal decision, though privately he responded—without committing himself. Kissinger drafted several secret messages for Nixon's signature which were then dispatched, not through American diplomats in Cairo, but by intelligence channels directly to Sadat through Hafez Ismail, his national security adviser. In these Nixon acknowledged the expulsion as an important act and pledged that his administration would concentrate on the Middle East as soon as the presidential elections and the Vietnam negotiations were concluded. The elections over, Vietnam dragged on, and Kissinger did not dispose of the negotiations until late in January 1973.

With Vietnam solved (or so it seemed), Kissinger opened his dossier on the Middle East. At the end of February, Hafez Ismail came to Washington. Kissinger spent a weekend in secret talks with that tall and taciturn Egyptian, expounding to him his notion of seeking a formula that would reconcile Egypt's sovereignty in Sinai with Israel's insistence on security, and he exhorted the Egyptians to produce practical ideas to advance the prospects of a settlement. All of this, he cautioned, would take time—and besides, nothing of substance could be achieved until after the Israeli elections scheduled for the following October. In his revealing book *The Road to Ramadan* (1975), the Egyptian editor Mohammed Hassanein Heikal recounts the Egyptian version of what happened between Ismail and Nixon and Kissinger:

Hafez Ismail was received by Nixon in the Oval Office. . . . Nixon then went on to say how much he had enjoyed his visit to Egypt in 1963 and what respect he felt for the late President Nasser. He said he wanted to play his part in the building of a permanent peace in the Middle East, though he could not say in advance what shape a final settlement should take. He did not wish to impose his ideas on anyone.

We had to remember, he said, that while Egypt wanted to keep its
sovereignty, Israel wanted to keep its security. (This theme, reducing
the whole problem to a simple equation between sovereignty and security, probably owed its origin to Kissinger, and was one which we were
to hear with increasing frequency.) He asked Hafez Ismail to give a
frank expression of Egypt's point of view and added: "In spite of all my
faults, not keeping my promises is not one of them."

Hafez Ismail then launched into his analysis of the situation—the
extreme danger of the present state of affairs; Egypt's historic role in
the area; her determination to keep out of spheres of influence, as
exemplified by the withdrawal of Russian experts. He said that the only
reason for differences between the United States and Egypt was the
total military and political backing which the United States gave to
Israel, and he warned the President that one day Israel would challenge America's position in the Middle East just as it had challenged
Britain's. He said that the main reason for the crisis in the Middle East
was the clash between two societies, the Jewish and the Palestinian,
and that it was essential Israel should try to settle directly with the
Palestinians. If Israel wanted peace, it would have to behave as a
Middle Eastern State and not continue to rely on support from the
outside world. It would have to put an end to immigration, cut its links
with world Zionism and abandon the claims of its citizens to dual
nationality.

Nixon said he thought that, as with China and a Vietnam settlement,
future discussions with Egypt should be conducted at two levels; one
through the State Department, where everything would be in the
open, and the other through secret channels supervised by Dr. Kissinger and without the knowledge of the State Department: that would
be the channel for a real settlement. Secrecy would have to be guaran-
teed so that Israel should not know what was going on, at any rate for
the time being. (He asked General Scowcroft not to record this passage
in the minutes, though we must now assume that the tapes were
running all the time.) Contacts with Kissinger should be continuous,
and we should talk to him frankly, just as if we were talking to the
President. Nixon ended by saying he would like to tell a personal story.
Two days previously he had been having dinner with his daughter and
asked her which of all the countries she had seen she would most like to
visit again. She had said Egypt. The impression which Hafez Ismail got
from his seventy minutes meeting with the President was that he was

extremely relaxed and that his expression of goodwill towards Egypt was genuine. Nixon, he felt, was eager to play a personal role in solving the Middle East problem.

The three secret meetings which Hafez Ismail then had with Kissinger in [Pepsi-Cola chairman] Donald Kendall's house [in Connecticut] on 24–25 February were not very productive, though they throw some light on the way in which Kissinger operates. He laid down three principles that should guide their dealings—mutual confidence, "no cheating," and complete secrecy. He said that America could not "impose" anything on Israel though there were ways of bringing pressure on Israel which Israel could not ignore and which his Government was prepared to use if a "moral basis" for their use existed and could be shown to exist to American public opinion. He said that America had no objection to Egypt's friendship with the Soviet Union, but that if Egypt thought it could throw a spanner into the relationship between America and the Soviet Union it would find itself mistaken. The United States was ready for a general discussion of Middle East questions with the Soviet Union, but when it came down to details it preferred to deal only with the parties directly concerned. Then he went on to his favorite sovereignty-security equation. He argued that any withdrawal by Israel would mean the abandonment of a concrete and material basis for security. Israel would have to be convinced that material security was not everything. The Egyptians would have to make up their minds what they were prepared to offer in exchange for some Israeli withdrawal. It was clear that Egypt, the country under occupation, was the one which was being asked to make concessions. Verbal guarantees, Hafez Ismail was told, were not enough. The concessions expected from Egypt were political and territorial.

Ismail was displeased by several of Kissinger's perceptions, and dismayed by the prospect of delay until after the Israeli elections in October, but otherwise he left the United States prepared to advise Sadat that at least the Americans seemed serious—finally—about promoting negotiations.

In Paris, en route home, Ismail read a *New York Times* report that Nixon had decided to furnish Israel with 36 new Skyhawks and 48 Phantoms. Through his secret channel Kissinger hastened to assure Sadat that the report was false, that the Israeli request (long since pending) was still "under study." Kissinger was furious at the leak because it undermined his conversations with Ismail; though the moving force of arms for Israel, he disapproved of piecemeal deliveries, favoring instead a single long-range commitment that, once rendered, would avert thereafter the discomfort of provocative announcements. The report, however, was not false, only premature. Nixon confirmed it in the spring, a month after Ismail's departure.

No matter the technicalities; the damage was irreparable. The abortive Ismail mission was the turning point on the path to war. In early April Sadat told Arnaud de Borchgrave of *Newsweek:*

> If we don't take our case into our own hands, there will be no movement. . . . Every door I have opened has been slammed in my face by Israel—with American blessings. . . . The situation is hopeless. . . . The time has come for a shock. . . . Everyone has fallen asleep over the Mideast crisis. . . . The Americans have left us no other way out. . . . Everything is now being mobilized for the resumption of the battle—which is now inevitable.

Kissinger dismissed the interview as bombast, but as the spring proceeded he brooded upon the Middle East and became progressively more uneasy. Secretly he met Ismail once more, in Paris, where he sought to penetrate Egyptian suspicion with pleas for confidence.* Sadat allowed the meeting chiefly as a cover, for he had taken his decision to wage war. Sheikh Zaki al-Yamani, the Saudi Minister of Petroleum, visited Washington and hinted that the "oil weapon" might be wielded if Washington did not move the Israelis and very soon—a threat that King Faisal echoed repeatedly from Riyadh. The Jordanians had

---

*Secretary Rogers deeply resented Kissinger's new role in matters of the Middle East. With Kissinger running the rest of American foreign policy, Rogers had struggled to reserve the Middle East as his personal province—but as of 1973 Kissinger took that from him, too. An official who served both Rogers and Kissinger told me that their relationship revealed "all the shabby traits of Henry's character—his secretiveness, suspiciousness, and vindictiveness. Henry wasn't content to undermine Bill's authority in every area of policy for intellectual reasons alone. Sometimes he did it just for laughs. It would make a great novel—or maybe a musical comedy. Rogers never really knew what hit him."

not tired of warning Kissinger that war was imminent. Kissinger confided to an eminent foreign correspondent that "the Israelis' intransigence is leading them to disaster." Nevertheless he thought he had time—as he had had time with Chou En-lai to repair relations with China, with Le Duc Tho to negotiate peace in Vietnam. Peace was a long and subtle quest, impervious to deadlines. Besides, Watergate was inching in on Nixon, shrinking his domestic power base and crippling his will to make decisions. Kissinger plunged into preparations for the summit meeting with Brezhnev, who in Washington that June seemed to agree with Nixon that the Middle East was not urgent. The summer of 1973 ensued with Watergate, an American veto of a resolution in the Security Council calling for complete Israeli withdrawal from the conquered territories, and drift.

In September, Kissinger replaced Rogers as Secretary of State (retaining as well his control of the National Security Council), thereby concluding his long intrigue against that forthright and ingenuous public servant. The General Assembly convened at the United Nations; on September 26, Kissinger called a press conference. His remarks on the Middle East read in retrospect like a self-fulfilling prophecy turned inside out, not only ironic but rather funny. "It is important," he said, "that foreign policy ... not be identified with one individual or virtuoso performances. . . . With respect to the Middle East, it would be a great mistake to assume that any one man can pull a rabbit out of the hat. . . . You cannot expect—and no one should ask us—to produce all the formulas and all the will as a substitute for that of the other parties."

Whilst in New York, Kissinger invited the Arab foreign ministers to lunch. The Arabs quarreled amongst themselves whether to accept, but in the end only the Libyans, the Iraqis, and the Southern Yemenis refused the invitation. Kissinger hitherto had avoided Arabs as best he could, and now was ill at ease because he fancied that his Jewishness might prejudice the dialogue. He decided to remove this barrier with a joke. "I recognize," he told his guests, "that many of you view me with suspicion. This

reminds me of a story which corresponds to our situation. The
Communists called a rally, and the police infiltrated it with an
informer. Then the police broke in and beat everybody up. The
informer protested and said, 'I'm the *anti*-Communist!' The
police said, 'We don't care what kind of a Communist you are—
you're under arrest!' "

Half the Arabs understood this as Kissinger's subtle way of
poking fun at his own Jewishness, of assuring them he was not a
Zionist, and they laughed. The other half had no idea of what he
was talking about. Anyway, he deflated the tension. "The problem of the Middle East is a complex one," he continued. "The
United States recognizes that it involves a legitimate concern for
security on one side and for justice on the other. Resolution 242
has many elements, but it is difficult and not practical to impose
theoretical and comprehensive formulas on the Middle East.
The problem should be approached gradually, piece by piece."
Already he had embraced the Rogers method; he had never
opposed it as such, only linking it explicitly to a defined final
settlement. He concluded by offering his friendship to the Arab
world. "We recognize that the present situation is intolerable to
the Arabs."

In chitchat during luncheon, Kissinger implied he would
launch a new American initiative before the end of 1973, not
dissimilar in rubric from those of Rogers, probably with Sisco
shuttling between the parties. Kissinger's style impressed the
foreign ministers. Nixon had never acknowledged that the Arabs
were seeking justice; no Anglo-Saxon secretary of state had displayed such warmth—*Semitic* warmth. Understandably pleased
with his performance, Kissinger left the luncheon confident he
had several months to come up with something.

The fourth Arab-Israeli war began less than a fortnight later.

Insofar as the United States contributed to causing it, the
errors of American policy can be identified primarily with two
men, for they alone possessed the power to have acted
otherwise—Richard Nixon and Henry Kissinger. Nixon's was
the higher responsibility; if as president he truly wished a set-

tlement, Kissinger as his resourceful servant would have wracked his brains and worked for one. True, Kissinger was a neophyte in the Middle East; his guilt was mitigated by his inexperience. But he was clearly culpable of neglect, vapid promises, and dubious strategical conceptions.

# 3

# Strike with Your Sword
# ... and Draw Honey

The October war was a surprise to Dr. Kissinger—and to Israel—though it should not have been. For a fortnight beforehand, American spy satellites, the Central Intelligence Agency, monitoring stations of the National Security Council, Israeli intelligence itself, kept feeding Kissinger evidence of Arab military preparations along the Suez and Syrian fronts. He did not ignore the evidence. Like the Israelis, and like the C.I.A., he misinterpreted it. Like the Israelis, and like the C.I.A., he assumed that the Arabs were too aware of their own technological inferiority—and of Israel's invincibility—to venture an attack.

Kissinger knew that the Russians had increased their shipments of MIG-21 jet fighters and T-62 tanks to the Syrians and the Egyptians, but he assumed that the movements on both fronts were defensive in purpose. The Egyptians had announced they were engaged in "autumn maneuvers." The Syrians deployed their SAMs closer to the Golan front, but the Israelis had shot down 13 Syrian MIGs in mid-September, and such precautions were not astonishing. Palestinian guerillas had kidnapped some Russian Jews in Austria in late September, and the Austrians had capitulated to their demand to restrict such Jews en route to Israel; this enraged the Israelis. In sum, Kissinger fancied that the Syrian and Egyptian armies were simply endeavoring to preclude retaliatory attacks on Cairo or Damascus or raids upon Palestinian bases. In fact, he feared that Israel might start a war, and he warned the Israelis that, if they did, they could not count upon American support.

Kissinger's warnings to Israel echoed those of General de Gaulle to Abba Eban, the Israeli foreign minister, in 1967 on the eve of the Six-Day War. "Don't make war," de Gaulle imperiously advised Eban. *"Vous serez considéré l'agresseur par le monde et par moi-même.* [You will be considered the aggressor by the world and by me.] *Vous allez faire entrer l'Union Sovietique plus profondément au Proche Orient, et Israël subira les conséquences.* [You will cause the Soviet Union to penetrate more deeply into the Middle East, and Israel will suffer the consequences.] *Vous allez créer le nationalisme palestinien, et ce nationalisme vous ne pourrez plus jamais vous en débarrasser.* [You will create a Palestinian nationalism, and you will never get rid of it.]" De Gaulle's warning was prophetic, but France was a second-rate power, and the Israelis ignored it. The United States was a first-rate power—Israel's fountainhead—and Kissinger's warning they could not ignore.

On October 4, the Russians hastily withdrew hundreds of their dependents from Cairo and Damascus. The omens of war loomed larger the next day, but though he was disturbed, Kissinger continued to misread them. During the darkness of that night, it dawned on the Israelis that Egypt and Syria were about to attack. Only then did the Israelis begin to mobilize—they did not "preempt" as in 1967 because of Kissinger's warning and above all because they were confident they could swiftly repel the Arabs on both fronts. Kissinger did not recognize that the war was imminent until two hours before it started, when he was awakened by worried aides at six o'clock in the morning in his suite at the Waldorf Towers in New York. Frantically he contacted the Russians, the Israelis, the Egyptians, and President Nixon, who was on holiday in Florida. But it was too late. The Arabs attacked at eight o'clock New York time—two in the afternoon on the Suez Canal—on the tenth day of Ramadan, the Moslem month of fasting, in the middle of Yom Kippur, the Jewish day of atonement, Saturday October 6.

Kissinger hastened back to Washington, as certain as the CIA that the Israelis would win the war swiftly. The Arabs, he thought, had made a wild mistake. For on the eve of the war he had won Israeli consent, and he fancied he had Egyptian concurrence (from Mohammed al-Zayyat, the foreign minister, then in New York) to begin "proximity talks" in November. Perplexed and angry, for several days he complained constantly to his aides of "irrational Arabs," "demented Arabs," and of the Arabs' "romanticism which leads them to impossible expectations." Convinced that Israel would crush Egypt, he feared that the Soviet Union would intervene, forcing the United States to intervene on the side of Israel and risking a war of the great powers.

On October 8 and 9, however, Kissinger's views began to change. After initial success on the Golan Heights, the Syrians were beginning to falter, but the Egyptians had crossed the Suez Canal, destroyed the Bar-Lev line, and now were entrenched several miles deep inside the Sinai desert. The Israelis had lost numerous tanks and aircraft, along with the legend of their invincibility; Kissinger was amongst the first to sense that the strategic balance was shifting away from them. He had no mind to restore it straightaway, because he recognized instinctively that the new balance tendered him an exquisite chance to use the war as an extension of diplomacy. If he allowed neither side to win decisively, then he might manipulate the result to launch negotiations, and—ultimately—to compose the Arab-Israeli quarrel. All of Kissinger's ensuing moves must be understood in this perspective.

Soon after the war began Kissinger proposed a cease-fire on

the lines of October 5, the *status quo ante*, partly because he foresaw the Israelis marching upon Cairo and Damascus, and he did not want that. As the war unfolded and it became clear that the Egyptians could retain their grip on territory, he attempted instead a cease-fire in place which would have enabled them to stay where they stood and negotiate thereafter from a position of strength and restored dignity. But Sadat believed he could go on winning; in retrospect he blundered badly by not stopping the war whilst he was still ahead. His alliance with the Syrians, however, constrained him to help them by keeping his own front active.

Much has been written about Dr. Kissinger's role in the re-supply of arms to Israel during the October war; he has been variously portrayed as a hero, valiantly struggling to overcome the obstructions of the Pentagon, and as a villain, malevolently playing games with Israel's fate. The evidence disavows such polemical interpretations. In keeping with his early perception that the war must be used to promote a settlement, Kissinger decided to withhold major deliveries to Israel so long as the Russians exercised restraint and so long as he hoped that Sadat would accept a cease-fire in place. Not only did he perceive an important opening to Egypt, he wished to prevent an oil embargo and a torrent of violent anti-American reprisals throughout the Arab world. Therefore early during the war Kissinger and Nixon devised a stratagem that became the source of many subsequent polemics. Nixon told the Pentagon to "play tough," to appear to impede major deliveries to Israel until such time as he and Kissinger determined otherwise. Neither Nixon nor Kissinger intended to be rushed by the Israelis, and both of them coveted the credit amongst American Jews should later circumstance constrain them to unleash an airlift. Secretary of Defense James R. Schlesinger, whose role in the matter was peripheral, later admitted as much: "There was a cover story in that period—that the source of resistance [to the airlift] was to be the Pentagon. This story was basically to protect the realities of national policy."

By the third day of the war, Israel began pressing for new provisions. Nixon authorized the release of some minor items to be sent clandestinely, and a few aircraft, but otherwise stuck to the cover story. The crisis with the Israelis intensified on October 10, when it became obvious that the war might drag on for weeks, but Kissinger persisted in blaming the Pentagon for obstructing major deliveries—the better to prevent Simcha Dinitz, the Israeli ambassador, from mobilizing American Jews against the administration. Dinitz swallowed Kissinger's protestations that the Pentagon bureaucracy was at fault, and held back his "shock troops" (Kissinger's description).

Kissinger was trying now to achieve the cease-fire in place; the Israelis angrily accepted it on October 12, and were rewarded with a slight crescendo of supplies. Sadat refused the cease-fire on October 13, the day the Soviet airlift to Egypt and Syria assumed major dimensions. We know now that many of the Russian planes were more than half empty, but American radar screens could not detect that. The Soviet airlift provoked Kissinger to cast his stratagem aside and release immense quantities of arms to Israel. He was resolved not so much to rescue Israel as to teach the Russians a hard lesson. For now this was not (to him) a conflict between Jews and Arabs; it was a test of wills between Washington and the Kremlin. In this, Kissinger reverted to his (and Nixon's) chronic obsession that Russian guns must never be permitted to prevail over the guns of the United States. Thus in the end American deliveries to Israel substantially exceeded those of Moscow to the Arabs, proving to the Russians—and to the world—America's physical capacity in crisis and the peril of seeking to challenge the United States in the Middle East or anywhere.

On October 17, two days after Kissinger unleashed the airlift, four Arab foreign ministers—Omar al-Saqqaf of Saudi Arabia, Abdul Aziz Bouteflika of Algeria, and their colleagues from Kuwait and Morocco—called at the White House. The ministers had been delegated to speak for the Arab countries in concert; they were tense, visibly apprehensive, as Kissinger received them in his office in the west wing. Kissinger acknowledged that the United States had paid insufficient attention to the problems of the Middle East. "We should have done more diplomatically," he confessed. "We recognize that this crisis is rooted in the lack of progress. You have made your point. The President and I will be more active as soon as the war ends. We shall undertake a major diplomatic effort. I shall personally conduct it. Of course, substantive progress will take time. As in our opening to China, many steps will be necessary. Our object is not to elaborate abstract principles—that would tie us all in knots. We will do better to concentrate on areas of agreement, to embark upon a process of accommodation and see where it leads.... Any cease-fire that would now take place would have to take into account the efficiency and valor of Arab arms.... We recognize the new realities in the Middle East." Whatever the new realities, the war had not altered Kissinger's philosophy of negotiations.

Saqqaf responded with the customary Arab plea for the implementation of Resolution 242, for the recovery of Arab and Palestinian rights, for the espousal by the United States of "a just and evenhanded policy." If the Arabs were angry about Kissinger's airlift, they were too polite—or too embarrassed—to press the point. This puzzled Kissinger. He turned to Bouteflika, all five feet of him, shod in Gucci boots, brandishing an immense cigar, his head cocked to his interpreter, who whispered incessantly in French. Kissinger had never met this North African zealot. "I know Your Excellency by reputation," he said. "I expected him to be more militant." Beneath his black moustache, Bouteflika simply smiled. "Please excuse me," Kissinger continued. "I must go to see the President. We're not used to dealing with reasonable Arabs." (Laughter.)

Kissinger briefed the President, and in ten minutes returned to escort the ministers into the Oval Office. Nixon rambled. Much as he had with Hafez Ismail, he evoked his pleasurable visitations to Araby. "When I was in your country... when I toured your country...." He reaffirmed Kissinger's philosophy of negotiation, and added, "We are not going to be constrained by domestic politics. We'll formulate our foreign policy on the basis of our national interests."

The Arab states proclaimed their oil embargo the same day. Two days later, on October 19, Nixon asked Congress for $2.2 billion in arms for Israel.

Even before the great airlift reached them, the Israelis were beginning to prevail in battle, not only pushing the Syrians back toward Damascus but destroying hundreds of Sadat's tanks in a single day. On October 15, the Israelis crossed the canal below Ismailia on the western bank, then later upon the eastern bank began to encircle Egypt's Third Army. On October 16, Soviet Premier Alexei Kosygin flew to Cairo for three days, with instructions to talk Sadat into ending the war. On October 20, Kissinger flew to Moscow, where he negotiated with the Russians the terms of Security Council Resolution 338, which called for an immediate cease-fire in place, the implementation of Resolution 242 in all of its parts, and immediate negotiations between the parties to establish "a just and durable peace in the Middle East"* The resolution was adopted at the United Nations on October 22, though the hostilities raged for several days more as the Israelis maneuvered to destroy the Third Army.

Kissinger had no intention to allow the Israelis to conclude the war with a smashing conquest. That would have disgraced the Egyptians as in 1967 and demolished the prospect of productive negotiation. Supported by the President, Kissinger applied intense pressure upon Israel to desist.

General Moshe Dayan, then the Israeli minister of defense, in subsequent speeches and interviews described this major crisis with Washington which foreshadowed further crises to come:

The Americans, in order to smooth the way with the Arabs, confronted us with an ultimatum to the effect that, if we would not enable the Third Army to receive food and water, we would find ourselves in a political conflict with them [the Americans]. . . .

*The text of Resolution 338, together with related resolutions 339 and 340, will be found in Appendix Three.

SMITH*: . . . You charged that the United States threatened . . . to fly supplies in to relieve the encircled Third Army if Israel refused to allow food and water through the lines. What actually happened there?

DAYAN: The United States moved in and denied us the fruits of victory. It was an ultimatum—nothing short of it. Had the United States not pressed us, the Third Army and Suez City would have had to surrender. We would have captured thirty thousand to forty thousand soldiers and Sadat would have had to admit it to his people. We might only have held them for a day and let them walk out without their arms, but it would have changed the whole Egyptian attitude about whether they had won or lost the war. It would have given us more cards in the practical negotiations.

SMITH: Would the Soviets really have intervened, as the Americans said they would at the time?

DAYAN: I don't think so. Not over the Third Army. If we had tried to take Cairo or Aswan, yes. Do you remember the U.S. alert on October 24th? [The Americans] thought the Soviets were going to land an airborne division near Cairo and link up with the Egyptians to try to drive us from the west bank of the canal. The Soviets were worried about Cairo and Aswan, not saving the Third Army.

During this crisis, Nixon and Kissinger warned Mrs. Meir they would suspend deliveries of American arms if the Israelis pursued their assault on the Third Army. Though no "contingency plan" for that purpose had been ordered, Kissinger did indeed threaten to send in food and medicine to the Third Army (by American helicopters) if Israel did not allow the Egyptians to establish their own relief corridor.

On October 24, an urgent message was handed to Kissinger in Washington from Soviet Party Chairman Leonid Brezhnev proposing a joint Soviet-American expeditionary force to save the Third Army. If the United States declined, Brezhnev warned, then the Soviet Union would intervene unilaterally. Already the Russians were marshaling airborne divisions. The message was intimidating, but Kissinger overreacted. He prevailed upon

*Terence Smith, correspondent in Israel of *The New York Times*, in an interview with Dayan published January 26, 1975.

Nixon to promulgate a "low" worldwide alert of American forces, including the nuclear-equipped Strategic Air Command. The Pentagon hastily prepared a plan to fly American troops to the battle zone to confront Soviet forces, then abandoned it six hours later as the crisis eased.

The "nuclear alert" appeared at the time to be a *deus ex machina* to divert attention from the domestic crisis of Watergate, but in truth it was part of the elaborate game Dr. Kissinger was playing with the Russians, the Israelis, and the Egyptians. In subsequent conversations with aides, Kissinger sought to justify his decision by calling it "our *deliberate* over-reaction." He had warned the Russians throughout the war that the United States would not tolerate an intervention of Soviet troops. The American alert dramatized the point. But the alert was aimed at Israel as well—to manifest emphatically that, whilst Washington would not countenance this Russian threat to shed Israeli blood, Israel must reciprocate by accepting American political imperatives and sparing the Third Army. Within a day, the Russians backed off. So did the Israelis—and the Third Army was spared.

Thus the war ended in deadlock—just as Kissinger had planned—with neither victor nor vanquished.

The October war revealed Dr. Kissinger at the apogee of his skill. Propelled by the vehemence of events, he recognized very early the paradoxical opportunities for peace, and he pursued peace without bending to the Russians, abandoning Israel, or irrevocably alienating the Arabs. More secretive than ever, he took care to insure that he alone was kept informed of all aspects of the conflict and that he alone was in communication with all of the parties—Israelis and Arabs, Russians, West Europeans and everyone else. For ten days he was deeply anxious, but by the eleventh day he had snatched control of events. With Nixon enmeshed in scandal (Vice-President Spiro Agnew's resignation and the Watergate "Saturday Night Massacre" took place at this time), Kissinger was in real measure running the world. His delay in releasing the airlift, his decision to save the Third Army, contributed to peace, and in so acting he—and Nixon—served the higher interest of the American republic.

True, the airlift, when it came, provoked the Arab oil embargo. Nixon's request to Congress on October 19 for the $2.2 billion in aid to Israel intensified the embargo. But these distasteful consequences were outweighed in Kissinger's calculations by the need to manifest to the Kremlin the constancy of American might. True, the airlift and the nuclear alert imposed severe strain upon the Atlantic alliance, just as the embargo made oil paupers of the Europeans. But the airlift did not burn Kissinger's bridges to Sadat; hardly a fortnight after it began, Sadat announced to the world press that American policy was "constructive." This statement, so much at variance with Nasser's vindictive accusations in 1967—and no doubt influenced by Kissinger's decision to save the Third Army—was the psychological breakthrough that Kissinger sought, a clear signal from Cairo that Sadat was aching to strike a bargain with the United States. In fact throughout the war, even with American weapons flooding into Israel and the Sinai, Kissinger marveled at the mildness of the Arab reaction—except for the embargo, no confiscations, no riots, no reprisals against American interests of any sort.

Sadat had concluded before the war was done that, though America remained the arsenal of his enemy, it wished also to be his friend; that the Russians could deliver arms but not peace; that for peace he needed the United States. There is an Arab saying, "*Adrub biseef wa taghada bil asal*" (Strike with your sword, and draw honey). Sadat had not drawn honey, but by waging war he had finally seized Dr. Kissinger's fascinated attention.

# 4

# An Arab Policy

"I never treat crises when they're cold," Dr. Kissinger once told a friend, "only when they're hot. This enables me to weigh the protagonists one against the other, not in terms of ten or two thousand years ago but in terms of what each of them merits at this moment." He meant, in particular, the Middle East, and his principle was put to a dangerous test on the morrow of the October war. Both Israelis and Egyptians expected Kissinger to rescue them from the impasse he had helped to contrive as the conclusion of that conflict.

The armies of Israel and Egypt were chaotically intertwined; the Egyptians still held fast in the northern sector of the Suez Canal's eastern bank, but in the south their Third Army was surrounded; on the western bank, the Israelis had thrust to within 60 miles of Cairo and had encircled the city of Suez. Sadat was demanding an immediate Israeli retreat to the lines of October 22 (as required by Security Council Resolution 338), then a peace conference to arrange total Israeli withdrawal from all of the Arab territories. Prime Minister Golda Meir, claiming that the October 22 lines were impossible to establish, demanded an immediate return to the lines of October 5, and a swift exchange of prisoners. The cease-fire threatened to collapse.

At the end of October, President Nixon invited Golda Meir to Washington; Sadat sent Dr. Ismail Fahmy, his irrepressible new foreign minister, without waiting for an invitation. As it happened, this enabled Kissinger to try his hand at instant mediation; he shuttled indefatigably between Fahmy at the State Department and Mrs. Meir at Blair House, though without palpable result. Fahmy insisted on the October 22 lines, Mrs. Meir upon her prisoners. Moreover, though the Israelis had desisted from destroying the Third Army, they still had not allowed a relief corridor.

At his first meeting with Kissinger, Dr. Fahmy observed that, as a result of the war, the United States and Egypt had reached a new "crossroads." Kissinger agreed, then explained his predominant problems—to preserve the cease-fire "and to get negotiations started. We have to reach beyond the cease-fire to an overall settlement"—as envisioned in Resolution 338. Quibbling with the Israelis over the lines of the cease-fire would impede rather than promote negotiations, he argued. Moreover "continuing [Arab] pressures on us—particularly the oil [embargo]—will make a settlement more difficult. We must create a certain confidence in each other. If there is no trust, the basis of our relationship will disappear. We will need confidence because it will take a long time to achieve a settlement. If we're threatened and criticized and pressured by the Arabs, we won't be able to convince our people that we should cooperate with the Arabs—we will have no support at home for this policy. . . . I'm the 'miracle man,' you think. Vietnam, you think. Remember, it took me four years of preparation to achieve a settlement in Vietnam, and two and a half years to prepare our opening to Peking. We need a long-range strategy."

Fahmy kept insisting—for such were his instructions from Sadat—on an Israeli retreat to the lines of October 22; he said the same to Nixon when Kissinger took him to the White House.

Fahmy's mission accomplished little of substance, but it did establish a new style in Arab-American relations. Before photographers and television cameras, Kissinger embraced the voluble, balding foreign minister—the first of many endearments he was to exchange publicly with the Arabs. Kissinger also drew up a working draft which provided in part for relief of the Third Army and an exchange of prisoners, and then, on November 5, flew off to the Middle East to deal with the belligerents on the scene.

He paused, en route, in Morocco and Tunisia to render his respects to King Hassan II and to President Habib ben Ali Bourguiba, but Cairo was the focus of his quest. Dr. Kissinger had been before to Israel but never to any part of Araby. Anwar Sadat, whose acquaintance he was about to make, he had long considered a bombastic clown. He could be pardoned for that assumption, for it corresponded—until the war—with the assessment of numerous Egyptians. President Gamal Abdel Nasser, whose own pigment was only faintly lighter, was reputed in his lifetime to have called Sadat "that black donkey." Little in Sadat's previous career appeared to have prepared him for the presidency of Egypt or for the sublime ordeal of matching wits with Henry Kissinger.

Sadat was a *fellah,* a peasant of the Nile delta, the son of a Sudanese mother who told me 20 years ago that "the West hates the Arabs because we are colored." He consumed much of his early life conspiring against the British domination of Egypt. As a boy of ten in his village of Mit Abu al Kom in the Nile delta, he discovered the works of Mahatma Gandhi; soon he could recite chapter and verse of British despotism not only in Egypt but, eastward across the Euphrates to beyond the Hindu Kush. "When he was still in primary school," his sister Sekina told me once, "Anwar began dressing up in a white sheet like Gandhi, and he would walk through the village leading a goat on a string. Then he would go and sit under a tree, pretending he did not want to eat."

Later, the Sadat family moved to the Kubri al Kubbeh quarter in Cairo, where Anwar turned to violence and attempts at terrorism. "In the middle of the night," Sekina remembered, "British troops and King Farouk's political police came crashing into our house, hurling us out of our beds, breaking furniture and crockery, tearing the place to pieces. They weren't at all nice. They were looking for Anwar."

That was during World War II. Sadat had graduated with Gamal Abdel Nasser from the Egyptian Military College at Abbassieh in 1938. They served together, upon graduation, at the same military post at Mankabad on the banks of the Upper Egyptian Nile, and nourished a common dream of a modern Egypt free of British bondage and a corrupt king. But if Nasser was cautious and brooding, Sadat was impulsive and bloodthirsty. By 1941, Sadat was concocting elaborate plots to expel the British army from Egypt.

In Cairo he consorted with the anti-British Sheikh Hassan al-Banna, Supreme Guide of the fanatical Moslem Brotherhood, and with General Aziz al-Masri, the former chief of staff of the Egyptian Army who had been sacked at the bidding of Winston Churchill. Twice Sadat tried to smuggle General Masri through to the German lines in the Sahara (where Masri was to advise the Germans how to outflank the British), but on the first endeavor the general's car broke down, and on the second his airplane crashed at takeoff. Sadat's subsequent intrigues with a pair of German spies in Cairo were betrayed by a belly dancer. He was court-martialed in 1942, cashiered out of the army, and dispatched to a prison camp in Upper Egypt.

He escaped, demanded an audience with the king, was recaptured, and escaped again—hiding out all over Egypt and in the teeming mosques of Cairo till the termination of the war. By that time he was demanding that Nasser's clandestine Free Officers movement adopt terrorism as a political tool, and he pleaded with Nasser for permission to blow up the British embassy. Nasser refused, but to keep Sadat happy he appointed him the head of a civilian auxiliary. Sadat then plotted to assassinate several pro-British politicans. He bungled an attempt on the life of Mustafa Nahas Pasha in 1945, but a year later some of his companions murdered Amin Osman Pasha, a former minister of finance, for declaring that the bond between Britain and Egypt was "as unbreakable as a Catholic marriage." Sadat was arrested for complicity, and sent back to prison. There he systematically improved his education; he improved his English, learned to speak German and Persian, and to read French. Released in 1948, he worked variously as a taxi driver, a baggage porter, journalist, short-story writer, a dealer in used tires, and almost became destitute.

Through the intercession of King Farouk's physician, Sadat's army commission was restored in 1950. He was ordered to act as a palace spy against suspected revolutionaries in the army, and gleefully he became a double agent, telling everything he knew not to the palace but to Nasser. By 1951, he was a lieutenant colonel and (so British intelligence has claimed) embroiled in yet another bungled plot—a mine was planted in the middle of the Suez Canal that failed to explode when a British ship bumped into it. In 1952, on the epochal night of the July 22–23 Revolution, Sadat was supposed to cut army communications in Cairo, but the signals got crossed; he took his family to the movies, and at the crucial moment Nasser could not find him.

For 18 years thereafter, beneath the shadow of his master, Sadat was a model of mediocrity and subservience. Nasser made him a member of the Revolutionary Command Council, the nation's new executive, but never entrusted him with important posts because he considered him incompetent. As editor of *Al Goumhouriya*, the government newspaper, and later as secretary-general of the Islamic Congress, Sadat composed polemics and delivered speeches so impassioned against the United States that even Nasser must have blushed.

I first met Sadat in 1956 at the Islamic Congress, a body that was intended to rally the world's 400 million Moslems to Nasser's banner but which never amounted to much. I was a young and callow journalist, very frustrated because no Egyptian official of importance deigned to receive me. "Go see Anwar

Sadat," someone said. "He'll see anybody." I found Sadat on
Zamalek island, an opulent precinct of Cairo surrounded by the
Nile, in a white villa shaded by palm trees. He was very brown,
very soft-spoken, and—I thought—very amusing. He was clad
in an immaculate white suit. "Ah, so you're a Roman Catholic?"
he asked. "Listen, I have just finished reading the four gospels of
Matthew, Mark, Luke, and John. As a result of my studies, I am
going to prove to the world that Islam and Christianity are identical. I shall leave it to the theologians to work out the details."
Sadat charmed me, but when I left the villa it was not with the
notion that I had just interviewed the next president of Egypt.

During those years of Nasser's ascendancy, Sadat developed
by degrees into an urbane, sophisticated, and—so his critics
contend—slightly venal man. Goaded by his elegant, half-
English wife, Gehan, he dressed in suits from Savile Row, dispatched his daughters to fashionable schools, honed away at the
rough edges of his character without discarding his earthy
charm. For half of him remained the village son—devoted despite his new sophistication to those millennial values of the
*fellah* that are rooted in the rhythms of prayer and hardship, in
closeness to the soil, and in the shrewdness which is the treasure
of the poor. Unlike Nasser, who grew up an urban schizoid in
Cairo and Alexandria, Sadat not only retained his roots in Mit
Abu al Kom, he returned there often to pray in the village
mosque, to mingle with the merchants, the butchers, the beasts
and toilers of the field. "Those visits have taught me something I
shall never forget," he told me in 1956. "They taught me how to
talk to the people—and how to listen."

Some of his old brashness reerupted from time to time. As
Speaker of the National Assembly in 1961, he went to Moscow,
where he engaged in a shouting match with Nikita Khrushchev
when Khrushchev attacked him for Nasser's persecution of
Egyptian Communists. The incident caused international re-
criminations, and provoked Sadat to observe that "even in
Moscow the Russians live like pigs." He meddled in the
Yemen—first urging Nasser to intervene in its civil war, and

then opposing the peace settlement he had himself helped to negotiate with Saudi Arabia in 1965. He made demagogic speeches in 1969, vowing that the army would cross the Suez Canal to push the Israelis out of Sinai, and vehemently he opposed the Rogers peace initiative before Nasser embraced it in 1970.

Nevertheless, Sadat mellowed and matured during his long years under Nasser's restraining hand. He traveled widely, all over the Moslem world, to America and Mongolia, and to so many remote corners of Egypt itself that he came to know his people more deeply than Nasser ever did. But he took pains never to stray too far from Nasser's shadow. Other Free Officers were falling from Nasser's favor because they belonged to cliques and aspired to power for themselves; Sadat never made that mistake. He eschewed the intrigues that flourished around the President, and—whatever his true opinion of Nasser's policies—kept his mouth shut. "*Sayed Nam*"—Mr. Yes—Nasser called him. "The Revolution," so the saying goes, "devours its own children." Not so with Anwar Sadat, since Nasser rewarded him, not with power, but with longevity. More naturally sly than Nasser, more preternaturally Egyptian, Sadat had learned that in politics patience can be as sharp a tool as cunning. In 1968, near the end of his life, Nasser named Sadat Vice-President of Egypt. It is the Sadats of this world who invariably survive—and succeed their masters.

But when Sadat succeeded Nasser in 1970, it did not seem he would survive for long. His rivals assumed he was a halfwit. This seemed to serve his purpose. Nasser had bequeathed to Egypt not only Anwar Sadat, but his goons as well. Nasser's goons—Presidential Affairs Minister Sami Sharaf, Interior Minister Sharawi Gomaa, *et al.*—gripped the rods of power in their own hands, particularly the pervasive intelligence apparatus, and they expected Sadat to do what they told him.

The Sharaf-Gomaa cabal considered themselves the rightful rulers of Egypt after Nasser's death. They were his younger heirs, and they wanted done with the old Free Officers such as

Sadat. While Nasser lived they were his tools ("Show me ten men I can trust," he used to say) and constantly he played off one against the other, keeping a black book of their misdeeds (they were nearly all corrupt) and even of their erotic escapades.* Now Sharaf and Gomaa were resolved to keep the intelligence apparatus beyond Sadat's grasp. Sadat made no move against them; he ignored them at first, and concentrated instead on building an alternative power base. He cut prices, eased restrictions, cultivated the press, the universities, the judiciary, the technocracy, and—above all—the army.

On radio and television Sadat spoke softly in vernacular Arabic, radiated rustic charm, and began to acquire charisma. The values he invoked were not visions of a Marxist utopia but the verities of the Egyptian village—above all, belief in God. As he gradually became more popular, he embarked on tiny probing operations of the intelligence apparatus, not daring yet to dismiss Sharaf and Gomaa, but insinuating one spy here, another there, the better to be informed of whatever their machinations. He embraced the Rogers initiative, invited Rogers to Cairo for conversations that we know led nowhere. Then, seven months after he succeeded Nasser, provoked by plots

*Nasser's suspiciousness bordered upon the pathological. He loved to terrify his underlings with displays of his intimate knowledge of their movements. My favorite story about him (possibly apocryphal, but it illustrates his character) involves a visit he made to Syria when he was president of that country during the unsuccessful Syrian-Egyptian union of 1958–61.

The drama department of Damascus University was staging *Macbeth*—in English—and invited the President to attend. Nasser accepted, and out of necessity most of Syrian officialdom (which, of course, could not speak English) showed up for the performance. The players waited for an hour, but still the President did not come. Finally, they began the performance without him. Close to the final act, Nasser walked in. The players rang down the curtain, and repeated the performance—from the beginning. A minor official at the rear of the hall (who had never met Nasser) slipped out in the darkness and went home to bed.

A year later, Nasser returned to Damascus. During a vast reception, attended by hundreds, the minor official was presented to the President. Nasser gazed at the man with blazing eyes, and said, "Ah. *Macbeth*—remember? Why did you walk out on me?"

amongst the goons (they were about to overthrow him), he *pounced*—turning the government on its head, packing Sami Sharaf and Sharawi Gomaa and all his other rivals off to jail.

This was, as I wrote then, "a marvel of political craftsmanship, a masterly lesson of how to proceed, step by modest step, from impotence to supreme power." But it did not solve any of Sadat's external problems. By the time of Nasser's death it had become obvious to any lucid Egyptian that the two pillars of Nasserist policy—Arab socialism and dependence upon the Soviet Union—had failed. Sadat knew that Egypt needed a new policy, but in struggling to concoct it he could not get anyone outside of Egypt—particularly the United States—to take him seriously. Dr. Kissinger, as we have noted, in practice ignored Sadat's dramatic cries for help and clung to his cozy theory that the only strategic ally he needed in the Middle East was Israel. But now the war had shattered that supposition, and as his aircraft turned from the Mediterranean to descend to the Nile delta, Dr. Kissinger no less than Sadat himself was in search of a new policy.

Their first encounter, on November 7, 1973—simply because it happened—was the food of history. Kissinger was apprehensive, for he was as dissimilar to Sadat as Talleyrand was to Wellington. Indeed, what greater contrast can we fancy than this plump Jewish professor in rumpled blue, and the lean, brown, erstwhile terrorist in khaki who welcomed him amid the gilded armchairs of Tahra Palace? Kissinger had brought Sisco and several other senior aides, but only to confer in the garden with Sadat's subordinates. Sadat he saved for himself; without even a note taker, the two of them retired to talk *tête-à-tête* for several hours.

Kissinger was touched at once by Sadat's urbanity and charm; Sadat liked Kissinger's incisiveness, so refreshing after the naïveté of Rogers. Besides, Kissinger possessed what Rogers never had—*power*. However, the reports of their instant romance (soon to be dramatized by their public kissing) have been exaggerated. Essentially we glimpse a pair of foxes, exchanging oaths of confidence, each of them intent on manipulating the other for his own purpose. Sadat, who considers himself a strategic thinker, stressed his wish to work with the United States, and he did not fail to evoke his hostility to the Soviet Union. He was to elaborate on the Russians in future meetings, but even now he urged that America and Egypt pursue a "common strategy" in the Middle East. They spoke of the peace conference, under joint Soviet and American auspices, envisioned by Resolution 338; Sadat urged a role for the Palestinians. Kissinger replied he would try to arrange some form of Palestinian participation—a significant departure from previous American indifference to the central place of the Palestinians in the Arab-Israeli conflict. The swiftest way to peace, Sadat went on, was a swift implementation of Resolution 242, meaning a swift Israeli withdrawal from all of Sinai. This was, of course, a maximal position, but Sadat imagined then that Kissinger could accomplish it, if not at once, in six months or a year at most. No longer, Sadat warned, would Egypt be put off with vague American promises.

Kissinger replied, "Look, I am a serious person. I shall keep what I can promise, but I shan't promise what I can't keep. If you expect from me broad and sweeping declarations, then I'm not your man." If Sadat persisted in voicing his demands in the ultimate language of Resolution 242, Kissinger continued, then the Israelis would not move an inch. Hinting that he sympathized with Sadat's objective of reclaiming all of Sinai, just as he sympathized with Israel's insistence on security, he defined the final goal as "mutually agreed borders"—a concept that could accommodate eventually Egypt's demand for sovereignty and Israel's for security. The ways and means to reconcile the two would be worked out in the peace conference, but there would never be a conference if Egypt insisted on a commitment from Israel for total withdrawal before negotiations started.

Furthermore Sadat had to understand the delicacy of Kissinger's domestic problems. Kissinger recognized that Sadat had to cope with internal pressures from the Egyptian army. The Israeli leaders suffered from similar internal pressures, and Kissinger was obliged to deal with a powerful Jewish lobby in the

United States. Kissinger could not be perceived as applying
pressure on Israel, though he was doing all he could to persuade
the Israelis to be reasonable. Sadat must not expect him to
mount pressure upon the Israelis in public—they would be all
the more obstinate if they felt Washington were forcing them to
the wall.

"We must put aside irreconcilables for the moment," Kissinger said, referring to the peace conference. "We must build
confidence, conceive a negotiating dynamic. We must set in
motion small agreements. We must proceed step by step."

But how was that possible, Sadat wondered, when the Israelis
wouldn't even return to the lines of October 22? "Nobody knows
where the lines of October 22nd are," Kissinger retorted. "If I
spend my capital with Israel on every point of the cease-fire,
there won't be any left for the peace conference. Look, instead
of wasting time on the October 22nd lines, why don't we try for
something bigger?" If Sadat would give him a few more weeks,
Kissinger would try to negotiate a "disengagement" of the armies along the Suez Canal. He would try to move the Israelis off
the western bank, then away from the canal and deeper into
Sinai.

Sadat puffed at his pipe and brooded. He was under intense
pressure in his own camp to rescue Suez and the Third Army;
each hour counted. Fahmy had been adamant, but now Sadat
overruled Fahmy and himself, and accepted Kissinger's proposition. This decision was crucial. It became the basis of their
friendship and the foundation of future American policy; it was
at that moment Kissinger decided he was dealing not with a
clown, but with a statesman. Moreover, Sadat accepted Kissinger's draft of six points, providing for a relief corridor to Suez and
the Third Army, to be followed by a full exchange of prisoners.
The modalities were to be determined by direct military talks
between Israelis and Egyptians at Kilometer 101, the point on
the Suez road where the Israelis sat entrenched, an hour's drive
from Cairo's gates. Sisco would leave forthwith for Israel, to win
Golda Meir's acquiescence. Finally, they agreed ("in principle")

to reestablish full diplomatic relations, suspended by Nasser during the Six-Day War.

The conversation was very cordial and very tough. The Egyptians claim that weaving through the dialogue, like a barely visible thread, was Kissinger's implied threat that he would unleash the Israelis on the Third Army if Sadat did not defer to his suggestions.

When Dr. Kissinger emerged from Tahra Palace, it was with something the United States had never really possessed before—an Arab policy. Its essence was a commitment to the Arabs that, so long as they understood the United States would not abandon Israel, Washington would truly wield its power to regain Arab rights. Henceforth Sadat was to serve as the keystone of that policy, the first recipient of whatever political, territorial, and financial favors Dr. Kissinger had the capacity to bestow. Henceforth Dr. Kissinger would undertake no initiative in the Middle East without first consulting the president of Egypt. "The enemy of my enemy is my friend," the Arab proverb says. In a single meeting Sadat had rewritten it to read, "The friend of my enemy is my friend, too."

That evening, at a dinner party at Foreign Minister Fahmy's residence overlooking the Nile, Kissinger met Mohammed Hassanein Heikal, the famous editor of *Al Ahram* who had been Nasser's gray eminence and was still (at that time) one of Sadat's closest strategic advisers. Heikal was vain, emotional, amusing, cunning, and very intelligent; his dark face and cool brown eyes exuded a self-assurance that could sometimes hint of arrogance. An exchange with Heikal was like an exchange with Kissinger. It was more than a conversation; it was an event. Kissinger's encounter with Heikal was predestined to produce a tournament of wits. On the morrow of the dinner party, Heikal composed a long account of their conversation for his weekly column in *Al Ahram*\*:

\*Kissinger subsequently denied its authenticity. In fact, at the conclusion of Miss Berger's birthday party in Jerusalem on August 23, 1975, Dr. Kissinger told me that he had only talked with Heikal for "ten minutes," and that Hei-

KISSINGER: I want to ask you about many things, because I want to know and understand from the Arab point of view more than the mere surface of the practical problems that the crisis forces on our attention. I had not yet opened the file of the Middle East crisis—I thought it would wait its turn. But the crisis has imposed itself on all, including myself, unexpectedly. In this you succeeded, and I am the first to grant you this success.

Heikal suggested that Kissinger's answer to one question was of paramount importance. What role was Kissinger representing in this crisis? In confronting previous problems, such as the Vietnam war or relations with the Soviet Union and China, Kissinger had acted on behalf of a party to the conflict. In the Middle East, however, the United States did not appear to be a direct party or even a negotiator in the conflict.

HEIKAL: You are the first to say that Israel has a will independent of the United States, and although you admit that you have a great deal of influence on her, in the end what you say means that there is a gap between the will of America and the will of Israel. You regard this area between the two wills as being extensive, and it may be that we have disagreed with you and found this area, by virtue of the closeness and the extent of the links, restricted—extremely restricted. But in any case there is an area and this area means that you are not exactly a *party* nor exactly a *negotiator*. If your role is not the role of the "other party," the "role of the negotiator," what exactly is your role? Is it the role of the "mediator"? Again, I do not think so—indeed I am sure not. The role of mediator requires neutrality between the two parties—or at least that the two parties should feel that this neutrality exists or could exist. We do not feel this. Your bias towards Israel needs no proof. The latest indication of it is the air and sea bridge which is bringing arms and ammunition from the United States to Israel. So you are not and

kal's "interview" was largely a fabrication. In Cairo a fortnight later, Heikal insisted to me he had talked with Kissinger not only at Dr. Fahmy's but that Kissinger had taken him back to his suite at the Nile Hilton, where they conversed "for at least another hour and a half." Who of the two was the more veracious, I cannot judge. I am reproducing Heikal's version of their dialogue in this book for a compelling reason: two of Kissinger's close aides told me that it echoed very accurately Kissinger's private statements at that time.

cannot be neutral; you cannot be a mediator. Then if you are not a negotiator because you are not a direct party, and if you are not a mediator because you are not neutral—what exactly is your role? I do not ask this question out of mere curiosity but because your answer to it will settle the whole tone of the talk between us.

KISSINGER: I have asked myself this question, and if the question is important to you for setting the tone of the talk between us, it is also important to me for setting the tone of the United States' approach to the crisis. I grant that I do not represent a direct party in the crisis; your conclusion is that I am not playing the role of mediator between the two parties in the crisis. Let us say, and agree to say, that I represent the role of the "concern" of the United States for a grave crisis which is taking place in an area that is sensitive as far as we are concerned, an area in which we have strategic, political and economic interests—and security interests—and we want to protect these interests. This is in addition, of course, to our concern for world peace and our strong desire for the friendship of the peoples of this area. Let us say the following:

*One*, we have strategic interests in the area.

*Two*, the other superpower—the Soviet Union—has interests in this area.

*Three*, we are trying to establish a new world order based on détente now that the era of cold war is past, but détente will not cause us to leave the area to the influence of the other superpower.

*Four*, we do not want any crisis to escalate to the extent of affecting détente, because the danger of that would be too grave for humanity to bear.

*Five*, we have a special relationship with Israel and we are committed to protect her security, and we believe that Israel's security can only be protected by respect for your sovereignty.

*Six*, if we have a special relationship with Israel, we do not regard it as incompatible with the friendship we want to promote and consolidate with you.

*Seven*, we do not want to be, either on our own or in partnership with others, guardians of this area. What we want is that the peoples of this area should build their own system of life and security in conformity with what they see fit and in harmony with world facts.

These are the elements of our attitude, as conceived by President

Nixon, and as conceived by me, and I agree with you that I am not a "party," nor a mediator. And perhaps you will agree with me that what I represent is American "concern" with the Middle East crisis, a concern that is trying to perform its role to protect its interests without conflicting with the interests of others. I know that I am dealing with a complicated and difficult problem. I find it more difficult than the problem of Vietnam, than opening the doors of China, or than achieving détente with the Soviet Union. The problem here is packed with conflicting and explosive elements—historical, national and psychological—old and new deposits, and innumerable attitudes inspired by suspicion and fear. I took on the problem knowing what was awaiting me, knowing that I do not constitute a "party" and that I am not a "mediator"; what I do claim is that I am an expression of American concern.

I want to tell you two things about the way I deal with problems. The first thing is that I do not like to approach a problem unless I feel that its basic elements, or at least a large part of its basic elements, are in my hand. This was the case in the Vietnam war; American public opinion wanted an end to the war. This was also the case in Peking and Moscow, because the facts of the new era were going in the direction I am going in. In the Middle East crisis I cannot exactly reckon which of the basic elements of the crisis are in my hand.

The second thing is that I hate failure. I have a credit balance of success and I do not want to throw it away—and I am not talking of the Nobel Peace Prize.*

Let me tell you a story. Some of my son's schoolfellows came to him saying: "Do you know that some of our friends are saying that your father doesn't deserve the Nobel Peace Prize, and we were angry with them and told them it wasn't true." But my son said to his friends: "What does it matter? My mother said the same thing."

So my problem in the Middle East crisis is as follows: I do not have enough of the elements of the crisis in my hand, and I hate failure and do not want to fail. The consequence is that I find myself in the midst of the crisis representing American concern for it, but all I have to depend on is my personal reputation, my personal credit balance. I

*Kissinger received the announcement of his Nobel Peace Prize in October at the height of the war in the Middle East, sharing the prize with Le Duc Tho, Hanoi's representative, for negotiating the peace agreement in Vietnam.

think that in spite of the difficulty of the circumstances there is a chance of success . . . but I want time. . . . I want the parties to give me their patience. . . . I admit that I am afraid of Arab romanticism. I fear that the Arabs fancy that the solution is just round the corner. It is my belief that we need a period of between six months and a year to reach the start of something reasonable.

When I met the four Arab foreign ministers during the recent war in the Middle East, one of them said to me: The man who succeeded in solving the problem of the Vietnam war, opening the door with China, and building détente with the Soviet Union can solve the Middle East problem. I said to them: I hope you are not thinking of the last two weeks in Paris, the venue of the Vietnam negotiations, or the last days in Peking or Moscow. Those days were preceded by long years of preparation and work to enable us to reach the decisive weeks and days. I told them that it was not in my power or any one else's to work miracles, and that international politics is not a series of conjuring tricks.

Some of you in the Arab world misunderstood the proposal put forward on the day after the fighting broke out in the Middle East—my proposal that the conflicting forces should return to the positions they were in before noon on October 6th. In making this proposal I was not biased towards Israel, as it seemed to some of you. I had different ideas.

I am going to tell you the whole story. Before October 6th all our information ruled out the possibility of war breaking out, and although there were persistent reports of your mobilization, the appraisal was that the mobilization was for maneuvers, not for war. Then all our experts thought that if you started the war Israeli military force would deal you a decisive blow. When the war did start and it was established that our information was wrong we still believed that our ideas on its outcome were correct. That was when I made my proposal for a cease-fire and for the conflicting forces to return to the lines they held before the fighting started. I thought that it was in your interests rather than in Israel's. Let me put the question to you in another way. If I told you that I was thinking of your interests only, you would think that I was deceiving you, and I do not want to do that, or try to do so, because you can discover the truth. My thinking was on the following lines: The Egyptians had embarked on a dangerous adventure, perhaps driven to it by despair, but Israeli military force would now crush them without mercy. What would happen after that? Egypt would turn to the Soviet

Union to rescue her, and there were two possibilities: that the Soviet Union would intervene in a way that would oblige us to intervene too, which would confront us with a terrible possibility—us and them together; or the Soviets would not intervene but would enter Egypt in such a way that they would never leave it. This too was a possibility we did not want.

It was not a question of concern for Egypt alone. First and foremost it was a question of concern for the facts and balance of forces of this era; this is why I made my proposal for an immediate cease-fire and the return of the conflicting forces to their previous positions. Two days later there was still violent fighting in Sinai; our information about your mobilization for war had been wrong, and it is clear that our ideas about your ability for war had also been wrong. I asked for the Pentagon's reports on the progress of the fighting and more than once I asked them: What exactly is going on in the Middle East? Their answer was that the picture looked very different from our previous ideas. I received report after report on your operation of crossing the Suez Canal, and on your soldiers' and officers' will to fight, and on the tank battles in the desert. And the fighting was still going on. I said at the time that circumstances had now become favorable for a cease-fire. The Egyptians had proved their ability to fight; they had changed the situation in the Middle East and there were now new facts which we must take into account. In my view there was no justification for continued fighting after that.

The political goal that the Egyptians had in mind when they accepted the risks of war had become clear. So it was incumbent upon us to strive for a cease-fire and take political action for a fundamental solution of the crisis. I contacted the Soviets; perhaps I have also told you that I sent a message to Cairo. My proposal at that time was for a cease-fire in place; I think that was on the tenth of October.

Here let me remind you of two points: the first is that you may have noticed that we have not given much attention to the question: Who fired the first shot? The second is that you may know that it was not easy to offer Israel a proposal for a cease-fire on October 10th or 11th. They were furiously angry with us because they estimated that now general mobilization in Israel was complete they were able to change the course of the fighting, but eventually they yielded. As for you, your words reached us through the Soviets—and the British too—to the effect that you were not prepared to accept. In brief, we were unable to achieve a cease-fire in circumstances that I regarded as favorable.

Let me tell you something about my views on the solution of conflicts. If we want to solve a critical conflict, the point we start from must be the point at which each party feels it has obtained something and that to stop there is not a defeat for it. Such a situation was offered us at the end of the first half of October. Egypt had crossed the Suez Canal, penetrated the Bar-Lev line and advanced some kilometers into Sinai east of the pre-October 6th cease-fire line. Israel had succeeded in checking the Syrian attack—which had been strong and intense—in the Golan, and advanced some kilometers northward from the pre-October 6th cease-fire line. Thus each side had obtained some part of what it wanted even if it had not obtained all it wanted. This then was the time to stop fighting and seek a solution by political methods.*

Kissinger then stressed the distinction between political emotions and political facts.

KISSINGER: We are today confronted with a *de facto* situation; whatever its causes, we must start confronting it.... It is still a situation favorable to a political solution. Your forces have crossed the canal, and they are in positions east of the Suez Canal. Israel's forces have crossed and they are in positions west of the Suez Canal. We can thus see that the time is still favorable for discussion of a solution—and we cooperated with the Soviet Union, with you and with other

---

*Dr. Kissinger told a rather different version of his efforts for a cease-fire to a group of American Jewish intellectuals in Washington on December 6, 1973. Then, according to the Israeli journal *Yediot Aharonot*, which published the notes of a participant, "Kissinger said he had warned the Israelis from the start [of the war] that the U.N. would order a cease-fire the moment the tide turned in their favor. Their strategy should therefore have been guided by political considerations: to get the maximum results before the cease-fire. When the pressure for a cease-fire began, the Secretary of State employed all the delaying tactics at his command. He flew to Moscow to gain time. According to him, he gained an extra 96 hours of fighting time for the Israelis—and they knew it. But Israel, he claims, failed to provide the U.S. with exact information about its military plans. He was told, for example, that the Israeli counteroffensive thrust (west of the Suez Canal) would turn north—instead, it turned south."

The discussion also showed that—at the time, at least—Kissinger urged rapid Israeli negotiation and rapid withdrawals from Arab territory.

For the full text of this discussion—very revealing for the way Dr. Kissinger talked to American Jews about his policies in the Middle East—see Appendix Four.

members of the Security Council so that a cease-fire resolution might be adopted.

I want to tell you something else. This time you have behaved differently from 1967. In 1967 you set the world against us—I am talking of what happened then, regardless of whether or not you were right—and the consequence was that a wave of violent hostility for the United States prevailed in the whole area. In this way you destroyed any desire on the part of the United States to perform a role it felt itself capable of performing.

In 1973 President Sadat behaved more quietly and, whether or not we were wrong, you made it possible for us to perform a role we desired to perform and felt ourselves capable of performing. The Soviet Union can give you arms, but the United States can give you a just solution which will give you back your territories, especially as you have been able really to change the situation in the Middle East. Do not imagine that Israel is pleased by what we are doing, but at the same time we do not imagine that you will be pleased by what we are doing. All the same politics in our age is not a question of emotions; it is the facts of power.

I now want to discuss with you your article on the importance of the American role in the crisis. You believe that, even if he wanted to, the American President would be unable to play any positive role in the Middle East crisis because of the internal pressures on him. Perhaps you will allow me to differ with you. There are problems confronting the White House, but I do not think that Richard Nixon will resign, or that he will be dismissed. The internal pressures on him are strong, but I still believe that the field of movement is open to him, even under these pressures. . . . Since when has Sinai been Egyptian?

HEIKAL: I will send you a number of love letters written on papyrus leaves five thousand years ago. They are from an Egyptian commander in the garrison of El-Arish to his wife, who was a Pharaonic princess, and he says: "I remember you in this distant place where I am waiting to repel the enemy from the frontiers of the sacred homeland." You are at present in the most ancient nation in history. . . .

KISSINGER: Is King Faisal prepared to go the whole way [in continuing the oil embargo]?

HEIKAL: You are on your way to Riyadh, and you will meet the King. You will find him firmer than many people have imagined—and I admit that I was one of them. He has been wounded by American policy, with which he has been connected for a long time. He is angry at your repeated promises that have not been kept. Also the Arab character of Jerusalem is a subject on which, in his view, there can be no discussion, and on this point the whole of the Arab nation is with him.

KISSINGER: Before leaving Washington I read all his correspondence with three Presidents—Kennedy, Johnson and Nixon—and I feel that Faisal is entitled to feel bitter. I am leaving for Amman and Riyadh tomorrow. I do not expect any problems with King Hussein. I expect all the problems to be with Faisal.

As a consequence of the conversation, Heikal reached the following conclusions:

1. Henry Kissinger is serious in his search for a solution, though I do not believe that he so far has a complete plan which he intends to carry out. What I felt about him is that he is trying to get things moving, and that through the movement he may find a way out.
2. That Henry Kissinger is a Jew will not restrict him; indeed, it may give him immunity against the Jewish pressure groups in American society.
3. Henry Kissinger has a good opinion, so it seemed to me, of his ability to move vis-à-vis the present American political situation and in the face of the immense pressures in American society—but for all this I shall be the first to wish him success if he tries and to congratulate him if he succeeds.
4. The Arab future cannot be allowed to depend on the efforts of one man in America, nor are the Arabs entitled to let themselves be dazzled by Henry Kissinger's success in other crises, even if Henry Kissinger is undoubtedly worthy of admiration.
5. There is a problem in his practical view of problems, for he comes from a school which believes that the truth is what we see at this moment, and not what we think or believe as a consequence of what has happened before. This is to underestimate the importance of history in major conflicts.
6. In his estimate, the facts of power take precedence over all other factors in calculations relative to crises. This point calls for vigilance, because the facts of power do not come to a stop at a precise moment, but are a constant debate between events. The practical application of this is that if Israel succeeds in changing the

power situation in the field, we may find ourselves called on to accept the new situation as a new basis, and this is exactly the problem that faced us after the Security Council cease-fire resolution of October 22nd 1973.

7. The importance of the time factor to us is different from the importance of the time factor to him. This is because we are under pressure from the present military, political and psychological situation, which pressures cause us anxious days and sleepless nights, whereas for him they are no more than memoranda written on paper, ideas, and possible subjects for discussion at the negotiating table.

8. I am not convinced, in spite of all he said, that the present American President is in a position to exert effective pressure on Israel. I think that if the American President in his present circumstances starts to exert pressure on Israel—supposing that he wants to exert such pressure—the forces of Zionism in the United States will lose no time in defaming him more than he has been defamed already. The American President will need outstanding courage to explain to American public opinion that there are groups in America that do not care if things reach the pitch of a nuclear confrontation which would drown the world in a flood of destruction if this is in Israel's interest. And this in spite of my belief, which has been confirmed by experience and never shaken, in the ability of the United States to exert pressure—indeed compulsion—on Israel to an extent not possible for any other quarter in the world, on condition that the President is leading and not being led.

9. World balances of power are a major factor in Kissinger's estimates; we must therefore recognize without ambiguity the importance of the Soviet role in the crisis. This role must not be an auxiliary or temporary element; it must be continuous and be consolidated in the form of profound Soviet-Arab understanding, and long-term friendship.

10. I do not believe that there is a definite and detailed Soviet-American agreement that we can rely on. Nor do I believe that there is an American guarantee that we can accept against Israel. If there is an American guarantee, I do not know what assurance there is for it except comprehensive Arab strength—political, economic and military.

Heikal had urged these views upon President Sadat; no doubt they lurked in Sadat's mind when he conferred with Kissinger on the morning of November 7. Nevertheless, the prospect of real friendship between Egypt and the United States dominated the first day that Dr. Kissinger ever spent in Cairo. Where this new friendship was to lead Egyptians and Americans had yet to be perceived, but the hopes of both were gleaming as Kissinger's blue and white Boeing flew away from Cairo to the east.

# 5

# "The Communists and the Jews!"

Dr. Kissinger proceeded to Amman, thence to Riyadh; he was bombarded in both places by messages from Sisco. Golda Meir was balking at Kissinger's six points, in particular the provisions for supplying Suez and the Third Army. She wanted to be certain that no weapons slipped through; her protestations foreshadowed the haggling that was to feature all of Kissinger's negotiations in future with the government of Israel. Words in the document were changed and rearranged, but no sooner was that accomplished than new messages came from Israel and Egypt, each accusing the other of violating the six points Kissinger had imposed upon them. Whilst all of this was happening, sleepless and exhausted, Kissinger drove to the royal palace, on the evening of November 8—for a dramatic audience with Faisal ibn Abdel-Aziz ibn Abdel-Rahman al-Faisal al-Saud, King of Saudi Arabia.

Anwar Sadat seems like Henry Kissinger's identical twin when we dwell upon the antimonies of Kissinger and Faisal. Kissinger was the Western secularist *par excellence;* Faisal was

Wahhabite theocracy incarnate. Scarcely seven decades before, Abdel Aziz ibn Saud, Faisal's legendary father, had galloped out of Kuwait with 40 companions mounted on camels and conquered the Nejd, the sandy wasteland in the heart of the Arabian peninsula. Abdel Aziz was more than a destitute Bedouin warlord; he was as well a religious reformer—the apostle of Wahhabism, a puritanical movement which preached a revival of Islamic simplicity and a fundamentalist fidelity to the precepts of the Koran.

The creed was uncompromising; it forbade all earthly pleasures save those of the marriage bed. Obscure and penurious though he was, Abdel Aziz brandished the Book, the sword, and his conjugal prowess with such tenacity that within 25 years he had united most of the Arabian peninsula under his rule and created a kingdom nearly thrice the size of Texas. He bound the tribes to his person by marrying their maidens and is said to have wed 300 times; he sired more than 40 sons who survived childhood. Intermittently the British paid Abdel Aziz a tiny subsidy, and when he expelled the Hashemite dynasty from the holy Hejaz, he inherited the tithes that pilgrims pay when they visit Mecca and Medina. But Abdel Aziz was always poor until the Americans discovered oil, at Dhahran in his eastern province, in 1938. Fifteen years later he died, almost the richest man in the world, confused and brokenhearted by what wealth had done to corrupt the Wahhabite austerity of his house.

He was succeeded by Saud, his eldest surviving son, who proceeded to make the monarchy a marvel of grotesque extravagance, whilst most of the populace remained in medieval want. Saud had already erected an immense concrete palace decorated in pink and gold, behind walled gardens with swimming pools and fountains, nightingales in gilded cages, mosaic terraces, multitudes of light bulbs amongst the rhododendron—a replica of the Moslem heaven—but he tired of that, tore it down and built another, neon-lit and more expensive. The swindlers of the Levant and parts beyond descended upon Riyadh and ensnared the royal family in a web of fraud. Saudi princes ventured more and more to the fleshpots of Europe and America, where they squandered fortunes on women, whiskey, and games of chance. By 1958 the monarchy was bankrupt, and Saud was constrained to install his half-brother, Faisal, as prime minister and *de facto* ruler to restore the kingdom's finances.

Faisal was the opposite of Saud in aspect and in character—frugal, untalkative, intellectual, infinitely patient. His career had been almost as fabulous as his father's. As an adolescent he had led a royal mission to the Court of St. James's; when he was scarcely twenty he had commanded an army which quelled rebellious tribes on the southern periphery of the kingdom. Whilst still a youth he became viceroy of the Hejaz, and foreign minister at twenty six. He had traveled widely and knew how the Christian democracies functioned. For years he corresponded with Lord Bertrand Russell. He detested ostentation, and inhabited a villa, not a palace. Saud had married a hundred times; Faisal preferred monogamy. (He was wed to the same woman, Queen Iffat, for more than 40 years.) Immediately he embarked upon reform, saving the kingdom from insolvency and the royal family from itself. In 1964 the royal family and the religious ulemas of the realm deposed Saud and proclaimed Faisal king.

Once upon the throne, Faisal pursued a heroic vision. As fervently religious as his father, he wished to prove, as his brother never could, that Koranic rectitude and fantastic wealth could flourish hand in hand. He aspired to avoid an incurable collision of Wahhabism with Western materialism, to bestow upon Arabia all the blessings of technology whilst he went on amputating the hands of thieves, to create for his people a welfare state whilst he protected them from the mischief of socialism, the godlessness of Communism, and the decadence of the liberal democracies.

To achieve this Faisal resolved to immunize the peninsula from every microbe of Marxian politics and to prevent at any price the radicalization of Araby at large. For that he needed an alliance with a great power, and perforce that power was the United States. With Hussein of Jordan, Faisal prefigured Sadat in choosing the patron of his chief enemy—Israel—as his own protector. The choice was imposed not only by America's primacy in the global conflict with Communism, but by the American corporate monopoly of Saudi oil. Faisal's friendship with Washington was never very happy, for in fact on the American side it was often blemished by false promises and mendacity. The issue, of course, was Israel.

In early 1945, on the Great Bitter Lake of the Suez Canal, dying President Franklin D. Roosevelt met old King Abdel Aziz aboard the *USS Quincy*. Roosevelt promised Abdel Aziz that he, as president, would never do anything hostile to the Arabs and that the United States government would make no basic change in its Palestine policy without consulting both Arabs and Jews beforehand; he confirmed the promises in writing. Two months later, Roosevelt was dead; within a year President Truman was telling his ministers to the Arab states, "I'm sorry, gentlemen, but I have to answer to hundreds of thousands of people who are anxious for the success of Zionism."

Faisal never forgot what seemed to him a breach of faith, though he did appear to forgive. He needed American technology to exploit his oil, and though he never ceased to assail its support of Zionism, he admired America as the arsenal of anti-Communism. He forged a friendship with Washington which came close to an alliance, accepted American arms, and seemed impervious to the accusations of radical Arabs that he was a reactionary and a "stooge." Following the Six-Day War of 1967, eager to maintain the flow of Saudi oil, Presidents Johnson and Nixon assured Faisal that they would press Israel to relinquish conquered Arab territory; nothing happened.

In the spring of 1972, Washington conveyed hints to Faisal that if he would help to persuade President Sadat to diminish the enormous Russian presence in Egypt, the United States would mount more serious pressure upon Israel. Faisal exhorted Sadat accordingly; for this and other reasons (as we have seen) Sadat expelled the Russians in July of that year. But Nixon ignored this momentous action. Faisal felt humiliated and betrayed.

The King had long resisted pressure from other Arab governments to wield his oil weapon against the United States, invoking the maxim that "petroleum and politics do not mix." Finally, in April of 1973, having despaired of a response from Nixon to the expulsion of the Russians—and aware that Sadat was preparing to resume war—the King dispatched Sheikh Ahmed Zaki al-Yamani, his minister of petroleum, on a special mission to Washington. Yamani was intercepted there by an American oil expert who urged him to warn the administration in blunt language of what he had already intimated in private— that Saudi Arabia would not increase production to meet America's needs unless Washington began working for Israeli withdrawal. Yamani thereupon saw Dr. Kissinger, Secretary of the Treasury George Schultz and his deputy, William Simon, Secretary of State Rogers, and Assistant Secretary Sisco. It was, Yamani later said, a dialogue of the deaf. Rogers and Sisco urged Yamani to enlist Saudi Arabia in common cause with America against the radicals and terrorists of the Arab world. Yamani suggested it might be more effective to attack the causes of terrorism, but the Americans did not seem to hear him.

Convinced that he had not been taken seriously, Yamani then decided to put the entire administration on notice, and he did so in *The Washington Post.* He phrased his warning positively, stressing that Saudi Arabia still considered itself America's best friend in the Middle East, and pledging fulfillment of its plan to increase production to 20 million barrels of oil a day by 1980 provided the United States "creates the right political atmosphere." Privately American officials retorted that Yamani had exceeded his authority and that he did not speak for the King.

On May 2, 1973, the King summoned Frank Jungers, the chairman and chief executive officer of the Arabian American Oil Company (Aramco), to the royal palace at Riyadh. There, in the presence of Yamani and several other ministers, Faisal solemnly informed Jungers that he could not much longer resist pressure from other Arab states, and repeated essentially the same warning that Yamani had conveyed to Washington. Jungers passed the message to the State Department and the White House. "It was ignored," Jungers told me subsequently. A few weeks after the audience in Riyadh, the King met Jungers and other oil company executives at Geneva, and talked not only of freezing production but hinted at reducing it. Again the message was passed to Washington. Again it was ignored.

Faisal habitually spoke in silences; the favorite game in Riyadh was fathoming his mind. Sheikh Zaki Yamani was a master of that, and he told me once, "His Majesty doesn't like to talk, but he loves to give hints. He's terribly intelligent, and has the ability to hide it. Some people say he reasons like a Bedouin, but that's not really true because the Bedu live from day to day and His Majesty excels in foresight." Frank Jungers of Aramco also knew Faisal well. "He never acts on whim," Jungers told me. "He never breaks his word. When he speaks, he never tells you anything unless he means it."

Washington knew this, or should have. Throughout the summer of 1973 there ensued a series of explicit warnings by Faisal, by two of his sons, by Yamani, and by other ministers that Saudi Arabia would ration its oil unless Washington adopted "a more evenhanded and just policy" in the Middle East. Faisal's declarations were made to *The Washington Post*, *The Christian Science Monitor*, and NBC-TV—but they were not sufficient to convince the administration.

In early September the King told *Newsweek* that "logic requires that our oil production does not exceed the limits that can be absorbed by our economy." To persuade the Saudis to exceed that limit, the U.S. would have to assist the kingdom to industrialize to create alternative income once its oil was depleted, and it would have to disavow "Zionist expansionist ambitions." If the U.S. did not respond, Saudi Arabia would act out of "exclusive . . . self-interest. In this case the resultant rise in prices may lead to an increase in income which would necessitate a cutback in production." And "a cutback in production would lead to a sudden and substantial rise in prices."

The statement was prophetic (*vide* oil prices today), but Washington continued to believe that Faisal was bluffing. Secretary

Schultz spoke of Arab "swaggering"; in a press conference Nixon ominously evoked the C.I.A.'s overthrow of Premier Mohammed Mossadegh in Iran two decades earlier and observed that "oil without a market . . . does not do a country much good." The Saudis perceived a threat of violence.

Meanwhile, Sadat was fashioning an alliance with Faisal—an axis between Cairo and Riyadh that with time became the paramount factor in pan-Arab politics. Under Nasser, Egypt and Saudi Arabia had been locked in chronic conflict. Nasser's method of achieving Arab unity was to impose it, by appealing to the street and through murky military intrigues. He committed his worst mistake in the Yemen—"my Vietnam," he later lamented—where for years his army was enmeshed in a war with royalist forces supported by the Saudis, and from which it emerged, enfeebled, to face defeat by Israel in 1967.

But Sadat ended the Arab cold war. With a sly skill that made Nasser seem clumsy by comparison, Sadat made unity by consensus the keystone of his Arab policy. Far from intriguing against governments that differed from his own, he accepted them as they were, established areas of common interest, then rallied them in quest of his objectives. Nowhere was this phenomenon more crucial than in the alliance he begot in 1973 with Faisal, who became thereafter the pillar of Sadat's foreign policy, and—for a price—his financier.

Faisal learned, or sensed, sometime in early 1973 that Sadat intended to go to war. Originally Sadat hoped to unleash hostilities at the end of April, but Faisal visited Cairo and talked him out of it. Diplomacy, the King argued, should be given a final chance. Sadat flew to Riyadh in August, pleaded that diplomacy had failed, and informed Faisal of his irrevocable decision to fight. Faisal preached prudence, then acquiesced. He agreed, should it prove necessary, to wield his oil weapon against the United States, but—in the beginning at least—only with moderation. He also promised Sadat $600 million (which he increased later) to help finance the war. The King was moved no doubt by sentiments of solidarity in the "great Arab struggle," but he was also pursuing Saudi Arabia's self-interest. War or no war, Faisal needed Sadat to sustain stability in the Arab east. From the beginning, Faisal made it clear that he had no mind to finance régimes that mingled Mohammed with Karl Marx; he expected Sadat to diminish Nasser's socialist model of development, to restrain radicals in his own camp and (as best he could) amongst the Syrians, the Iraqis, and the Palestinians. Since he embraced Faisal, Sadat has—for his own self-interest, too—consistently labored for those objectives.

When the war began on October 6, Faisal fulfilled his financial bargain with Sadat, but still he hesitated to impose an oil embargo. He sent Yamani to a meeting of Arab petroleum ministers in Kuwait with instructions (so Yamani told me) to resist the radicals. The Iraqis proposed nationalizing all American oil companies on Arab soil, the withdrawal of all Arab funds from American banks, a total embargo of the United States—and when Yamani refused, the Iraqis walked out.

Faisal was in secret communication with Nixon and Kissinger. He anticipated that Nixon would replenish Israel with arms to compensate for the Soviet deliveries to Egypt and Syria, but he warned the President that a massive, public bequest to Israel would make Saudi forbearance impossible before Arab opinion. On October 19, Nixon asked Congress for $2.2 billion in military aid to Israel. Faisal's forbearance vanished. The Americans, he decided, had taken him for granted for the last time. He slashed oil production and imposed an embargo on the United States. In so doing, as though by accident, Faisal outflanked the revolutionaries and restored conservatism to the Arab vanguard.*

---

*After the October war, whilst the hardships of the oil embargo were bearing down, and the United States was losing billions of dollars in Gross National Product, Dr. Kissinger admitted to aides that the administration had erred in announcing the $2.2 billion in arms for Israel. "I made a mistake," Kissinger confessed. He considered it his only big mistake throughout the war. He regretted it above all because it provoked Faisal—whom he realized too late had not been bluffing—to abandon (temporarily) his alliance with Washington and to adopt (for a period) a hostile policy.

Kissinger assigned some of the blame to President Nixon. Before the request

Such were the circumstances on the evening of November 8, 1973, as Dr. Kissinger and his aides entered the royal study at Riyadh. Faisal sat in an overstuffed armchair amidst his robed entourage, beside a table with a white telephone. In Cairo, Kissinger has asked Sadat what to expect from this master of much of the world's oil and the mightiest Arab of a millennium. "Well, Dr. Henry," Sadat replied, "he'll probably preach to you about Communism and the Jews."

KISSINGER: ... I recall Your Majesty's visit to the United States early during President Nixon's administration, when Your Majesty pointed out to the President some of the dangers in the Middle East. Many of Your Majesty's prophecies have come true.... I wish to explain our actions in the war of last month. Your Majesty may not approve, but he must know why we acted as we did. We were motivated by a desire to prevent an increase of Communist influence, and when the Soviets began to send in arms we had to react. In any case, the war is over now, and we were instrumental in arranging the cease-fire and ... the resupply of the Third Army.

As Dr. Kissinger spoke, the King hunched in his chair, his hooded head surmounted by a band of woven gold, his remarkable mouth frozen with distaste, his long, speckled fingers plucking at lint on his cloak. When he answered, his voice was high-pitched, like a lamentation.

FAISAL: Thank you for your explanation. I wish to remind you of what I said to President Nixon and to Secretary Rogers. It is essential to press Israel to withdraw from occupied territory. As you know, the Communists want the situation to remain critical. The United States used to stand up against aggression—you did that in World War II and

---

for $2.2 billion, it had been decided to send the Israelis arms worth $850 million—which the Pentagon considered perfectly adequate. If we're condemned for a sheep, why not for a lamb? Nixon reasoned. The Arabs would be angry anyway, he reasoned. Once the Soviet airlift assumed major dimensions, and once he cast aside the stratagem that delayed the American airlift, Nixon raised the bequest to Israel to $2.2 billion—to reap extra credit from Israel and American Jews, and (most important) to impress the Russians. The President said, in so many words, "If we're going to do it, let's do it big." That, remarked an aide of Kissinger's, "was pure Nixon."

in 1956 during the Suez war. If the United States had done the same after 1967, we would not have witnessed this deterioration. I speak as a friend, and I want you to know how painful it is for me to take steps which injure our friendship. Ever since 1967 the Communists have been exploiting the situation and in particular spreading false stories about Saudi Arabia because they know that Saudi Arabia is the biggest obstacle to Communism in the Middle East. Israel is advancing Communist objectives. It is unfortunate that among those of the Jewish faith there are those who embrace Zionism. Before the Jewish state was established, there existed nothing to harm good relations between Arabs and Jews. There were many Jews in Arab countries. When the Jews were persecuted in Spain, Arabs protected them. When the Romans drove the Jews out, Arabs protected them. At Yalta, it was Stalin who said there had to be a Jewish state. This is not a question of racism, but a question of love for one's own country. It is necessary to establish in Palestine a mixed Jewish-Moslem state. Most of the immigration to Israel is from the Soviet Union, and they want to establish a Communist base right in the Middle East. Communists have no faith. They don't believe in God.

KISSINGER: Your Majesty, our problem now is how to proceed from the present situation—which we know is intolerable—to genuine peace.

FAISAL: That's easy. Make Israel withdraw.

KISSINGER: I agree that there must be Israeli withdrawals, but this is a complicated problem for the United States—and not just a foreign-policy problem. We have decided to make a major effort to achieve a settlement. We've made a beginning in Egypt, and we've agreed with President Sadat to convene a peace conference. We wish to establish good relations with all Arab countries that desire them with us. I mentioned Syria to Your Majesty at the dinner table.

FAISAL: I asked a Syrian friend if Syria would object to a visit by Your Excellency. The Syrian said Syria would welcome him.

KISSINGER: We don't intend to exclude Syria from our high-level contacts, and we'll take steps to establish them. Your Majesty will see that in the coming months we'll make a major effort to achieve progress.

FAISAL: I hope it will only take weeks.

KISSINGER: Well, that raises the question of Your Majesty's oil embargo. We understand the emotions that led to the embargo.

FAISAL: That is why you must move as quickly as possible—so that we can rescind the embargo. It was very painful for me to have been forced to take this action against our American friends.

KISSINGER: Your Majesty's decision had a serious effect, coming as it did from an old friend.

FAISAL: That's why I've suffered even more than you have.

KISSINGER: But now we face a new situation. Those who oppose peace seek to portray the Arabs as hostile to the United States. They are trying to turn opinion against our peace efforts. It will be difficult for us to go ahead if we face a continuing oil embargo. We can absorb the economic impact of the embargo, but the psychological impact worries me. I'd like to suggest that Your Majesty take steps to limit the application of the embargo.

FAISAL: I should like to rescind it immediately. I, too, am in a difficult position. It would be easier if the United States would announce that Israel must withdraw and permit the Palestinians to return to their homes.

KISSINGER: Such a dramatic announcement would produce very strong reactions. We must move step by step. . . . I should like to urge Your Majesty to reflect. I do not ask for a decision right now, but I urge Your Majesty to reflect on it.

FAISAL: Our predicament is the other side of the coin. The Communists are accusing some Arabs of bowing to American pressure. To those who accuse you of bowing to Arab pressure, you can reply that the only reason the Arabs are doing this is because you support the enemy of the Arabs.

KISSINGER: Your Majesty, it doesn't work that way in the United States. Our best argument is not to say that we're anti-Israeli or pro-Arab, but that we want peace in the Middle East and that we're pursuing the interests of the United States. If we try to put it on the basis of the merits of the Arab-Israeli dispute, there will always be more people defending Israel than the Arab side. So we have to put it in terms of American national interests.

FAISAL: I appreciate your reasoning, but I hope that you can appreciate ours. The embargo was a common decision of the Arab family. To urge an end of the embargo, I must be able to go to the other Arab governments with an argument. Therefore I need swift action from you. You need to announce your position.

KISSINGER: If we announce this before negotiations, we will undermine our effectiveness in the negotiations. I don't want to promise
anything I can't deliver.

FAISAL: We hope you will achieve your goal, and we wish you success. We pray to Almighty God that He will continue to give you
success in your noble efforts. I have spoken frankly to Your Excellency
because I respect his ability and wisdom.

KISSINGER: I don't want to tire Your Majesty.

With that exchange of courtesies, the conversation ended—at
an impasse. During the royal pronouncement on the Jews, Kis-
singer remained serene. Earlier, at dinner, it had been a bit
more difficult to digest. The American ambassador to Riyadh,
James E. Akins, sat separated from Kissinger by several senior
princes, but through the veil of robes and the click of coffee cups
Akins caught snatches of the princes' discourse. ". . . Israel . . .
Zionism . . . Jewish Communist conspiracy. . . ." On the way out,
Kissinger whispered to Akins, in his deepest Teutonic accent,
"That was your idea of light dinner conversation?"

I met Faisal five weeks after Kissinger's first audience with
him, and in retrospect my own experience with the King seems
very similar. I was not, to be sure, so confident I would be
received. I was asked to wait in an antechamber of the royal
palace, until the King arrived there that morning from his private residence. Soon I heard the harbinger of sirens, then the
doors of automobiles being slammed shut. I gazed to the entrance hall, where beneath a blazing chandelier scores of men in
flowing robes rose reverently to attention. Through that forest of
shrouded heads I perceived a tall man, clad as the others save for
a headband woven of gold, stride pensively into the palace. He
was approached by the assistant chief of royal protocol, who
handed him a piece of paper with my name, then whispered into
his ear. The tall man lowered his hawklike profile, hesitated, and
nodded. The assistant chief of protocol turned and beckoned to
me, and I advanced from the antechamber, beneath the chandelier, to an immense room with a yellow carpet and painted

green walls. There, sitting in an overstuffed armchair, waiting
for me, was Faisal.

I bowed, and said, "*Es salaamu aleikum, Jalaltak.* May peace
be upon Your Majesty." The King motioned me into another
armchair. The room was thronged with retainers, petitioners,
soldiers, but now in a magical migration of whispering robes
they vanished, leaving me alone with the King, the assistant
chief of protocol, and a servant who brought us glasses of sweet
tea. The King exuded an exquisite sadness. His nose was
aquiline and large; his eyes, like his beard, commingled brown
with gray and protruded slightly at the lower lids; his face was
deeply furrowed, as though ravaged by suffering so long endured from a diseased stomach. Most extraordinary was his
mouth, congealed as if with permanent disdain for the burden of
his kingdom's fortune and the follies of the human race.

He spoke to me of Jerusalem and of the Jews. Jerusalem was
his special concern, the holiest city of Islam after Mecca and
Medina. He had often said that his great wish before he died was
to pray there, at the Mosque of Al Aqsa. "Praised be He," says
Sura XVII, verse one, of the Holy Koran, "Who did take His
servant Mohammed,/For a Journey by night,/From the Sacred
Mosque of Mecca,/To the Far Mosque of Jerusalem,/Whose
precincts We did bless,/The better to show him,/Some of Our
Marvels." According to the *Hadith,* which supplements the
Koran as a source of Islamic revelation, the Prophet Mohammed
hitched his horse Buraq near the Mosque of Al Aqsa, then ascended from Jerusalem with the Angel Gabriel to each of the
seven heavens, where the Prophet met Adam, Abraham, Moses,
Zacharia, and Jesus. Israel's continuing occupation of Arab
Jerusalem enraged Faisal. "Only Moslems and Christians," he
told me, "have holy places and rights in Jerusalem. The Jews
have no shrines in Jerusalem."

But what, I wondered, of the Wailing Wall? "Under the
League of Nations," the King continued, "a commission was sent
to Jerusalem to inquire into the battle of Jews and Moslems for
the Wailing Wall. The commission decided that the Wailing

Wall was only a part of the wall of the Mosque of Al Aqsa. The commission reported these conclusions. Therefore the Jews have no rights in Jerusalem. Another wall can be built for them, and they can wail against that."

Again, as he spoke, as always when he spoke, the King hunched in his chair, his long, speckled fingers plucking at lint on his cloak. For me, the scene of Faisal was like a dream, so vivid it recurs from time to time, in dreams and in dreams of dreams.

And yet, whilst half of Faisal's head was filled with primitive rage against Jews and simplistic notions that with a wave of the hand Dr. Kissinger could dismiss the Israelis from Arab territory, the other half was exquisitely subtle. For all of its intransigence his first audience with Kissinger contained the seeds of a remarkably compliant policy. The King's allusion to Syria was crucial. After the audience Omar al-Saqqaf, the minister for foreign affairs, urged Kissinger to visit Damascus, revealing Faisal's conviction that Syria was the key to peace. In subsequent missions to Riyadh for more than a year thereafter, Kissinger practiced every persuasion to soften the Wahhabite pope. True, Faisal went on protesting about the Jews, nor did he rescind the embargo until the spring, but in mid-December 1973 he assured Kissinger he would do all he could to promote negotiations—particularly in Syria. Crucial.

I was present for a few moments, taking snapshots, when Kissinger entered the King's cabinet for his audience of December 14, 1973. Faisal stood apart, impassive, waiting. He smiled at Kissinger's Palestinian-born interpreter (an old friend), but he did not smile when he greeted Kissinger. The encounter this time, however, proved to be more friendly. Kissinger spoke of his hopes for the conference at Geneva. "Your Majesty must trust me," he said. "I cannot deceive you. If I did, you would know within a few months." Whether Faisal ever truly trusted Kissinger I know not, but in fact as time passed and it became clear to the King that he could not hope for total Israeli withdrawal quickly, he became the financier of Kissinger's interim diplomacy throughout the Middle East. He subsidized Sadat, seduced the Syrians, bribed the Beiruti press. His horror of radicalization prevailed over his hatred of Zionism.

Besides, Faisal needed the United States to modernize his kingdom. Kissinger knew this, and he played the card shrewdly. On December 15, at the height of the oil embargo, he had a revealing conversation in Riyadh with Hisham Nazer, the minister of state for planning, and several important princes.

NAZER: When I was in Washington, I talked to Bill Simon about an American development mission to Saudi Arabia. Actually I think we should send a mission to the United States, because the missions that come here get rather tiresome.

KISSINGER: What kind of industries are you planning? How much of your population is rural and Bedouin?

NAZER: There is more of a shift to settlement and urban living.

KISSINGER: I assume that the shift has political implications, since urban populations tend to be less traditional. How can the United States relate to the Saudi development process?

NAZER: There are two conditions. First, peace, and second, help in organizing our industrial sector. If we produce oil, we must invest the revenues productively, and here you can help particularly by providing technology. Specifically, you have the technology of desert agriculture which we could use.

KISSINGER: Are the present mechanisms for cooperation adequate?

NAZER: We've never had trouble going directly to the American private sector, but we need help in tapping the resources and technology of the United States government.

We glimpse here the essence of Dr. Kissinger's parallel Middle East policy, for in fact his diplomacy always proceeded on two levels. The first level was the containment of the Arab-Israeli conflict, which he considered almost intractable. The second level was the promotion of American technology, which all of the Arabs (including the radicals) craved and which helped him to buy time whilst he coped with the first problem. In effect he was saying to the Arabs, "I know what you want—your territory—and I'm working on it. Meanwhile I'll give you *everything else* you want to compete in the twentieth century."

For the Saudis, this has meant a vast commitment by the American government to play a major part in fashioning their "infrastructure" and to sell them over the years arms worth billions of dollars. Whole cantonments and towns—at Tobuk, at Khamis Nusrayt, at Al Batin—have been and will be constructed for the Saudis by the U.S. Army Corps of Engineers (this began before Kissinger); today there are nearly 20,000 Americans in the kingdom; tomorrow there may be twice that.

For the Egyptians the parallel policy has meant American diplomatic support, American money, encouragement of American investors and of the oil princes to rescue Cairo's economy—not to mention encouragement of the West Europeans to sell arms to Sadat, since it was also Kissinger's long-range plan to eliminate the Soviet Union as the chief source of weaponry amongst the Arabs. The parallel policy has even succeeded to an extent in such militant states as Syria and Iraq, which still depend upon the Russians for their guns but are as covetous of American technology as the Saudis and the Egyptians.

# 6

# Saladin and
# the Crusader

Dr. Kissinger flew from Riyadh to Peking on November 9, 1973, to see Premier Chou En-lai and Chairman Mao Tse-tung. Whilst he was en route, Israel accepted his amended six points. ("If Israel accepts them, we'll call it the 'Kissinger Plan,'" the Secretary had jested. "If Israel rejects them, then it's the 'Sisco Plan.'") The six points:

1. Egypt and Israel agree to observe scrupulously the cease-fire called for by the U.N. Security Council.
2. Both sides agree that discussions between them will begin immediately to settle the question of the return to the October 22 positions in the framework of agreement on the disengagement and separation of forces under the auspices of the U.N.
3. The town of Suez will receive daily supplies of food, water, and medicine. All wounded civilians in the town of Suez will be evacuated.
4. There shall be no impediment to the movement of nonmilitary supplies to the east bank.
5. The Israeli checkpoints on the Cairo-Suez road will be replaced by U.N. checkpoints. At the Suez end of the road Israeli officers can

participate with the U.N. to supervise the nonmilitary nature of the cargo at the bank of the canal.

6. As soon as the U.N. checkpoints are established on the Cairo-Suez road, there will be an exchange of all prisoners of war, including wounded.

Sadat's earlier insistence on an Israeli retreat to the lines of October 22 had been subsumed, under his agreement with Kissinger, into the framework of discussions for a broader disengagement of forces. I was in Egypt for part of the October war, and during those weeks after the war I visited Kilometer 101 on the Cairo-Suez road, where the Israeli and Egyptian armies confronted each other. It was a weird scene. On the desert hills around, Israeli tanks loomed, their guns trained upon us; in foxholes by the road, Israeli soldiers tinkered with thier machine guns or lay flat on their backs atop their sand bags, reading pulp novels in Hebrew. By the barricade of oil drums and wire, Egyptian and Israeli soldiers, towheaded Scandinavians of the United Nations Emergency Force (U.N.E.F.), commingled with one another, laughing, exchanging gossip as best they could through that other barrier of language (though some of the Oriental Jews spoke Arabic), posing for our snapshots with arms and shoulders interlocked. Was this, I wondered, an auspice of fraternity one day between Israel and Araby?

The Egyptians were robust and copper-skinned, short-maned beneath their starched caps, trimly turned and lean of body. The Israelis were a motley bunch, as long-haired and slovenly as hippies—no reflection upon their martial capacities; they were, after all, but a stone's throw, a rocket's thrust, from Cairo's gate. Near the oil drums and wire was pitched a large tent, wherein Egyptian and Israeli officers, under the chairmanship of a Finnish general, squabbled about the application of Dr. Kissinger's six points.

When a convoy of Egyptian trucks arrived on scene, the Israelis dismantled the cargo, searching amongst the bundles of food and medicine for concealed guns and ammunition, spreading even blood plasma upon the sandy pavement, where we watched it bubble, like the blood of St. Januarius at Naples, in the heat of the desert sun. Kissinger's final formulation of the six points resolved this problem with the sort of sophistry that he often summoned in subsequent negotiations: Suez town and the Third Army stranded on the east bank of the canal were supplied thereafter with the necessities of life over a road controlled by the Israelis but punctuated by United Nations checkpoints. Thus Sadat could pretend it was a U.N., not an Israeli, road. Sadat's card was his Israeli prisoners: he would not release them until the U.N. checkpoints replaced those of the Israelis.

That done, the exchange of prisoners was consummated. But the military talks between Israelis and Egyptians at Kilometer 101 eventually reached deadlock on the issue of Israeli withdrawals. The Israelis proposed a return to the lines of October 5, though now with the provision that the United Nations fill the vacuum of the retreating armies; the Egyptians demanded that Israel relinquish nearly half of the Sinai.

Such were the *official* positions of Israel and Egypt. In fact, General Aharon Yariv, the Israeli negotiator, and General Mohammed Abdel Ghany al-Gamasy, the Egyptian chief of staff, came much closer to an agreement on the basis of informal proposals each had been authorized to discuss. General Yariv offered a withdrawal of six to seven miles from the east bank of the canal in exchange for an Egyptian commitment to limit forces for a depth of 20 miles on the west bank; a reopening of the canal with access for Israeli ships; and other advantages to Israel. General Gamasy proposed an Israeli retreat of about 22 miles from the canal; a U.N. buffer zone; a reopening of the canal at a later stage when Israel had withdrawn nearly 40 miles; and a timetable for the complete evacuation of the Sinai. Yariv and Gamasy were struggling to reconcile these formulations when the Israeli government instructed Yariv to desist—and to return to the original Israeli proposal.

Why? According to the Israeli journalist Matti Golan, in his book *The Secret Conversations of Henry Kissinger* (1976), Dr. Kissinger himself prevailed upon Golda Meir to sabotage the negotiation. Kissinger felt that if Yariv and Gamasy achieved a disengagement at Kilometer 101, there would remain nothing to negotiate at Geneva. "Kissinger's opinion," Golan contends, "was that jumping straight into the peace negotiations [at Geneva] could break up the conference very early. He looked for something less pretentious, something that had a chance of immediate success. A disengagement-of-forces agreement between Israel and Egypt seemed ideal. . . . If they were given a chance, Yariv and Gamasy might well have been able to reach the same agreement, on their own, that Kissinger arranged with so much media fanfare [seven weeks] later."

Mr. Golan's claim is essentially correct. To cite one of Dr. Kissinger's friends, "If you take Henry out of context, he's an abomination."* Golan interprets Kissinger's intervention in the Kilometer 101 negotiations somewhat out of context, however. Kissinger felt that the first Israeli-Egyptian disengagement should be a model for future negotiations on the Syrian and the Jordanian fronts. He feared that, if the Israelis and Egyptians reached an agreement independently, without his mediation, future efforts on the other fronts might founder because the proper international forum for negotiations had not been established. Thus the forum, the format, the process, the *context* of the disengagement were as important as the disengagement itself—even though, as events proved, Geneva was not to prosper as the site of substantive negotiations. Kissinger easily persuaded the Israeli government of his logic. Golda Meir was in no hurry to give territory away before the Israeli elections of December 31, and there is no certainty she would have encouraged Yariv to conclude an agreement quickly.

---

*He is very much an abomination in Mr. Golan's book. Golan's portrait of Kissinger is venomous. The Secretary is depicted, on practically every page, as perfidious to Israel. Golan has Kissinger constantly "shouting" at the Israelis—simply not so. Read from the perspective of the American interest in the Middle East, the portrait of Kissinger is rather more complimentary than Golan seems to have intended. On the other hand, his portrait of Yitzhak Rabin—read from any perspective—is devastating.

This said, it has to be acknowledged that Dr. Kissinger's professional and personal vanity were also involved. He wished to keep the United States in control of the negotiating process—and if there was to be a disengagement, *he* coveted the credit.

By early December, Kissinger concluded he was again needed urgently in the Middle East. On the eve of his departure, December 7, General Dayan called at the State Department. There, amidst the gold brocade, the Persian carpets, the potted rubber plants of Kissinger's immense office on the seventh floor, Dayan sought substantially more weaponry—tanks, aircraft, armored personnel carriers—than Israel was already receiving. Kissinger protested the drain on American reserves. "We have a problem with our own armed services," he said. "We've done so much for Israel already. It's not our policy to weaken you militarily, but there are limits." Dayan kept pressing him, citing the Soviet replenishment of Egypt's arsenal. "The Egyptians have more than two thousand tanks," he claimed. Kissinger countered that perhaps he could spare 200 American tanks. Not enough, Dayan protested. "We destroyed 1,300 Syrian tanks, and before we knew it they were replaced." Kissinger put him off.

Dayan thrust forward with another problem—the blockade the Egyptians had earlier threatened to impose at the Bab al-Mandab (the Gate of Lamentations) at the mouth of the Red Sea. During negotiations for the six-point agreement, Sadat had implicitly promised not to press the blockade, but the ghost continued to distress Dayan. The problem, he insisted, concerned not only Israel but the United States. "Do you intend," he asked, "to stand by and allow the blockade of international waterways as a matter of principle?"

"I don't disagree with your question," Kissinger answered blandly, "but the United States is unlikely to go to war for an abstract international principle—unless vital American interests are involved, as a practical matter."

Behind his thin smile and black eye patch, Dayan clearly felt frustrated. He turned to the canal. "If we leave the canal, the east and west bank, we want to know what the regime will be. Are the Soviets to control it?" Again Kissinger was evasive. "We can discuss such questions when I come to Israel," he said, "—not in isolation. . . . When I come to Israel, we should work out a common strategy. We're at the end of one era and the beginning of another."

Dr. Kissinger was wielding with the Israelis much the same tactic as he did with the Arabs, or for that matter with the North Vietnamese before them—he wished to keep them guessing. Now he focused on a favorite theme, that Israel consider ways to assist the United States to relieve the Arab oil embargo, and the pressures upon both Israel and America from the Europeans, the Japanese, and the Third World. (Conversely, as we have observed from his first audience with King Faisal, Kissinger never tired of telling the Arabs that they must rely on diplomacy, not upon the pressure of their embargo, to produce Israeli withdrawals from conquered territory.) Vaguely Kissinger reassured Dayan that he would maintain Israel's capacity for war, but he expected in exchange Israeli concessions at the negotiating table. (Only later would he lament that he did not extract the concessions before he provided Israel—as he was to do—with further quantities of arms.) Dayan replied that his government was prepared to negotiate a separation of forces—"but we don't feel under great pressure to do it." He was not squandering promises, either—until Kissinger informed him what Israel would receive for them.

The meeting concluded desultorily. They resumed later that afternoon, whereupon Dayan described his personal notions of an Arab-Israeli peace—which were, in fact, rather more subtle than those of his government. If peace came, he said, it would come in three stages: *one*, through the separation of forces so as to stabilize the cease-fire; *two*, through some sort of subsequent agreement to station troops of the United Nations between the opposing sides (he had Egypt and the Sinai uppermost in mind); and *three*, by addressing eventually the issues of the Palestinians, Jerusalem, and (by implication) the final borders.

Dayan recognized that Egypt might never wish to consummate the third phase—final peace—all by itself. Egypt could achieve phases one and two with Israel, but because of the obstacles thrown up by Syria, the Palestinians, and the other Arabs, Egypt would eschew phase three. He implied that in its own interest Egypt should pursue a final settlement alone, but he doubted that Egypt would ever dare without the blessing of its brother Arabs. No such blessing would be bestowed without large Israeli concessions to them as well—and to Syria and the Palestinians, Israel was not prepared to be so generous. Therefore Dayan foresaw no final settlement for the indefinite future. Instead, he wished stability in the Sinai desert, with Egypt operating the canal, detached from Israel by a U.N. buffer zone—until such distant time as new generations of Arabs, upon the Jordan, upon the Golan Heights, were resigned to ceding territory.

DAYAN: Another thing bothers me. Israel's best card is our continuing occupation of the pocket west of the canal, and we have to give that up just to get to the second phase. If we have to pull our forces back from the canal, then we must receive something of real value—such as assurances of no more war.

KISSINGER: You'll never get that in this phase. You're asking for the impossible. You're being unrealistic. . . . I'm going to Cairo, and I'll talk to Sadat about all of these ideas.

Ambassador Dinitz, who was also present, spoke of the Israeli elections of late December—and of the Palestinians.

DINITZ: I have Golda's instructions to get an understanding between the United States and Israel on Geneva.

KISSINGER: I'll be in touch with you, especially on the problem of Palestinian participation.

DINITZ: Golda cannot go into the elections if there's any doubt on the Palestinians at Geneva.

Kissinger repulsed the Israeli demand for immediate Egyptian nonbelligerency—it would bedevil him again and again—but he capitulated straightaway on the issue of the Palestinians.

Faced with Israel's refusal to go to Geneva if the Palestinians were present, he instructed his ambassador in Cairo to inform Sadat that now he did not favor Palestinian participation at the convening of the peace conference. Israel would permit "safe" Palestinians of King Hussein's regime to sit on the Jordanian delegation, but would not tolerate a separate delegation dominated by the Palestine Liberation Organization (P.L.O.). In late November the Arab summit meeting at Algiers had endorsed negotiations with Israel and designated the P.L.O. as the "sole representative" of the Palestinians at Geneva. Yasir Arafat, head of the P.L.O., had arrived at Algiers from Moscow, where the Russians had prevailed upon him to accept the original United Nations plan of 1947 which partitioned Palestine into Jewish and Arab states. To demand the 1947 U.N. borders could only have been a negotiating position; but that Arafat was willing to advance it meant a *de facto* recognition of Israel's right to exist—as would his very presence at a peace conference with Israel.

True, an invitation to Arafat to participate at Geneva would have provoked a violent debate within the P.L.O., and he might have demurred in the end; true, the Jordanians as well as the Israelis opposed the P.L.O. Nevertheless, in excluding the P.L.O. from the start, Kissinger excluded from the process of peacemaking the very essence of the Arab-Israeli quarrel. This lost opportunity was lamentable, for as difficult as it may have been to confront the Palestinian dilemma in late 1973—on the morrow of the war when Arab confidence was high, when old rigidities were less inflexible and possibilities were more fluid— it became vastly more difficult as time slipped by.

Dr. Kissinger flew to Brussels for a NATO convocation, thence to Algiers for his first encounter with President Houari Boumedienne. Kissinger was unfearful of such courtly sovereigns as Kings Hassan and Hussein, but he had a phobia of "radical" Arabs. He considered Boumedienne one of them.

Was there, indeed, any chief of state in Araby as tenebrous, as brooding, as cold, as uncomely, as implacable as that monk-soldier Colonel Boumedienne? He had emerged from Algeria's war of independence as head of the army, but even then he hovered in the shadows, for he had a horror of fame. Tormented and ambitious, he acquired power by degrees; for three years he watched whilst the megalomaniac Ahmed Ben Bella, Algeria's first president, made a mess of running the country. Ben Bella favored a flamboyant and costly internationalism that preached revolution throughout Africa; Boumedienne preferred to focus upon the revolution within Algeria itself. He suspected that the Egyptian intelligence apparatus was manipulating Ben Bella, and he was wary of the President's Marxist fantasies.

By June of 1965 Ben Bella had ruined the economy, and Boumedienne overthrew him in an easy *coup d'état*. From that moment Algeria retrenched as Boumedienne embarked upon ambitious schemes of industrialization flavored with "Islamic Socialism." Several subsequent attempts to murder him— contrived, one may assume, by old comrades he had deposed from power—only hardened his resolution. He lacked Ben Bella's gifts as a demagogue, and—unlike Nasser—he possessed no "charisma." His smile was crooked; his teeth were atrocious; he was so sensitive about his teeth that he hid from the gaze of his people. Finally a French army dentist was summoned to fix his teeth. Boumedienne grew more gregarious, but remained inscrutable. I watched him once, in Algiers, at a large reception. From time to time a laugh illumined his lengthy face, but it was his suspicious brown eyes I found astonishing. They seemed to roll in their orbits, and they hinted of something deeper than cold passion. They made me afraid.

Boumedienne was called, by some of his compatriots, "the Sphinx of Algiers." For him, Islamic Socialism was an applied science, wherein the state inexorably seized all remnants of imperialist (French) wealth, wherein the poor eternally revolted against the rich, the better to establish a kingdom (or a republic) of God upon earth. He was also deeply influenced by the black revolutionary philosopher Frantz Fanon: "Everything is possible for us so long as we do not ape Europe." Boumedienne helped finance and train militant Palestinians, whilst his press pronounced impassioned denunciations of American foreign policy in the Middle East, in Indochina, and far beyond. And yet, if the French had taught the Algerians (and Boumedienne) anything, it was how to draw careful Cartesian distinctions: Washington's foreign policy was one thing, commerce with the Americans quite another. For paradoxically, in order to fulfill his Fanonian fantasies, Boumedienne needed American money. Publicly he opposed Dr. Kissinger's diplomacy in the Middle East, but he had long since contracted to sell Algerian natural gas and crude oil to the United States, for many billions of dollars over the years to come—and he needed more.

Kissinger recognized this dualism and resolved to invoke his parallel policy—technological diplomacy—as a method to accommodate it. Despite his phobia, he was fascinated, too, by the need to deal with an Arab "radical"; even before meeting Boumedienne, he respected him as a tough leader, as a luminary in a large constituency that overreached the borders of Algeria. For example, Boumedienne was close to the Syrians; if Kissinger could influence Boumedienne, perhaps he could influence Syria. Therefore, though Boumedienne was not a party to the negotiations in the Middle East, it was essential to Kissinger to dissuade this militant Algerian from obstructing his gradualist diplomacy.

Boumedienne, clad in a black cloak, received the Secretary on December 13, in a white villa, the old Ministry of Defense, where he resides, high in the hills which gaze upon Algiers bay. Kissinger was at pains to explain his strategy of step by step, to expound the reasons that massive and immediate Israeli withdrawals were not possible, aspiring at the least to neutralize the Algerian if not to convert him altogether. They turned eventually to bilateral relations, which gave Boumedienne the chance to expound upon his program for development and his need for further capital. Kissinger suggested his hopes for promoting ever greater exports of American trade and technology to Algeria. He did not need to add that a moderate Algerian policy in the Arab-Israeli conflict would advance that vision.

Boumedienne got the point. He did not disavow his theology of Arab rights and Israeli wrongs, but he implied he would do what he could to persuade the Syrians to give Kissinger a chance. He agreed to reestablish formal relations with Washington in his own good time and authorized his foreign minister, Abdul Aziz Bouteflika, to make a statement at the airport that endorsed Kissinger's diplomacy. All of this served Boumedienne's interest; he had probably made up his mind before Kissinger came to Algiers. In so acting he detached himself from the Arab radicals, aligned himself with Sadat and Faisal, and in that company increased his power in Arab councils and his stature upon the world stage.

Dr. Kissinger remained in Algeria only a few hours, then flew to Cairo. Sadat, still clad in khaki, received him amidst jasmine shrubs and banyan trees, outside his spacious villa at the Barrages, near the Nile north of the capital, on December 13 and 14. In the villa they talked, alone, into the night, then resumed the next morning. Only for the final quarter of an hour was Fahmy—very upset for being left out—invited to join them.

The President was distressed by Kissinger's failure to arrange a role for the Palestinians at Geneva, but acquiescent. "We look upon you as the principal Arab leader," Kissinger reassured him, "and our purpose is to strengthen your position—in Egypt and throughout the Arab world." They discussed the arrangements for the Geneva conference and agreed that its first goal would be to separate the Egyptian and Israeli armies. The Secretary explained what he considered attainable from the Israelis at that stage—not much, in fact, in terms of territory—and the two men pored over maps. Sadat's confidence in Kissinger was still strong, but he was ill at ease, uncertain as to where Kissinger's diplomacy would lead.

Sadat (as I have suggested) fancied himself a gifted strategic thinker; like Kissinger, he loved to play with conceptual propositions. Kissinger was quick to perceive this and happy to massage Sadat's strategic vanity; Sadat reciprocated. In this and in subsequent conversations Sadat returned to the need for a "common strategy" between Egypt and the United States—which he elaborated largely in terms of removing Soviet influence from the Middle East. He wished to push the Russians out of Syria, Iraq, South Yemen, even Somalia, not to mention the remnants of their influence from Egypt itself. Such an exodus could only be accomplished by strengthening the American position throughout the region, by reviving and magnifying the hegemony the United States had enjoyed during the late 1940s and early 1950s. There existed, in fact, almost a magic formula for achieving that—rapid implementation of Resolution 242, meaning total Israeli withdrawal from Arab territory.

Sadat's concept was clear, though not very subtle. Kissinger listened, but did not bite. Of course, Kissinger wished to diminish Soviet influence—he had always said so—but he was at pains to avoid any conspiracy with Sadat to expel the Russians from the Middle East. He needed at least their passive assent if step by step was to prosper, and he reminded Sadat that Moscow had legitimate interests in the region—the United States had to respect them. The chief American interest in the area was oil—access to it and reasonable prices. The surest way to preserve access—and to prevent Soviet hegemony—was to preserve political stability. For that, Egypt and the United States could and must cooperate; their consultation must be close and frequent, conceived *ad hoc* as problems arose, including problems with the Russians.

I am summarizing exchanges that took place, not only in December 1973 but in the year or so that followed. More recently Sadat has expanded his strategic vision to conceive of a local, triangular hegemony in the Middle East, an axis composed of the three predominant anti-Communist powers—Egypt, Saudi Arabia, and Iran.

Sadat no doubt dramatized his anti-Communism because he assumed it would please Kissinger, but equally Kissinger could not have questioned Sadat's authentic anti-Soviet phobia. Sadat resented the long years that Egypt had squandered under Russian tutelage, and he brooded constantly upon his grievances. As a soldier, he resented the arrogance of the Russian officers that Moscow sent to train his army, and the inadequacy of their equipment in the face of American generosity to Israel. He remembered the humiliations of running to Moscow to beg Leonid Brezhnev for more arms.

In an extraordinary address he delivered on September 28, 1975, to the People's Assembly, Sadat relived the contemptuous treatment he had endured from the Soviet leaders:

I contacted the Russians [in early 1971] and asked them, "Where are the [SAM antiaircraft] batteries for Upper Egypt? There are barrages there, and without protection half a million *feddans* will be flooded." The Russians replied, "Yes, they are coming. They are on the way." I said, "Good!" We even prepared the trains to take the equipment to Upper Egypt straightaway, so that we could defend the vital installations of Upper Egypt.

February 18th came, but nothing arrived. February 22nd came, but nothing arrived, and not even a word about why the supplies were delayed, or about when they would come. I sent a message [to Moscow] in late February. On March 1st and 2nd, I paid my first visit to the Soviet Union as President, secretly. I sat with the three Soviet leaders in the Kremlin. "Why?" I asked. "You know about the deadline I fixed for March 7th. What about Upper Egypt?" How was I to defend Upper Egypt? "The batteries are ready and will be sent to you," I was told. We realized that the Russians were going to have a Congress on March 31st. On such occasions they behave in an intolerable fashion. They try to present themselves as guardians of others, and they think that we are hotheads, that as soon as we received the batteries we would open fire, dragging them in, and then go and lose the battle. They did not want this. They would not say no, but they would not send the batteries.

I told the Russians that nobody could accept such treatment. "Do not always leave me ten steps behind Israel," I said. "I am the one being attacked. Leave me two steps behind Israel but not ten steps." Israel was boasting that its long arm could reach the heart of the Arab nation. Israel was right because with the Phantom plane it could reach any part of my country while I did not have a single weapon to deter it. I told the Russians, "I want weapons for deterrence. I won't use them unless I am attacked." This fell on deaf ears. It was a very violent meeting.

Sadat disliked Brezhnev, who even lacked Khrushchev's spontaneity and warmth—or rather, he conveyed a warmth that Sadat suspected was put on. Brezhnev oozed the manner of a boorish bureaucrat, doing violence to Sadat's diligently acquired sophistication and good taste; he told flat, often vulgar Russian jokes, which Sadat laughed at only to be polite. Even in his salesmanship, when Brezhnev talked of emotions his own emotions seemed to emerge from a machine-like mind, and even when he grew angry he was acting, or so Sadat observed to intimates afterwards. What bored Sadat above all was Brezhnev's predilection for reliving his memories of World War II, an art he had far from mastered; Sadat felt that Brezhnev was engaging in some sort of posthumous competition with his old boss, Nikita Khrushchev, who excelled in war stories.

Brezhnev sometimes evoked his wartime experiences as a means of relieving tension in the bargaining sessions with Sadat, particularly when Sadat pressed him for offensive weapons; the punch line was invariably, "You're asking for too much." Sadat seldom lost his temper. He would shuffle through some papers, remove his horn-rimmed spectacles and remark, "That was a marvelous story about Stalingrad, Mr. Chairman. Now, if we may get back to this question of supersonic bombers..." But Sadat returned home from one meeting after another virtually with empty hands. True, the Russians replenished him with MIGs and tanks not long before the October war, but from the morrow of the war he railed at them again for not replacing and increasing the equipment he had lost.

Moreover he was convinced that the Russians hated him, that they wished to replace him with a leftist such as Aly Sabry, the former vice-president whom he had sent to jail in 1971 with Sami Sharaf and Sharawi Gomaa for plotting to overthrow him. Above all, the Russians offended Sadat's Egyptian nationaalism—and his Islamic fundamentalism. He distrusted the Soviet Union and detested Communism primarily because he was deeply religious and they were atheistic. In the Moslem Middle East, such a motivation can be obsessive, more so than most Western liberals can comprehend. A leftist intellectual who was confined to the same prison as Sadat in 1946 (when Sadat was there as an anti-British terrorist) told me that Sadat would not even approach the Communist prisoners for fear of contamination. Since then, he has grown more cosmopolitan, but his basic beliefs have not changed.

Sadat could have pursued an essentially anti-Soviet policy in Egypt and throughout the Middle East without gratuitously insulting the Soviet Union in his speeches, but as the months passed after the October war, he seemed to revel in publicly abusing the Russians. His advisers—even Fahmy, an architect of his pro-American, anti-Soviet policy—cringed. "Where are we going to get arms?" they asked him. "Why do you trust all to Kissinger—when you're not even sure he can deliver?" To such alarums Sadat replied, not long after the war, "Late one night I decided to sever relations with Moscow. Only in the morning did I change my mind."

Eventually (in March 1974) *Pravda* itself assailed Sadat's exclusivist policy of intimate relations with the United States and of diminishing the socialist system established by President Nasser. *Pravda*'s warning echoed Brezhnev's anxiety for Russia's immense material investment in Egypt (where just the war debt to Moscow exceeded $4 billion) and his rage at Sadat's ingratitude. There was no compelling reason that Sadat could not have balanced his opening to Washington with continuing cordiality to Moscow, the better to avoid a strategic cul-de-sac. But his strategy was to heap his eggs in Dr. Henry's basket, as though determined to embarrass him into fulfilling his ends.

Much of this was yet to come. During his meeting with Sadat in mid-December of 1973, Kissinger's great objective was to convene the peace conference at Geneva on December 18. He had Sadat in hand, but now he had to convince the Syrians to attend as well. Kissinger proceeded to Riyadh—where King Faisal bestowed his benediction upon the negotiations and hinted he might ease the embargo—and then, on December 15, to Damascus at last.

Save for Iraq, no nation in the Middle East had so tempestuous a past as Syria. It was the cradle of Arab nationalism, the cauldron of sublime ideologies that enchanted the Arab mind, then caused contradiction and pain when Syrians set out to apply them. Syria seemed to be ungovernable. Its soul yearned for Arab unity, but its body was an incongruous collection of sects, tribes, clans, families warring constantly amongst themselves. From the moment of independence from France following World War II, the governments of Damascus were a murky comedy of musical chairs as *coup* succeeded *coup*. Finally, in 1958, as though to rescue Syria from themselves, the politicans sought refuge in the arms of Nasser and united Syria with Egypt. Nasser did not do so badly in ruling Syria—he did worse, implanting all the impedimenta of a police state and so disillusioning his new subjects that conservatives mounted another *coup* and dissolved the union in 1961. For a while the right governed, only to be overthrown by the socialist Ba'ath (Resurrection) party, whose civilian and military branches henceforth flogged each other for supremacy. In late 1970, Hafez al-Assad, commander of the air force and minister of defense, seized power in a bloodless *coup*.

Assad was a leading Ba'athist, a mountain boy from the north of Syria, an Alawite who appointed other Alawites to key commands to maintain himself as president. Curious, since the Alawites number hardly more than a tenth of Syria's populace. Nominally they are a sect of Shi'a Islam, but the cult is clouded in secrecy and clandestine rites. Alawites revere Ali, the husband of Fatima, the Prophet's favorite daughter. Ali is immersed in light, for he is the Prince of Stars, but in history the Alawites would do anything to obscure their true convictions from Christians and orthodox Moslems alike. Persecuted for centuries, they made cunning their armor.

The French used Alawites as Janissaries in the colonial army, and since independence Alawites have dominated the officer corps. This phenomenon helps to explain Assad's rise to power, but it does not explain his longevity—for in fact he has ruled Syria longer than any of his predecessors and ruled it rather well. Self-reliant and shrewd, humorous, stubborn, unforgiving, not very cultured, a night worker who never seemed to sleep, Assad learned much from his own mistakes. He had been minister of defense and commander of the air force in 1967. Israel's conquest that year of the Golan Heights, and the destruction of two-thirds of Syria's air force on the ground, was largely Assad's fault. In fact, he considered himself personally responsible for the defeat. In September of 1970, Assad ignored his superiors and refused to commit the air force to the Palestinian guerrillas fighting King Hussein of Jordan, for he knew that such audacity might invite American and Israeli intervention. As president, he modified militant Ba'athi socialism and revived the private sector, opening Syria to Western trade, stimulating the repatriation of vanished capital and rekindling the loyalty of the merchant class. Assisted by the Soviets, he launched the construction of an immense dam on the Euphrates river to multiply farms and food.

With political freedom Assad was more frugal, for he had to balance a precarious coalition of Sunni and Shi'a Moslems, Alawites and Christians, Nasserists, Communists, urban entrepreneurs, rural conservatives, extremist Ba'athi ideologues within and without the army. The militants amongst these constrained Assad almost as much as he constrained them, and on Israel they were implacable. Hatred of Israel was far more fierce in Syria than in Egypt. During the October war, the Syrians snatched back much of the Golan Heights, but then the Israelis bombed vital centers of Syria's infrastructure—a major power station, the port at Latakia, the oil refinery at Homs—and marched beyond the Golan almost to the suburbs of Damascus.

Assad recognized the reality of Israel; he accepted U.N. Resolution 338 following Soviet assurances that Israel would withdraw from all occupied territory and recognize the rights of the Palestinians. But he was wary of Kissinger, whose gradualist diplomacy appeared to him as just another stratagem to strengthen Israel. Suspicion is perhaps the predominant Syrian trait. It hovered in the halls of the presidential palace on that evening of December when—beneath an oil painting of Saladin's victory over the Crusaders—Assad welcomed Dr. Kissinger and his party.

Typically, Kissinger began by being funny. Through the interpreter he said, "I should teach you English, Mr. President. You'll be the first Arab leader to speak English with a German accent. Did you meet Mr. Sisco? I had to bring him with me—if I left him in Washington, he might mount a *coup d'état.*" Assad laughed. Kissinger assumed that the Syrians, like other Arabs, were intrigued by his success with women, so he talked about women and repeated some lecherous pleasantries. There ensued a seminar on world affairs, Kissinger reverting to his role of Harvard professor—analyzing China, the Soviet Union, American domestic politics—the President of Syria his attentive pupil.*

Kissinger observed that he was the first American secretary of state to visit Syria in more than 20 years, since John Foster Dulles, in fact.

"The United States is responsible for the delay," Assad rejoined.

The Syrian foreign minister, Abdel Halim Khaddam, had already pointed that out, Kissinger responded. "The Foreign Minister was polite, but I don't wish to suggest his views lacked strength. Weakness is not a Syrian attribute."

Assad brushed aside the compliment, and invited Kissinger to be clear and blunt.

"It's not our policy to divide the Arabs," Kissinger said. "I'll always tell everyone I talk to the same thing."

"That's difficult to do," Assad said, "but in the long run it's better."

KISSINGER: We must have confidence in each other.... We must get a peace conference started to establish a legal framework for

_____
*Perhaps I am exaggerating. Assad told me recently that "I never was Dr. Kissinger's pupil." He laughed at my suggestion. "Neither Kissinger nor anybody could do that to me."

negotiations. With that, we'll work for a disengagement agreement, first on the Egyptian front, then seek to do the same on the Syrian front. The immediate problem is the letter of invitation to the conference. We've been talking of opening on the eighteenth, but we may need a few more days. What are your views?

ASSAD: They depend upon our talk today. . . .

KISSINGER: We have no peace plan of our own. It's easy to make specific proposals—the important thing is to take practical steps. We and the Soviets agreed only that there should be a peace conference. Eventually it will have to deal with all of the questions—withdrawals, security, borders, Jerusalem, and the Palestinians. . . . Is it true you have not yet decided to attend the Geneva conference?

ASSAD: We've not decided *not* to attend.

Kissinger produced his draft letter of invitation to the conference, to be sent simultaneously by the United States and the Soviet Union to the United Nations Secretary-General. He pointed to the crucial sentence: "The parties have also agreed that the question of other participants from the Middle East area will be discussed during the first stage of the Conference"—i.e., the Palestinians were to be excluded from the initial phase of negotiations.

KISSINGER: Israel didn't want a reference to the Palestinians at this point. We recognize that you will not solve this problem without taking Palestinian interests into account, but we think it would be a mistake to take up the Palestinian question at the beginning of the conference.

ASSAD: I understood that an earlier text had referred to "the question of the Palestinians."

Assad was alluding to his exchanges with Sadat. Through interminable cups of Turkish coffee and sweet tea, the conversation dragged on; two hours and a half had been scheduled; after six hours they were still talking, and in Amman the King of Jordan expected Kissinger for dinner. Rattling his amber worry beads, Assad began a long exposition of Syrian policy, assailing the United States for its support of Israel.

KISSINGER: I think we should talk now of the practical problems of convening the Geneva conference.

ASSAD: Does the United States agree, first, that Syria cannot surrender territory in a settlement; second, that there can be no settlement without a solution for the Arab people of Palestine; and, third, is the purpose of the peace conference to carry out these two objectives, or to use up time without achieving a solution?

KISSINGER: ... We're prepared to discuss with you the withdrawal of Israeli forces in the first stage, and we recognize that there would have to be further withdrawals in later stages.... It's evident there won't be any settlement that you don't agree to.... Now we must move into the disengagement phase.

ASSAD: Any disengagement must involve all of the Golan Heights.

KISSINGER: That's out of the question.... The first problem is the territory occupied in the October war—and whether Israel will withdraw from *that*....

ASSAD: Before Geneva convenes there ought to be a disengagement agreement.

KISSINGER: For Israel, it's important that Syria provide a list of Israeli prisoners of war, permit the Red Cross to visit them, and release wounded prisoners....

ASSAD: Why should I give up this card? What am I getting for it? Brezhnev never mentioned that to me. The disengagement ought to involve the whole of Golan because the whole of Golan is very small.

KISSINGER: Look, it took me four years to settle the whole Vietnamese war. You're asking for the impossible.... I thought we were going to discuss the date for convening Geneva.... What about the language regarding "other participants"?

ASSAD: Anything in that letter that you and President Sadat agree upon is agreeable to me.

KISSINGER: But how will you answer the letter?

ASSAD: There should be disengagement before the conference convenes.... The text of the letter is not accurate. It says Syria has agreed to attend the conference. I have not agreed. First I have to know if we must give up territory.

KISSINGER: I can't give you answers to these kind of questions at this stage.

ASSAD: Then perhaps you should postpone the conference.

# Kisses and Mangoes

After midnight on December 16, Dr. Kissinger arrived finally at Amman to dine with Hussein ibn Talal al-Hashem of the Hashemite Kingdom of Jordan. He was greeted at the airport by Zeid al-Rifai, the urbane and balding young prime minister and foreign minister who had been his pupil at Harvard. ("I attended his seminar on American foreign policy," Rifai told me recently. "Dr. Kissinger was different from the other professors. His seminar had a unique way of disseminating a great deal of information with humor and sarcasm. I was his only Arab student. We engaged in constant arguments. He had no tendency to Zionism and no grasp of the Middle East. After I left Harvard I lost contact with him until we assumed similar positions—I as His Majesty's political adviser, he as President Nixon's most powerful counsellor.")

Drums rolled; bagpipes blew; *kaffiyeh*-clad troops of the Arab Legion presented arms; the rooftops swarmed with police and soldiers manning machine guns and submachine guns. Dr. Kissinger and his party—Assistant Secretary Sisco, his deputies

Alfred (Roy) Atherton, Harold Saunders, *et al.*—must hardly have noticed. They were all by now nearly comatose with fatigue, somnambulists of diplomacy stumbling by reflex from one capital to the next. On they journeyed to Basman Palace, which beyond high walls, orchards, and pine trees stood at the summit of a hill overlooking the valleys of Amman, like Rome itself, a city of seven hills.

King Hussein had kept the dinner warm, but did not serve it until he had conferred with his guest. Alone of the Arab leaders, Hussein had known Kissinger before the October war, for he visited Washington regularly. Kissinger liked the diminutive Hashemite, and flattered him, each time they met, for his fortitude in his war with the Palestinian *fedayin* in 1970. ("We were all inspired by Your Majesty's extraordinary courage during that crisis"—Kissinger's ritual encomium to the King.) Jordan had not joined in the October conflict, but Hussein was as covetous of Arab Jerusalem and the rest of his conquered territory on the west bank of the River Jordan as Sadat and Assad were of theirs. The King and his advisers—Crown Prince Hassan, Zeid Rifai, Abdel Moneim al-Rifai (Zeid's uncle and a former prime minister)—wished above all to discover Jordan's place in Kissinger's new diplomacy.

"What does 'disengagement' mean?" Zeid Rifai asked. "Does it include Jordan?"

"It refers primarily to the belligerents of the last war," Kissinger replied, "but it should not exclude Jordan. It means, first, creating buffer zones between the belligerents of the last war. After that, there would come a second stage." In other words, until Kissinger had disposed of disengagement on the Egyptian and Syrian fronts, Jordan would have to wait.

The Jordanians, to their later regret, did not that night press for their proper disengagement, though Zeid Rifai expressed his concern that "Egypt will make its own agreement with Israel, and Jordan will be left out."

"It's all right to discuss details separately," the King added, "but the peace settlement should be a package."

Abdel Moneim Rifai wondered if Kissinger contemplated a disengagement phase for Jordan; his nephew suggested that "we should at least have a few kilometers on the west bank."

"I'm not sure that's possible," Kissinger said. "Nevertheless, it's important for Jordan to go to Geneva to establish that it's a party. Israel will not give up the west bank to Arafat."

Hussein assured him that a Jordanian delegation, headed by Zeid Rifai, would be present at Geneva. The conversation was significant, not for what it accomplished—save for the King's assent to the Geneva conference, it accomplished nothing—but for what it postponed. Kissinger assumed that he could deal with Jordan in his own good time, and he persisted in that supposition until it was too late. (We shall, in due course, have much to say about that.) The party repaired, toward two or three in the morning, to the royal table, where, struggling to stay awake, they dined upon overcooked rice and mutton.

Kissinger retired to the royal guesthouse at about four; he rose about six, and left later that morning for Lebanon. Beirut had been his intended destination, but the capital was throbbing with anti-Kissinger demonstrations mounted by Palestinians and leftist Moslem Lebanese. So he detoured to an air-force base near Rayak, in the Bekaa valley, a few miles from the Syrian border, for a luncheon with Suleiman Franjieh, the president of Lebanon. Since Lebanon had never substantially engaged in war with Israel, it was not a direct party to Kissinger's diplomacy and it did not need to participate at Geneva, but Kissinger wished to inform Franjieh of his plans and to win his sympathy and support.

Franjieh—white-haired, stubborn, not very intelligent—was an erstwhile assassin, a veteran of the tribal vendettas that are the flesh and blood of Lebanese history. Earlier in his life he had participated in a shoot-out in a mountain church, joining members of his Maronite clan in gunning down a rival family during a funeral Mass. This notorious incident was partly the reason he was president, for the Christians of Lebanon intended it as a warning to the Palestinians that Franjieh would crush them brutally if they violated Lebanese sovereignty and provoked a war with Israel across the southern border.

Franjieh urged Kissinger to create a Palestinian state with all dispatch, so that his several hundred thousand Palestinians would leave Lebanon, allowing it to live in peace. Such a state was not one of Dr. Kissinger's priorities, and the ensuing upheavals in Lebanon are a measure of his myopic neglect of that elementary problem—the future of the Palestinian people.

That afternoon Kissinger returned to Jerusalem. He had Egypt's and Jordan's agreement to convene at Geneva, but not Syria's—and not Israel's. The Israeli populace was hostile. Much of the press—convinced that Kissinger's promises to protect Israel were insincere—doubted that a peace conference could accomplish anything. The Secretary dined that evening at Abba Eban's residence, a rather modest stone house with a wealth of books. Golda Meir presided, assisted by Eban, Deputy Prime Minister Yigal Allon, General Dayan, Ambassador Dinitz, Minister of Finance Pinhas Sapir, and their advisers; Kissinger brought Sisco, Atherton, Kenneth Keating (his ambassador to Tel Aviv), and several other subordinates. "Pork chops for dinner?" Kissinger jested. No—though the food, as usual in Israel, was dreadful, hardly more delicious than Hashemite mutton chops.

Kissinger regaled the Israelis with an uproarious account of his conversation with President Assad—who seemed the soul of reason, Kissinger said, until he announced, at the very end, that Syria would not be represented at Geneva. Assad's concept of disengagement, he added, was immediate recovery of the whole Golan Heights. The Israelis roared. The rest of the evening, and the next day, were less convivial.

Mrs. Meir pressed Kissinger on the Israeli prisoners of war in Syria. "Assad was very hard on this," Kissinger replied, whereupon Allon informed him that the government had promised the Knesset (the Israeli parliament) not to negotiate with Syria until Assad delivered his list of POWs. Hardly more than several scores of Israeli prisoners were involved, but legally the Syrians were violating the Geneva Convention, and the issue had traumatized Israeli public opinion. Dayan warned flatly that Israel would not go to Geneva until the list was handed over.

"You should consider the international consequences if you refuse to go," Kissinger replied. "Israel is in a difficult position. You need maneuvering room. I'm not suggesting that your position is wrong—it's morally right—but you must weigh the consequences." He turned to Egypt, and to Sadat's intention, once disengagement was achieved, to begin economic reconstruction and reopen the Suez Canal—"but he wants to keep some forces on the east bank."

MRS. MEIR: Why . . . if he wants peace?

KISSINGER: His view is that he can't afford to withdraw from his own territory which he has reconquered. We have to relieve the oil embargo, the threat of renewed hostilities. Time is critical. Faisal can't lift the embargo alone—without losing all he's gained by supporting the overall Arab position.

The dialogue leaped aimlessly from topic to topic, and came to rest on Jordan. Allon observed that most Arabs on the west bank favored Hussein: "Our concern is that there will be pressure to turn the west bank over to the Palestinians." Dayan conceded that Palestinian pressures might prevent Jordan from concluding a final settlement, "but it might be possible to reestablish some form of Jordanian authority on the west bank."

Kissinger urged the Israelis to make a dramatic move to strengthen Hussein's position. "You should appear," he urged, "to be taking the initiative, and not simply to be doing things grudgingly under pressure." As we shall see, the Israelis ignored this advice—eventually to their own (and Kissinger's) great regret.

As for the United Nations, it was then, as it is now, immensely unpopular in Israel; if there was to be a peace conference, Mrs. Meir insisted, the role of the U.N. had to be minimal. Moreover, the Israelis were unsatisfied with Kissinger's letter of invitation to the conference, and they dissected every phrase. Finally Kissinger fell back upon a favorite device. "Accept the letter as it is," he told them, "and then explain your own interpretation in a statement to the Knesset." It was after midnight when the Israelis bowed.*

That left—or so it seemed—only the issue of Israel's refusal to go to Geneva should the Syrians produce no list of Israeli POWs. It was one o'clock in the morning. "We can't solve that tonight," Kissinger sighed, and he went home to bed.

They resumed next morning, in the conference room of Prime Minister Meir's modernistic offices near the Knesset; now General David Elazar, the Israeli chief of staff, and General Aharon Yariv, a former chief of intelligence, joined them.

Dr. Kissinger focused on the theory and application of an Israeli-Egyptian disengagement pact. A disengagement was clearly in Israel's interest, he argued—it would produce an early negotiating success, avoid discussion of Israel's final frontiers, and assuage pressures upon Israel and the United States. Above all, disengagement would render it very difficult for the Egyptians to resume war. "I've discussed disengagement with Sadat," Kissinger continued, "and he's accepted the general concept. He will thin out his forces on the east bank of the canal, limit arms in that area, and accept a buffer zone under the U.N. I made it clear to him that it's important to Israel to retain the [Mitla and Gidi] passes in the Sinai."

"The passes," Allon replied, "can be discussed as part of a final settlement." Allon's remark was but a faint foreshadowing of what was later to become a savage quarrel between Kissinger and the Israelis. For the moment, the Israelis insisted upon an effective and permanent United Nations force, upon a severe limitation of Egyptian SAMs, upon guarantees against the resumption of war. Kissinger exhorted them to avoid a fixation upon military details: "We must keep in mind the *strategic purpose* of a disengagement. You have to remember what is at stake—you have to make a correct assessment of the overall situation. If we don't get an agreement quickly, by the end of

*The full text of the letter—outlining the legal framework of the Geneva conference, and convening the conference under the auspices of the United Nations—will be found in Appendix Five.

January, then all of the pressures—the oil embargo, the Russians, the Europeans, the Japanese—will be brought to bear on us." If the disengagement was not achieved, and very soon, then Sadat might abandon American mediation, and Israel itself would be immeasurably worse off. Israel might bargain hard, Kissinger implied, but it should not make its price too high. The world would not stand still for Israel.

KISSINGER: Look, Sadat has already changed his position. Initially he demanded El Arish, then the evacuation of the Sinai passes. I think a lot of these details are negotiable with Sadat, but you have to establish your own priorities. . . .

MRS. MEIR *sharply*: You've painted a realistic picture, but what you call disengagement is really just a withdrawal of Israeli forces, and there's nothing reciprocal about *that*.

KISSINGER: . . . He will restore the civil populace to the canal zone—a guarantee against hostilities.

MRS. MEIR *passionately*: We're going to a peace conference, not to a disengagement conference. What does Sadat say about peace? This is just the first step back to 1967. After this agreement everything will be the same—except the world will have its oil.

KISSINGER *mischievously*: That would make a big difference.

Mrs. Meir was upset, and she meant to speak her mind. The Arabs might impose their embargo again, she warned, whenever they wanted something. Did Dr. Kissinger forget 1970, when the military standstill went into effect upon the canal—and the Egyptians moved their missiles forward? "Reality," she said, "is whatever the other side wants, *we* have to accept."

Kissinger protested that the cease-fire upon the canal had lasted for two and a half years, then pleaded anew the benefits to Israel of a successful disengagement—but the Prime Minister was not to be deterred. "What do we do if the Syrians send no list of prisoners?" she demanded. "Doesn't the Geneva Convention require that?"

"We negotiated four years with the North Vietnamese without getting a list," Kissinger shot back. "We kept invoking the Geneva Convention, too. All you're being asked to do is to go to Geneva, not to make any commitments."

Mrs. Meir was outraged. "The Syrians have been mistreating our prisoners," she said. "There must be a limit somewhere. There must be *some human feeling*."

More calmly, Allon suggested that Kissinger persuade President Assad that Israel, in return for the list of prisoners, was prepared to negotiate—and that the negotiations would have a territorial dimension.

"I already told him that," Kissinger said, "and he turned it down."

The meeting concluded as indecisively as it had begun. Kissinger fussed about briefing the press, contrived the customary euphoria for a joint communiqué: ". . . friendly, useful talks . . . agreement on all issues relating to the convening of the peace conference, and some of the principles to be involved in the disengagement phase."

He was clearly attempting to force the Israelis' hand. Golda slapped him down. "That won't do," she said. "The cabinet hasn't agreed to say that we're going to the conference."

"We can say we agreed on *procedures*," Eban suggested.

"We should add that you agreed that the first item at the conference should be separation of forces," Kissinger said. "We have to say *something*."

It was by now already the afternoon of December 17, the very eve of the day Dr. Kissinger had intended to convene the peace conference. He knew that his deadline would elude him—that further exchanges were essential with Sadat, with the Syrians, the Jordanians, the Russians, the Secretary-General of the United Nations—but he was prepared to move the planets to assemble all of the parties at Geneva several days before Christmastide. In a nightmarish (indeed phantasmagoric) migration, he flew off from Tel Aviv to Lisbon, from there swiftly to Madrid, from there swiftly to Paris, conferring in each capital with the leaders of those nations, maintaining all the while a fusillade of communications with the principals of the peace conference. At the Ritz Hotel in Lisbon, Sisco and Atherton, sleepless for several nights themselves, woke Kissinger at three in the morning with a message from Fahmy that required an instant response. Sadat had still been struggling to persuade the Syrians to be present at Geneva, but the next afternoon the Syrians formally announced they would stay away, and accused both Israel and the United States of "maneuvers that would lead us into an endless wilderness." The Israeli cabinet, however, endorsed Israel's participation and dispatched Eban to Geneva. Kissinger arrived at Geneva on the evening of December 20 and plunged instantly into clearing from the scene all final complications.

Kissinger prevailed. The peace conference opened on December 21, 1973, in the Palais des Nations, once the home of the League of Nations. Israel was there, with Egypt and Jordan—but not the Syrians or the Palestine Liberation Organization. Officially the conference was convened by Dr. Kurt Waldheim, the United Nations secretary-general, but—as the Israelis wished—he was only a decorous bystander. Nominally the co-chairmanship was shared by the United States and the Soviet Union, but the Russians were surprisingly serviceable and Kissinger stage-managed everything. In his address, perhaps the most eloquent he has ever delivered, Kissinger recognized the obstacles but voiced ambitious hopes:

We are convened here at a moment of historic opportunity. . . . For the first time in a generation the peoples of the Middle East are sitting together to turn their talents to the challenge of a lasting peace. . . . Either we begin today the process of correcting the conditions which produced [the Arab-Israeli] conflict, or we doom untold tens of thousands to travail, sorrow, and further inconclusive bloodshed. When the history of our era is written, it will speak not of a series of Arab-Israeli wars but of one war broken by periods of uneasy armistices and temporary cease-fires. That war has already lasted twenty-five years. Whether future histories will call this the era of the twenty-five-year Arab-Israeli war, or the thirty-year war, or the fifty-year war, rests in large measure in our hands. . . .

We are challenged by emotions so deeply felt—by causes so passionately believed and pursued—that the tragic march from cataclysm to cataclysm, each more costly and decisive than the last, sometimes seems preordained. Yet our presence here today, in itself a momentous accomplishment, is a symbol of rejection of this fatalistic view. Respect for the forces of history does not mean blind submission to those forces. There is an Arab saying, *Elli Fat Mat*, which means that the past is dead. . . .

People on both sides have had enough of bloodshed. No further proof of heroism is necessary; no military point remains to be made. . . . One side seeks the recovery of sovereignty and the redress of grievances suffered by a displaced people. The other seeks security and recognition of its legitimacy as a nation. The common goal of peace must surely be broad enough to embrace all these aspirations. . . . Our final objective is the implementation in all its parts of Resolution 242. This goal has the full support of the United States. . . . A peace agreement must include these elements, among others: withdrawals, recognized frontiers, security arrangements, guarantees, a settlement of the legitimate interests of the Palestinians, and a recognition that Jerusalem contains places considered holy by three great religions.

Peace will require that we relate the imperative of withdrawals to the necessities of security, the requirement of guarantees to the sovereignty of the parties, the hopes of the displaced to the realities now existing. . . . There is a measure of safety in power to prevent aggression, but there is greater security still in arrangements considered so just that no one wishes to overthrow them. . . .

The great tragedies of history occur not when right confronts wrong, but when two rights face each other. The problems of the Middle East today have such a character. There is justice on all sides, but there is greater justice still in finding a truth which merges all aspirations in the realization of a common humanity. It was a Jewish sage who, speaking for all mankind, expressed this problem well: "If I am not for myself, who is for me, but if I am for myself alone, who am I?"

There was a quarrel about seating arrangements (the Arabs refused to sit beside the Israelis), a predictable exchange of polemics between Ismail Fahmy and Abba Eban (Fahmy accused Israel of "atrocities" against the Palestinians, Eban accused Syria of torturing Israeli prisoners), but otherwise Kissinger's scenario was observed. After the ceremonial overture, an Egyptian-Israeli working committee embarked upon discussions of disengagement, and the conference adjourned— supposedly to come alive again soon after the Israeli elections. It has yet to reconvene. Some had foreseen the conference as a kind of Arab-Israeli Congress of Vienna, but in retrospect it amounted to little more than a short cartoon, mildly entertaining, vivacious now and then, but ephemeral and insubstantial.

"It was the most peculiar conference I ever attended," Prime Minister Rifai of Jordan lamented to me recently. "I expected it would be based on Resolutions 242 and 338. But it had no terms of reference, no rules of procedure, and no agenda. The first two meetings were reserved for televised speeches. At the third meeting I was surprised to hear the suggestion for the joint Egyptian-Israeli committee on disengagement, which should have been discussed *before* Geneva so we could get on with a global settlement. I put a request on the record for a disengagement on the Jordan-Israeli front, but the conference broke up and Dr. Kissinger busied himself with the Israelis and Egyptians." Several members of the Jordanian delegation were Palestinian, but the conference did not consider the concerns of the Palestinian diaspora. In fact, on December 20, the day before the conference, Kissinger passed to the Israelis a secret and very significant "Memorandum of Understanding" promising that no other parties would be invited to future meetings at Geneva "without the agreement of the initial participants"—which meant an Israeli veto on participation by the P.L.O.

Prime Minister Rifai was not the first to suggest that Dr. Kissinger staged the conference mainly as pomp and circumstance, as a public-relations drumroll for a mouse-sized marvel—the first Egyptian-Israeli disengagement. In justice to Kissinger, however, it should be remembered that *at the time* he considered Geneva might subsequently serve a useful purpose as the site for negotiations.

Golda Meir's Labor government was returned to power with a reduced majority; in the Knesset, it lost seats to the rightist and recalcitrant Likud. In early January 1974, General Dayan returned to Washington to confer with Dr. Kissinger. Though a "hawk," Dayan was the most creative of the Israeli leaders; implicitly he conceded an Israeli withdrawal into the Sinai, and now he produced his "five-zone" concept. The area of disengagement should cover five zones, he said—a U.N. buffer (zone one) between the Israeli and Egyptian armies, whose forces in those zones (two and three, respectively) would be severely limited. Beyond zones two and three, there should extend on either side of the Suez Canal zones four and five, respectively, each 30 kilometers deep, where surface-to-air missiles would likewise be forbidden.

This became the conceptual foundation of the accord that was soon to follow. The idea was Dayan's, not Kissinger's. Dayan invited Kissinger to return to the Middle East; Kissinger contacted Sadat, who urged him to come at once. On January 12, Kissinger reached Aswan, where Sadat was recovering from bronchitis. They conferred at the President's rustic villa, surrounded by a tropical garden overlooking the Nile not far from the high dam (which Foster Dulles had refused to finance, thereby provoking Nasser's nationalization of the Suez Canal, the eruption of the Suez War, and the Soviet penetration of Egypt). Sadat exhorted Kissinger to undertake an immediate "shuttle" and to conclude the disengagement forthwith. Kissinger had hitherto planned to mediate the principles, then defer to the Egyptian-Israeli military committee to resolve the particulars at Geneva. "Why Geneva?" Sadat asked. "You can do it all here."

Kissinger returned to Aswan next day from Jerusalem; on January 14, Sadat accepted Dayan's conceptual framework and added, "Let's go fast. I want you to remain in the area until the agreement is signed. I won't quibble over details." In Washington and Jerusalem, Kissinger had already determined the scope of the Israeli withdrawal; now the problem focused on limitations of force. "It's difficult for me," Sadat said, "to sign a document which limits the forces in my own territory."

That afternoon, Kissinger proposed to enshrine the disengagement in two documents—a formal agreement to be signed by Israel and Egypt, and a separate letter from the United States to each government stating its understanding of the limitation of forces. The formal agreement would only allude to the limitations; the American letter would define them. With this sophistry Sadat could claim that Israel had not *imposed* the limitations upon Egypt. Sadat assented in a *tête-à-tête*; later, to Sadat's subordinates, Kissinger slyly suggested that the idea was Sadat's.

By evening, the American team had produced the two draft documents. The Egyptians refined them, then Kissinger flew to Israel. He negotiated mostly with Allon, Eban, Dayan, Dinitz, and Elazar because Golda Meir was ill with shingles. Describing to the Israelis his *tête-à-tête* with Sadat, Kissinger illumined the President's motivations. "Tell me seriously," Sadat had said, "what Israel can and cannot accept, and for Egypt I'll tell you the same." Sadat recognized the benefits and disadvantages of a swift negotiation. Swiftness avoided interference from the Russians and the radical Arabs, and eluded the peril of another war. Nevertheless, Sadat had said, with swiftness "you may not get the best deal on every issue because you can't stop to haggle over each detail."

Exceedingly sensitive to force limitations, Sadat had asked Kissinger to camouflage Dayan's five-zone framework. Sadat agreed to specify five zones in the agreement, but only three on the map—for Egypt, Israel, and the United Nations, respectively. "All right," Dayan told Kissinger, "there will be three zones. We'll produce a new map you can take back to Aswan." The Israelis further dissected Kissinger's drafts, and with virtuosity Kissinger managed to accommodate their fixation on legalisms. We glimpse him interpolating, scratching out, scribbling all over the drafts: "Paragraph one could be divided into two paragraphs. The next three paragraphs—no problem. Paragraph five probably won't survive in this form."

By the fourth day of the shuttle, the agreement was assured. Kissinger was already quibbling with Dayan about the timing of the announcement. Dayan wanted to brief the Knesset first; Kissinger had a horror of leaks and wished to unveil his victory as a bombshell for the evening telecasts in the United States. Some technicalities remained to be negotiated. At Aswan, General Gamasy, the Egyptian chief of staff, told Kissinger "We must keep some artillery on the east bank. The 122-mm. howitzer is organic to our units." Kissinger returned with this complication to Jerusalem.

"May I suggest something constructive?" Dayan said. "We'll agree to howitzers—but we'll specify a range limitation."

"Well, let's say a range of no more than 12 kilometers," Kissinger suggested. And so it was.

The agreement was announced by President Nixon at the White House on January 17, 1974, and signed by General Gamasy and General Elazar at Kilometer 101 the next day—less than a week after Kissinger's appearance at Aswan.* It contained all of Dayan's essentials—indeed, Dayan can be called its secret father. The Israelis were to withdraw into Sinai to a line roughly 15 miles from the Suez Canal, protected by a U.N. buffer, leaving the Egyptians a thin ribbon of territory on the east bank, where reciprocally they would diminish their army from 60,000 to 7,000 men; symmetrically beyond either line, no missiles for 30 kilometers. Sadat gave no promise of nonbelligerency, but neither did he get a timetable for further Israeli withdrawals, and secretly he promised the United States to permit nonmilitary Israeli cargoes to transit the canal as soon as it was cleared. The agreement was public; the American letter defining the limitation of forces was secret, though the Israelis leaked it straightaway.

Additionally Kissinger gave the Israelis a secret bilateral Memorandum of Understanding in which the United States conveyed Egypt's promise to clear the canal, rebuild its cities, and resume peacetime activities in that region. The United States also agreed in the memorandum to insist in the Security Council, should the issue arise, that the withdrawal of the U.N. Emergency Force (U.N.E.F.) from the buffer zone required the consent of both parties. Egypt and Israel had accepted American aerial reconnaissance of the disengagement area; the memorandum concluded that "the United States will make every effort to

*The full text of the agreement will be found in Appendix Six.

be fully responsive on a continuing and long-term basis to Israel's military equipment requirements."

Dr. Kissinger's predominant emotion in this shuttle should be
obvious—*it was easy*. He applied minimal pressure on either
party, since by now both Israel and Egypt needed the agreement badly. Israel had to demobilize or face bankruptcy. Sadat
had to save the Third Army and prove that the war had won him
territory.

Not that Sadat's subordinates were satisfied—Fahmy felt that
Kissinger could have delivered more territory; General Gamasy
considered the agreement militarily unsound, a great impediment to the resumption of war should diplomacy fail in the
future and leave Israel in possession of most of the Sinai. Other
generals were disturbed as well that the Soviet Union had not
even been consulted. They were good soldiers, however, and,
like Fahmy, they acquiesced when Sadat pronounced his will.
Mohammed Hassanein Heikal, who appeared at Aswan at the
end of the negotiation, protested that the agreement would
freeze the situation to Israel's advantage. Heikal refused to acquiesce, and quickly fell from the favor of the President, who
dismissed him from his editorship of *Al Ahram*.

Sadat treated his subordinates as Kissinger treated Sisco—as
mere technicians, to be entrusted only with details. Fahmy was
deeply vexed to be excluded from the *tête-à-têtes*, but Kissinger craved privacy with the President to convince him of
his views—above all, the narrow perimeter of the possible.
Fahmy and Gamasy, Kissinger feared, might have maneuvered
for more, and protracted the negotiation. In Israel, the agreement required approval by the cabinet, but Sadat made every
crucial decision alone with Kissinger.

As Dr. Kissinger took his leave of Aswan, beneath the mango
trees of the tropical garden, Sadat kissed him. "You are not only
my friend," the President said, "you are my brother." No doubt
the Secretary was moved, and amused. Of the Israelis he had
said, "The reason they don't get better treatment is because
Eban doesn't kiss me."

# 8

# Farewell, Miss Israel

The swift success of the Israeli-Egyptian disengagement confirmed Dr. Kissinger's belief that step-by-step diplomacy was the best—indeed the only—method for containing the Arab-Israeli conflict. By now Egyptians and Israelis were well schooled in the dynamics of that method. Kissinger avoided essence—*viz.* the Palestinian problem—and clung to the periphery, for in his view rearrangement of the periphery alone was possible. On the periphery he encouraged the belligerents themselves to provide the points of reference; that done, he identified the components, then skillfully composed them. His great function—he has said so many times—was to explain persuasively to each party the constraints upon the other.

Further patterns of Kissinger's diplomacy were becoming clear. On the one hand, the Arabs expected him to pursue a final settlement which would somehow include the Palestinians, and to push the Israelis back to their old frontiers with deliberate speed. On the other, the Israelis expected him to confine his diplomacy—at least for some time—to readjustments of the

113

cease-fire lines, to relieve international pressures upon Israel, and in the meanwhile to fortify Israel with an unrelenting flow of arms. Kissinger did not promise the Arabs to restore their 1967 frontiers, though he permitted them to believe he would eventually endeavor to do so; he did not promise the Israelis they could retain substantial portions of conquered territory, though he was at pains to point out to them that they would not need to consider final frontiers for some time to come. Did Kissinger wish a stalemate? On the contrary. Nevertheless, as we have seen, he argued to the Israelis that limited disengagement agreements would appease for a period the Arabs' appetite for territory, create a climate of momentum and progress, and allow Israel the leisure to postpone agonizing decisions indefinitely.

Ambiguity was Kissinger's most useful tool, for beneath the umbrella of that ambiguity both sides could claim victories. Ambiguity also protected Kissinger's domestic flank, for he knew that, should American Jews perceive him as endangering Israel's vital interests, he might not be able to conduct any Arab policy at all. As for a grand strategy of the future that gazed beyond ambiguity, beyond rearrangements of the periphery in the here and now, Kissinger did not seem to have one. True, at Geneva he had defined the elements of a final peace—withdrawals, recognized frontiers, security arrangements, guarantees, a settlement for Jerusalem and the Palestinians—but these were vague aspirations drawn from Resolution 242 and previous American policy statements, and he appeared to possess no tangible notion of how to achieve them.

As a Spenglerian, as a "historical pessimist," Dr. Kissinger doubted philosophically that any deep problem could be solved. He seems to have concluded that to seek solutions soon of basic problems in the Middle East was hopeless, beyond his reach, and thus in compensation he pursued immediate, minor triumphs so as to diminish the crisis. For their war, Kissinger owed the Arabs that much. But if anything, his tactic of  ambiguity—of peripheral readjustment, of postponing for the undefined future the resolution of the great questions—

predominantly favored Israel. Nevertheless, argue (and later rage) with them as he might, he could not convince the Israelis that his policy served their interest.

There were other patterns and other problems. By hastening back and forth between Arabs and Israelis to arrange marginal solutions, by entangling himself in the most intricate mechanics of cease-fires and disengagements, Kissinger established Kissinger as indispensable to future peace. Had he devoted that energy to a swifter consummation of broader objectives in a general peace conference, his method might be easier to defend, but by his own choice he became enmeshed in a minefield of detail impossible to elude thereafter. He would protest that no other diplomat could have done it, that no deputy possessed prestige or power in sufficient measure to untangle even issues of detail; but by committing his personal intervention from the very first, even to the resolution of trivia, Kissinger became the prisoner of his own method.

The Sinai disengagement also helped to kill the Geneva conference. Sadat was loath to negotiate with Israel alone; he could not risk returning to Geneva until Syria like Egypt had regained some territory in disengagement. Moreover Israel—tormented by a cabinet crisis—was in no mood to negotiate affairs of substance. En route home from Aswan, at Sadat's behest, Kissinger called again at Damascus, where he found President Assad furious at Sadat for accepting disengagement but more willing now to consider disengagement for himself. Assad reduced his demands and asked for only half of Golan. This gave Kissinger a point of reference; he passed it to the Israelis, who refused to negotiate until Assad produced his list of Israeli prisoners. Kissinger returned to Damascus in February (1974), then delivered the list of 65 prisoners to Golda Meir, who wept with relief and gratitude. Israel and Syria dispatched negotiators to Washington, where Kissinger found their positions still immensely far apart.

In the meanwhile Kissinger was grappling with the oil embargo. As part of his bargain with Kissinger for the Sinai disengagement, Sadat endeavored to persuade the oil princes to end the boycott, but his good offices were not enough. During December and January, Nixon and Kissinger played "impeachment politics" with the Saudis, warning that the embargo would weaken the embattled President and diminish his power to promote peace. The warning was buttressed by murky hints of American military intervention in the Persian Gulf. When neither ploy worked, Kissinger threatened to publish previous correspondence with the Saudis which might embarrass them before the other Arabs. The American ambassador to Riyadh, James E. Akins, had already clashed with Kissinger in November, threatening to resign should Kissinger exclude him from the audience with King Faisal; Kissinger relented. Now Akins refused to convey Kissinger's message to the King, and sought out Omar Saqqaf, the minister of state, instead. Saqqaf warned against informing the King; Saudi Arabia, he suggested, could also publish correspondence which might embarrass the United States. Kissinger reconsidered, and the message Akins transmitted to the King was more gracious.

But Kissinger sustained his pressure. Though the Arabs had vowed to lift the embargo only when Israel withdrew completely, by February they were alarmed by Europe's penury and plagued with doubt. Syria urged a prolongation, but the oil princes sent Saqqaf and Ismail Fahmy to Washington to strike a bargain: do something for Syria, they told Nixon and Kissinger, and the embargo will stop. Kissinger promised to try; in March the embargo was suspended. Kissinger subsequently denied the "linkage," but in fact his Syrian shuttle was the price he paid to end the embargo—and (in terms of substance) not a high price at that. (He would have undertaken the shuttle anyway—to strengthen Sadat and to end the war of attrition on the Golan Heights.) The Saudis were rewarded with a grandiose American commitment to industrialize their kingdom and to sell them large quantities of modern tanks, naval vessels, and fighter aircraft.

On the last day of April, Dr. Kissinger flew back to the Middle

East to embark upon the new negotiation. He called first at Alexandria to see President Sadat, who had become by now his chief adviser on Arab affairs. Kissinger wished to know how to deal with Assad; Sadat explored with him those vagaries and prepossessions of the Syrian's character which Sadat felt might influence the negotiation. Assad was stubborn but cunning; he loved to take decisions at the eleventh hour, and above all he would not make concessions unless he could convince his power base—the Syrian military establishment and the luminaries of the Ba'ath party—that compromise with Israel would serve Syria's and their own interest. After he left Alexandria, Kissinger exchanged constant messages with Sadat, who provided shrewd counsel on how to cope with Assad. Moreover, throughout the ordeal that followed, Sadat urged Assad to accept Dr. Henry's definition of the possible. Toward the end of May, when it appeared that the negotiations would collapse, Sadat dispatched General Gamasy to Damascus to exhort the Syrians in his name and to explain to them how U.N.E.F. functioned in the Sinai as a model for a buffer force in Syria.

In Jerusalem, on May 2, the Israelis' position had not evolved—they were ready only to divide the salient they had captured in October, retaining half of it for themselves and the whole of Golan, too. Moreover, the matter was vexed by internal Israeli politics—Golda Meir would remain in office only long enough to negotiate the disengagement, to be succeeded by Yitzhak Rabin as prime minister. In Israel, Kissinger did not enjoy Egyptian secrecy; at times he must have felt he was negotiating with the whole country. His own team (Sisco, Atherton, et al.) were essentially the same, but now they faced not only the previous Israeli negotiators but Rabin, Shimon Peres, the minister of defense-designate, and General Mordechai Gur, the new chief of staff. Gur began with a military briefing that stressed Israel's strategic need to maintain positions on Mt. Hermon, which abutted the Golan Heights on the north and overlooked Damascus, and the hills near Kuneitra, which dominated the rest of Golan.

KISSINGER: This problem cannot be dealt with in military terms alone. . . . This is a geopolitical problem . . . and you must weigh the alternatives you'll face if we fail to get a disengagement. . . .

GUR:   [But] the Israeli settlements are almost against the [pre-war] line.

KISSINGER: This isn't an argument that will carry weight with world opinion. Those settlements are in occupied territory.

Privately Kissinger has described the Golan settlements as "the worst mistake the Jews have made in 2,500 years." Yigal Allon, the foreign minister-designate, passionately defended Israel's need to retain all of Golan for the security of Galilee and the Hula Valley.

KISSINGER: There are really two issues. One, where will the line be? Two, how will the forces be separated, and what kind of buffer and what kind of limitation on those forces? . . . The minimum essential for the Syrians is to get back Kuneitra. . . .

MRS. MEIR:  . . . None of our neighbors—certainly not Syria—is prepared to negotiate real peace. . . . All the Syrians want to talk about after two wars in six years is the disengagement of forces—[so] we can't just brush aside the military arguments [of our] chief of staff. [Besides,] regimes change in the Arab world. . . . Suppose something happens to Sadat and someone more anti-Israeli and pro-Soviet comes to power? What happens then to all these agreements?

KISSINGER: It's obviously true that everything we do can be lost by the overthrow of a government, but even in that case a great deal [would] depend on how reasonable [Israel] has been in negotiations. . . . The extent to which the United States [could] help you . . . would depend on the nature of the crisis and how it came about.

This is one of the basic arguments Dr. Kissinger has constantly wielded with the Israelis—the scope of future American commitments to Israel will be determined by Israel's readiness to rise above narrow military advantage and take risks for political reasons. But in this conversation he could not even get them to propose a line closer to Kuneitra, the old capital of the Golan Heights near the cease-fire line of 1967. With no more than an agenda from the Israelis—prisoner exchange, force limitations, nature of the U.N. buffer zone, etc.—Kissinger next day departed for Damascus, expecting the negotiations to last perhaps a week, certainly not a fortnight.

Sadat was not the Secretary's only counsellor on how to cope with Assad. Distressed that he had failed with Assad in December, convinced that he possessed no sense of Syrian psychology, Dr. Kissinger in preparation for this new adventure had done considerable research. He had profited, in particular, from the advice of his Arabists about the Syrian bargaining psychology. From conversations with several American officials, I have reconstructed the substance of the counsel Kissinger received. Foremost was the distinction Arabs were wont to make between bargaining for rugs and negotiating the restitution of wrongs. For the first, the casbah mentality prevailed; for the second, the Bedu syndrome.

Like the Palestinians (to whom they were bound by bonds of blood and intermarriage), the Syrians were Levantines. Syria itself was in history a crossroads of commerce, ideas, peoples, and armies—a crossroads which produced a clash between desert and town, between the townsman and the Bedu. Out of that collision, the Levantine mind was born. From the Bedu, the modern Syrian inherited his code of honor, hospitality, revenge, love of language and of poetry. But for all that the townsman of Syria—socially, culturally, politically—was a merchant, a man of the marketplace whose predominant ethos was the casbah syndrome, composed of common sense, accommodation, a love of haggling no less than love of profit.

Bargaining in the casbah—for a carpet or a coffee pot—was not a game of halving the merchant's asking price, then haggling to the middle ground. Between a Levantine and a foreigner, yes, but between Levantines themselves both the buyer and the seller recognized the real worth of the carpet or the coffee pot. The purpose of the exercise was not to haggle over the basic price, but over the margin of profit the buyer was prepared to concede. First, there must be probing to establish if each party knew the approximate value of the object and the perimeters of profit. Coffee is served, chitchat exchanged. Once it is clear that each party understands, the real bargaining begins.

In that contest, each party must know what it wants and approximately what it is prepared to pay; moreover, it must know that the other side knows also. But in the midst of bargaining there must develop as well a personal bond between buyer and seller—a covenant of confidence and trust that excites the sentiment of friendship. (As we have observed, in his previous dealings with the Arabs, Dr. Kissinger already had displayed some working knowledge of these principles. He was, after all, a Semite.)

But a rug or a coffee pot was one thing, redressing an injustice quite another. Dissect any Syrian, and you will discover the casbah and Bedu syndromes constantly at war. Affairs of right and wrong could not be bargained over—at best one weighed the wrong and sought the proper moral and material compensation. For example, a family whose son has been murdered by another will not deign to meet the offending family. A mediator—a *wasit*—is summoned; as in the casbah, he endeavors to establish trust between the parties before demands are transmitted, compensation proposed. Only after the mediator resolves all the particulars of what is essentially an affair to save face will the injured party confront the villain and embark upon reconciliation.

Dr. Kissinger was the *wasit* between Syria and Israel. His Arabists predicted that he would find President Assad a compound of Bedu and casbah—outraged by the real and imagined wrongs of Israel, warily prepared to strike bargains on troop withdrawals, demilitarized zones, and—ultimately—compensation for the Palestinians.

On May 3, at the presidential palace, beneath that painting of Saladin vanquishing the Crusaders, upon those Persian carpets and carved wood chaises longues, Assad and Kissinger began the bargaining, or rather the prebargaining. Coffee was served, chitchat exchanged. Kissinger pretended he had nothing to do but gossip of irrelevancies, for he knew there was no hastening the protocols of Arab politeness. They drifted from tangent to tangent; eventually he described Israel's unstable internal situation, then inquired casually about Andrei Gromyko, the Soviet foreign minister, who was expected soon in Damascus. "I can see the scenario," Kissinger said. "Your foreign minister will meet Gromyko at the airport, then take him to lunch. Then they will make a statement condemning the United States and 'partial solutions.' Then Syria will get some more MIG-23s."

Assad was amused. Kissinger's eye came to rest on Abdel Halim Khaddam, Assad's fire-breathing young foreign minister. "Such pretty blue eyes," he said. "Won't you come back with me to Israel? I want to fix you up with Golda." (On another occasion Kissinger produced a black notebook from his pocket, and told Khaddam, "This has the hottest telephone numbers in Washington. When you sign the agreement, it's yours.") Presently he asked Assad if he would exchange wounded prisoners with Israel before the negotiations were finished—"this would help the atmosphere," he said. Assad darkened. "That would be interpreted by my people," he responded, "as a premature concession." Then Kissinger produced the Israeli map, with its proposed line dividing the salient. "It does not seem," Assad replied angrily, "that Israel wants peace. The line is unacceptable. It proves that Israel is expansionist."

Kissinger returned to Jerusalem and urged the Israelis to be realistic. For weeks the Syrians had been waging a war of attrition across their lines with Israel; the cease-fire, Kissinger's diplomacy itself, were at stake.

KISSINGER: It's necessary to give back Kuneitra, plus a bit of the areas west of the [pre-October] line. We need a line that's negotiable, or the negotiations will collapse very soon. . . . Israel should understand the Syrians' perception. You're sitting on their territory, and you argue how little to give back.

MRS. MEIR angrily: . . . We didn't just get up one day in 1967 [after all] the shelling from the Heights and decide to take Golan away from them. . . . In October we had eight hundred killed and two thousand wounded in Golan alone—in a war they started. And now they say we

Israelis are being outrageous. They say this is *their* territory. Eight hundred boys gave their lives for an attack the Syrians started. [Assad] lost the war—and now we have to pay for it because he says it's *his* territory!

KISSINGER: Each side has its own definition of justice. Remember what this is all about . . . to keep the negotiating process alive, to prevent another round of hostilities which would benefit the Soviet Union and increase pressure on you, on us, and [on] Sadat to rejoin the battle. . . . I think Assad is serious [about] reaching an agreement. . . .

DAYAN: I think the next stage [after the disengagement agreement] should be the one before the last. The next stage should be the end of belligerency. The last stage [should be] real peace. . . . Maybe we could divide Kuneitra. . . .

KISSINGER: It won't work.

DAYAN: . . . To protect our positions in the fields and hills west of Kuneitra, we have to have positions in Kuneitra.

MRS. MEIR: There's a cabinet meeting tomorrow—we must ask for authority to propose a new line. We'll have a big fight in the cabinet and [in] the Knesset and [with] our people who live on the Golan Heights.

The Secretary encountered some of the Golan settlers outside his hotel, screaming *"Jew boy, go home!"*—a reference apparently to Nixon's reputed remark describing Dr. Kissinger in that idiom. The cabinet relented, and Mrs. Meir proposed a new line. The concept, of course, came from Dayan, soon to relinquish his defense portfolio. Now the government agreed to give back the salient, and a slice of Kuneitra, proposing to divide that city into three zones—for Israel, the U.N., and Syria, respectively. In Damascus, Assad rejected this proposal. ("Oh, bring me my pen!" he exclaimed with sarcasm. "I'll sign it straightaway!") For the next three weeks, Kissinger shuttled back and forth, struggling to reconcile the contradictions.

On May 8, in Damascus, before resuming the negotiation, Dr. Kissinger donned anew the toga of a Harvard sage and treated the President of Syria to a seminar on global politics. The topic was President Nixon's forthcoming summit conference in Moscow with Chairman Brezhnev. "We'll have three categories of agreements," Kissinger began, "trade, economic cooperation, and arms control." There ensued a discussion on the limitation of ballistic missiles. Assad mischievously suggested that the United States and the Soviet Union should distribute all of their weapons equitably in the Middle East—"We'll store them for both of you." Kissinger laughed, then asked about the dialogue between the Arab governments and the European community: "Any European who agrees to meet in the same room with 20 Arab leaders is crazy!"

They rambled on, about the European security conference, and the imminent presidential election in France; they agreed that Monsieur Giscard d'Estaing would defeat Monsieur Mitterand. Assad was fascinated. There were, after all, not that many Harvard professors in Syria he could ordinarily consult, and he pleased Dr. Kissinger because he—so parochial in his origins and training—clearly wished to improve his knowledge of the world. He asked penetrating questions.

I have, as I suggested in my prologue, often reflected upon the phenomenon of these seminars that the Secretary of State conducted for General Assad. This perhaps because I am a devotee of Harvard seminars myself, though I did not attend that institution as an undergraduate and I had hardly heard of Dr. Kissinger before he went to work in the White House. But since assuming residence at Harvard, I have been bemused by what I can only call "the academic fantasy"—a disease of some (though not all) professors of politics, government, and diplomacy. The fantasy they entertain is to see their theories acted out upon the real proscenium of power. Most of their theories never shall be. Professor Kissinger has realized his academic fantasy, acted out his theories more extravagantly than, a mere decade ago, he might ever have imagined. He has assumed pride of place amongst that minuscule fellowship of pedants who successfully made the leap from academe to the pantheon of power. His former peers in academe (particularly at Harvard) have many of them opposed him because they honestly disdain his policies. But beneath that (it seems to me) they will never forgive him for having wielded power at all. In applying his theories, Professor Kissinger has committed many errors, but at the least he has the satisfaction that historians (and he is one himself) will cover the pages of their books with the chronicle of his deeds. More than that, he kept giving seminars—to chiefs of state.

All of which is by the way. By May 12, Kissinger had become so exasperated with the Israelis he said, "Assad is no longer demanding half of Golan—we're negotiating on your line, and you're arguing about a few kilometers or a few hundred yards here and there. You're always looking at the trees, and you don't see the woods! If we didn't have this negotiation, there'd be an international forum for the 1967 frontiers."* The Israelis improved their map slightly, but not enough to satisfy Assad—"he must have some breathing space around Kuneitra," Kissinger told them. Israel insisted on retaining the hills outside Kuneitra; this outraged Assad. On May 13, Kissinger warned the Israelis the negotiations might collapse.

Next day, to Assad and his chief aides—General Mustafa Tlas, minister of defense; General Hikmat Shihabi, chief of intelligence; General Nadji Jamil, chief of the air force—Kissinger tried to put the best face upon the Israeli proposal. "There are demonstrators in the streets," he said, "crying 'Don't give up an inch of Golan!' Look, the Israelis have made considerable concessions—no salient, back to the pre-October line, and now they'll get out of all of Kuneitra and draw the line at the edge of the town. There will be Syrian civilians inside Kuneitra." The

---

*According to Matti Golan, Kissinger at one point burst out: "Such bargaining is not dignified for an American Secretary of State. I am wandering around here like a rug merchant in order to bargain over one hundred to two hundred meters! Like a peddler in the market! I'm trying to save you, and you think you are doing me a favor when you are kind enough to give me a few more meters. As if I were a citizen of Kuneitra. As if I planned to build my house there!"

Other Israeli habits, I know, offended Dr. Kissinger—such as their appetite for fruits and nuts. The Israelis kept a bowl of dried fruits and nuts on the negotiating table. During the intensity of the discussions, they gobbled them down—leaving none for Kissinger. This, as the saying goes, drove him "up the wall."

generals said, "No." Assad protested, "Kuneitra a pocket surrounded by Israelis north, south and west? Unacceptable."

On May 15, Palestinian guerrillas attacked Maalot, near the
Lebanese border, killing 16 Israeli adolescents; this hardened
the cabinet. Next morning, to the Israeli negotiators, Kissinger
expressed his sorrow, and presently—perhaps to relieve the
tension—told a story about his masseur at the King David Hotel.

MASSEUR: We support your efforts. We must have peace.
KISSINGER: What are you willing to give up for peace?
MASSEUR: Nothing. Not an inch.
KISSINGER: Shall I break off the negotiations?
MASSEUR: Absolutely not. I would give up ten years of my life for
peace.
KISSINGER: How many kilometers would you give up?
MASSEUR: Not a kilometer.

This exchange, Kissinger mused, echoed the attitude of the
Israeli government. In desperation, throwing out an idea that
had emerged from discussions with his staff, he suggested that
perhaps Israel could continue cultivating the fields around
Kuneitra—so long as they were demilitarized and placed within
the U.N. zone.

Allon, Rabin, and Gur picked this up, promising to discuss it
with the cabinet. Kissinger's idea revived the negotiations, for it
became the basis of the crucial Israeli concession. But for
another fortnight the haggling did not cease. Assad, furthermore, would not hear of Israeli outposts remaining on Mt. Hermon. "I'll take Khaddam back with me," Kissinger jested wear-
ily in Damascus. "He can convince Golda." Drafting the documents was a crucifixion. With the Syrians, Kissinger did not
betray his frustration, but with the Israelis he was less civil. On
May 23, in conference with the Israelis, Kissinger contrasted
Sadat and Assad: "Sadat has a fixed determination to overcome
obstacles and move toward peace. He makes big moves and
breaks impasses. With Assad, each issue when you get to it
becomes major, and you have to bargain hard over every point.
It's so time-consuming! Sadat makes command decisions. Assad

had his lieutenants there, and I had to convince them, too." In describing Assad, Kissinger was also describing the Israelis to themselves.

So the haggling went on—and with it the war of attrition. In Damascus recently President Assad told me that during the negotiation "the Israelis were exploiting Dr. Kissinger's aircraft when he took off from Tel Aviv toward the sea. Their warplanes flew in the shadow of his wings, and at a certain point they parted—then struck at targets in our territory." The haggling went on—about the location of the line, the cultivation of the fields, a village here, a crossroads there, the width of the buffer zone, the limitation of forces and artillery (another American letter to resolve that!), the length of the U.N. mandate, the exchange of prisoners wounded and unwounded, the quantity of Syrian police to be permitted in Kuneitra. The Syrians wished only observers in the buffer zone; the Israelis insisted on an armed force; the issue was resolved by calling them both—the United Nations Disengagement Observer Force (U.N.D.O.F.). The talks nearly collapsed again at least twice, and Kissinger kept threatening to go home. Nixon—who needed the agreement as much as anybody—told him to stay, and started calling up Golda Meir.

The Israelis knew from the beginning that they would be obliged to relinquish Kuneitra, but they were resolved to extract the best possible bargain for themselves—to haggle over each grain of sand, over every blade of grass. Sometimes they knew what Assad had told Kissinger even before Kissinger returned to Jerusalem. Unbeknownst to Kissinger, let alone to Assad, Israeli intelligence possessed extraordinary means to discover the contents of Assad's messages to other Arab governments.

Assad relied on less complicated ruses of his own. An audacious poker player, constantly bluffing to improve the pot, he retracted his previous assent to the Israeli line. On May 27, Assad and Kissinger composed a communiqué announcing the collapse of the negotiations. On the way to the door, Assad touched Kissinger's hand and said, "What a pity. We've come so far and we've not succeeded. Can't anything be done about the line? Go back to Jerusalem—and try again."

Two days later the agreement was achieved. It was modeled on the Israeli-Egyptian disengagement—in effect five zones, embracing the U.N. buffer; two zones of ten-kilometer depth for Israel and Syria each where troops, artillery, and tanks were severely limited; symmetrical zones 20 kilometers deep where missiles were proscribed. (As in the Sinai, this proscription favored Israel; the Israelis favored their air force, not air defense, whereas for the Arabs SAMs were paramount.) The new Israeli line roughly corresponded to the cease-fire demarcation of 1967, except that Syria regained Kuneitra, which was placed inside the buffer zone. Just beyond the town's periphery, the Israelis could continue to cultivate the fields within the buffer, and they retained their settlements and the strategic hills. Israel was not obliged to abandon all of its outposts upon Mt. Hermon, but the posts were open—as were all the zones—to inspection by U.N.-D.O.F. American memoranda were conveyed to both sides. Assad had refused to agree in writing to prohibit "paramilitary" (Palestinian) operations from his soil, so the American letter to Israel sanctioned—in the event of such incursions—Israeli retaliation.*

In the euphoria of the achievement—hailed then as the diplomatic miracle of our time—the torment of the experience almost seemed to be forgotten. Dr. Kissinger had spent nearly five weeks away from Washington, struggling as well during sleepless days and nights to run the entire State Department from his Boeing or the King David Hotel. On May 14, President Assad had told him, "From this negotiation it's clear to me that, even if we get an agreement, the future will be very difficult. I'm worried about the new leadership in Israel. Those who are new to responsibility must flex their muscles." By the end of the bargaining, Assad had lost his taste—if he ever had any—for

*The full text of the agreement, the protocol, and the published memorandum to Israel, will be found in Appendix Seven. Dr. Kissinger did not relinquish his black notebook to Foreign Minister Khaddam.

step-by-step diplomacy, and that portended discomfitting consequences for Kissinger.

After the negotiations, Kissinger privately described the Syrians and Israelis as "the only peoples in the Middle East who deserve each other"—but in truth he did not feel quite that way about Hafez Assad or Golda Meir. He admired Sadat, and respected Faisal, but he grew fond of Assad. The Freudians of diplomacy might explain this as Kissinger's familiar compulsion to identify with adversaries, and that may indeed be part of it. But Assad also fascinated Kissinger as the embodiment of that Arab romanticism he used to curse, as a sometimes too simplistic man of steel who could compete with him on his own terrain of humor and dissimulation, as a despot of high principle who in fundamentals—for all his Alawite cunning—said what he meant and meant what he said.

"As a diplomat I like Sadat," Kissinger has remarked. "As a historian, I prefer Assad." In fact, he considered Assad more straightforward than Sadat. There is an Arabic saying, *"Keef ala kadamaik tuma atlob"*—"Stand on your feet, and say what you want." At bottom, that was Assad.

As for Golda Meir, President Assad observed to me that "one of the weaknesses I discovered in Dr. Kissinger was his special love of that woman. It struck me as strange that this university professor and secretary of state was unable to conceal such a furious affection. And for your information he used to describe her as the beauty of Jerusalem and as 'Miss Israel.'" To others Kissinger has called her "that preposterous woman." Mrs. Meir's tantrums, her volcanic obstinacy, drove Kissinger crazy—but there was no doubt of his deep affection. She was a woman of steel, and she alone in Israel, once her word was given, could enforce discipline and deliver the cabinet. Now, she was stepping down, but in the year to come Dr. Kissinger would yearn for Miss Israel.

In her last appearance as prime minister, Mrs. Meir tendered a reception for Dr. Kissinger. The Secretary kissed her. Rabin and the others roared with laughter, but Golda wagged her finger. "I never knew," she said, "that you kissed women."

# 9

# Of Promises
# and Doom

Dr. Kissinger emerged from the Golan disengagement—and onto the cover of *Newsweek*—as "Super K," the owlish marvel in horn-rimmed spectacles and blue tights who belied his own protestations that he did not possess "the power to work miracles—international politics is not a series of conjuring tricks." Ah, but he *was* a conjurer, thought many Arabs at the time; some Israelis thought likewise. Israeli wits had their own way of describing his diplomatic method, and one of their fables seemed almost true.

A matchmaker (Dr. Kissinger) approached a pauper in his village to tell him that he had a beautiful bride for his son.

"Sorry," said the pauper. "I never meddle in my son's affairs."

"Ah," said the matchmaker, "but you don't know the girl. She's the daughter of Lord Rothschild."

"Well, in that case..."

The matchmaker hastened to Lord Rothschild. "I have the ideal husband for your daughter."

"But my daughter is too young," protested His Lordship.

"Ah, but you don't know the young man. He's the vice-president of the World Bank."

"Well, in that case . . ."

The matchmaker hastened to the president of the World Bank. "I have the perfect vice-president for you."

"But I have two vice-presidents."

"Ah, but you don't know the gentleman. He's the son-in-law of Lord Rothschild."

Alas, the Golan disengagement was the last of Dr. Kissinger's great prestidigitations. It marked the high noon of his gradualist diplomacy in the Middle East. Thereafter we begin to remark lengthening shadows, faltering steps, frustration, recrimination, paralysis, and doubt.

In mid-June 1974 Dr. Kissinger returned to the Middle East—with Richard Nixon. The President resented Kissinger's glory; he considered the agreements in Sinai and on the Golan Heights as equally the result of presidential power and supervision. Nixon coveted his share of Kissinger's luster—and for that his tour was largely ceremonial, undertaken not only to dramatize the American commitment to peace but to portray the President in his statesman's toga as he struggled to elude impeachment. Nevertheless, during his peregrination, Nixon made significant promises to the Arab chiefs of state.

They involved the American interpretation of United Nations Security Council Resolution 242. On the territorial dimension of 242, Kissinger has sometimes been accused of making contradictory promises to Arabs and Israelis, but in fact such duplicity is difficult to establish. He had stated often that the United States would labor for the fulfillment in all its clauses of that ambiguous resolution, but he was evasive when anyone asked him to define it. On December 15, 1973, to Hisham Nazer and the Saudi princes, Kissinger replied, "Whatever a settlement brings, it will involve Israeli withdrawal from Arab land. We know that a settlement will have to be in accord with the interests of the parties. I recognize that you must see some results within a measurable period of time, but to give you a precise answer would only make the process more difficult. Arabs have always wanted a proclamation about the principles of a settlement, but it is better to have progress first, the proclamation afterwards."

We know that Kissinger said essentially the same to Sadat on the previous November 7, and on May 18 during the Golan disengagement shuttle he repeated it to Assad: "My predecessor once stated publicly his interpretation of 242, and for four years he was beaten over the head. Obviously for a settlement you have to agree, but for us to take a position on final borders would destroy our capacity to conduct negotiations. So we must proceed step by step."

"Would the American public object," Assad pressed him, "if the United States government said it wanted complete Israeli withdrawal?"

"That," Kissinger replied, "would start an incredible fight." In other words, by publicly favoring the 1967 frontiers, the United States would provoke a tempest of unbearable domestic pressures and emasculate its own capacity to influence Israel.

Certainly Kissinger *allowed* the Arabs to think that, implicitly at least, he favored complete or substantial Israeli withdrawal. In January 1974, during a visit to Abu Dhabi, President Sadat told me, "I have assurances from Kissinger" on total withdrawal, but this may have been Sadat's wishful exegesis of Dr. Henry's conundrum.

Kissinger's replies to the Israelis resembled his opacity with the Arabs. On May 2, 1974, at the beginning of the Golan negotiation, Rabin and Eban probed him for his views on final borders. "I can't predict how it will all come out," he answered. "What's important is the process itself—to keep negotiations going, to prevent them from freezing." Kissinger was more explicit in his meeting on December 6, 1973, with American Jewish intellectuals. Then, according to the Israeli journal which published the notes of a participant, he said that Israel would not have to withdraw to her 1967 borders; he believed that more favorable frontiers would be agreed upon in the negotiations. But even on that occasion he stressed that Israel would be obliged to return "substantial territories."

Nixon was uncomfortable in Egypt. Perhaps he was preoccupied with presentiments of his doomed presidency, but he suffered physically as well. He was, in fact, seriously ill. En route to Cairo, at Salzburg, his physicians had discovered phlebitis in his throbbing left leg; whereupon they urged him to abandon his tour of the Middle East, since exertions of state might release the clot from his leg to his lungs or to his heart and kill him. But not even the threat of death would deter the President from the metaphysical satisfaction of (what was to be, and he must have sensed it) his last grand triumph. He endured intense pain, in the midst of millions who acclaimed him.

Before the mob—in silhouette together against the pyramids of Giza, waving from the window of their luxurious train between Cairo and Alexandria—Nixon was convivial with Sadat, but that was mostly theater. Privately the two presidents groped for words; their silences were long and awkward. Occasionally Nixon would revive and say, "Nice day. . . ." At Alexandria he was so nebulous in his meanderings that Kissinger often felt obliged to interrupt so as to sharpen the discussions. Sadat, not such a facile conversationalist himself, was delighted to have the President of the United States as his guest, and quite content (as were most Egyptians) to focus upon Nixon's fairness since the October war, forgiving his favoritism to Israel during the previous five years. Reciprocally, both Nixon and Kissinger, intent on strengthening their Arab policy, heaped public praise and promises—of economic assistance, of a peaceful nuclear power plant—upon Sadat. Nixon brought a large, opulently appointed military helicopter to Cairo and bestowed it upon the President. But of personal rapport, there was almost none; barely two months before his last disgrace, Nixon could hardly communicate with anybody.

Nevertheless, in reply to Sadat's questions, Nixon did tell his host that the American objective in the Sinai was to restore the old Egyptian international border. Dr. Kissinger was sitting there when Nixon said it. Moreover, Sadat probed Nixon about American recognition of the Palestine Liberation Organization. Nixon answered to the effect that, at some appropriate future time, the United States would endeavor to bring the P.L.O. into the negotiating process. His response was cautious, but that much was clear. (Evidently in reference to this statement, and others from Kissinger, Sadat told the Lebanese magazine *Al Hawadess* in February 1976 that he had "more than a pledge from the United States to recognize the Palestine Liberation Organization, but I am not in a position to reveal it.")

Afterwards, at Damascus and Amman, also in Dr. Kissinger's presence, again in response to questions, Nixon informed President Assad and King Hussein, respectively, that the United States favored the substantial restitution of the 1967 frontiers on the Golan Heights and on the west bank of the Jordan within the framework of a general peace. With all three chiefs of state, it was clear from the context of the conversations that Nixon expected these Arab governments to confer full peace and recognition upon Israel in return for the old frontiers.

President Assad told Nixon emphatically (as he had often told Kissinger) that Syria would never relinquish territory to Israel upon the Golan Heights. Nixon replied, "We understand you . . . we know what the end is"—and then went on to employ a vivid image. The purpose of interim diplomacy, he said, was to nudge the Israelis backwards upon the Heights, step by step, "until they reach the edge, then tumble over."

Dr. Kissinger has orally repeated to President Sadat President Nixon's position on the 1967 frontiers since Nixon stated it in June 1974. President Ford reaffirmed Nixon's position on the final frontiers to Sadat in June 1975, during their meeting at Salzburg.*

*My sources for these secret statements of Presidents Nixon and Ford on the 1967 frontiers are primary ones—participants in the meetings, not all of them Arabs. When I originally published a portion of these disclosures in the spring 1976 issue of *Foreign Policy* magazine, both Dr. Kissinger and President Ford subsequently denied them. Mr. Bernard Gwertzman, writing in *The New York Times* of Saturday, March 6, 1976, reported that "State Department officials said privately . . . that they believed that Mr. Sheehan's comments on the final borders were based on Mr. Sadat's interpretation of deliberately ambiguous comments made to him by Mr. Nixon and Mr. Ford that expressed sympathy with his desire for the recovery of all the occupied land but no commitment to help him fulfill it."

In a subsequent dispatch in the *Times* of Thursday, March 18, 1976, Mr.

Of course the Arabs wish to have these declarations in writing, but that is the sort of memorandum that Nixon and Ford and Kissinger have—so far—refused to render up to them. In any case, why this change in tactics? As the clock continued to tick after the conclusion of the October war, and Israel stood firm upon most of her conquests, the Americans evidently sought to sustain their credibility with the Arabs by resorting once again to oral reassurances.

There emerges from all of this yet another demonstration of Kissingerian ambiguity. And duplicity, as well? In the topography of step by step, Kissinger obviously emphasized different

---

Gwertzman reported President Ford's reaction. At a meeting in the White House with a group of American Jewish leaders on March 17, according to one of the participants, President Ford—evidently referring to my article—"flatly denied . . . that he had told Mr. Sadat that the United States favored the return to Egypt of all land seized by Israel in the 1967 war. . . . Mr. Ford, according to another participant, opened the meeting by asserting that he had been careful never to commit the United States to anything more than support of the ambiguously worded United Nations Security Council Resolution 242 of 1967, which called on Israel to withdraw from occupied territory while still possessing 'secure and recognized borders.' This is taken by Israelis to mean they can keep some of the occupied lands, and Mr. Ford said the final borders should be negotiated by the parties."

I respectfully submit that the secret statements by Presidents Nixon and Ford in 1974 and 1975 went palpably beyond the ambiguous position stated by the President on March 17, 1976. A dispatch from Tel Aviv in *The New York Times* of March 8, 1976, reported that "three ministers [of the Israeli cabinet] submitted questions to . . . Prime Minister [Rabin] about the veracity of Mr. Sheehan's assertion[s]. . . . Mr. Rabin said that [Ambassador] Dinitz had made an official approach to the State Department in the matter and that Mr. Kissinger had assured him that the United States adhered to its stand that final borders should be determined in negotiations between the parties as provided in Security Council resolutions. But informed Israelis said that they gave credence to the Sheehan account."

I am not astonished that informed Israelis should do so. In fact, in November 1975, a senior Israeli official told me that he had "heard" of the secret statements by Presidents Nixon and Ford that I have cited. He did not deny their authenticity, though he denigrated their seriousness. "Polite chitchat over cocktails," he called them. "Moslems don't serve cocktails to visiting Presidents," I observed. "Very well then," the Israeli official said, "—over Turkish coffee."

phenomena to each party. To the Israelis he stressed the hills, to the Arabs, the valleys. But duplicity?

In the strict sense there was duplicity only if Nixon, Ford, and Kissinger had rendered contradictory promises to the Israelis— that they could *keep* substantial portions of conquered territory in a final settlement. There is no evidence that such assertions were ever made.

In July 1970, during a press conference, Nixon did endorse "defensible frontiers" for Israel; the endorsement was repeated in the aftermath of the October war to induce the Israelis to accept American peacemaking proposals. (Nixon and Kissinger also promised, after the war, that the United States would not interpret Resolution 242 in a sense that would alter "the character of the State of Israel"—a pledge to oppose a massive repatriation of Palestinian refugees to Israel under a peace settlement.) To the Israelis, "defensible frontiers" connotes expanded frontiers, but Nixon never defined what the phrase meant to him or to the government of the United States. To the Arabs, American diplomats defended "defensible frontiers" as simply consistent with the clause in Resolution 242 calling for "secure and recognized boundaries." Ambiguity, surely—but duplicity?

# 10

# King of Jerusalem?

Are oral reassurances worth anything—to Jordan, for example? The Hashemite Kingdom, and the Palestinians who resided there and in parts beyond, assumed a critical importance during the final summer of Richard Nixon's presidency—though curiously Dr. Kissinger did not seem to notice.

Kissinger, like Nixon and President Johnson before him, took King Hussein for granted. Jordan, after all, was nearly an American protectorate; but unlike Israel, it possessed no American constituency and thus had to be content with whatever scraps Washington might care to cast its way. In 1967, Hussein had lobbied amongst the other Arabs for their acceptance of Resolution 242, in return for which he received hollow promises from Johnson (and then Nixon) that the United States would persuade Israel to relinquish its conquests.

True, Nixon very nearly intervened on Jordan's side in September of 1970—when a Syrian tank force invaded the north of the kingdom to aid the Palestinian *fedayin* who were at war with Hussein, whereupon Israel at Kissinger's request agreed to repulse the Syrians. In their biography of Kissinger, the Kalb brothers provide some particulars of that crisis:

Nixon had made up his mind that Hussein would not be toppled, that the balance of forces in the Middle East would not be changed. . . . [Soviet Chargé d'Affaires Yuli] Vorontsov was again told that there would be an acute danger to peace unless the Syrian tanks retreated. No option would be ruled out. . . .

Israel was planning a pincer attack against Syrian forces concentrated in the Irbid area [near the Syrian border]. . . . Hussein would be assured that Israeli forces would be withdrawn from Jordan the moment the operation was completed. . . . Syria would be another matter. . . .

[Ambassador] Rabin told Kissinger solemnly that if Syria sent fresh reinforcements into Jordan and if, as expected, the Jordanian army began to collapse, Israel would agree to Hussein's request, as transmitted by the Americans. The Israeli air force would be ordered into action against Syrian tanks. But Israel reserved the right to send combat troops into Jordan if such additional action were considered necessary. Moreover, Israel would not limit her military action to Jordan. Air and ground attacks into Syria might also be required to secure the "political goal" of saving Hussein's pro-Western regime. . . .

Syria moved a small number of additional tanks across the border, and it appeared that a mass movement could be underway. The Jordanian army could not dislodge the Syrians from Irbid. The commandos were staging more daring attacks against the King's troops. Hussein sent another appeal [to Washington] for "urgent help." . . .

Kissinger and Rabin met once again. The Israeli Ambassador . . . repeated that Israel wanted Nixon's word that the U.S. would either deter or prevent any Soviet intervention resulting from an Israeli move into Jordan or Syria. . . . This time Nixon gave his approval. Their understanding was stark and historic: Israel would move against Syrian forces in Jordan; and if Egyptian or Soviet forces then moved against Israel, the United States would intervene against both. . . . Israeli tanks, in great number, moved toward the Jordan River. The Golan Heights came alive with visible preparations for war. At military airfields throughout Israel jet engines were revved up and missile racks and bomb bays were loaded. An American aircraft carrier eased to within sixty nautical miles of the Israeli coastline. . . .

Suddenly, on Tuesday, September 22 [1970] the tension snapped.

Reassured by the American-Israeli coordination, Hussein launched an all-out attack against the Syrians. His tanks moved north toward Irbid, and his . . . jet fighters cracked hard at Syrian armor surrounding Irbid. And, to Kissinger's relief, there were reports by nightfall (midday in Washington) that . . . Syrian tanks had begun to swing around and head north toward the border.

To this it must be added that the crucial reason for the Syrian retreat was General Hafez Assad's refusal (partially from fear of American and Israeli reaction) to commit the Syrian air force to the battle of Irbid. Prior to that turning point, Hussein in desperation—for his rule of Jordan was at stake—was prepared to countenance Israeli intervention. The King did not covet Israeli armor or ground troops inside Jordan—Israel's promises to Kissinger notwithstanding, he feared that, once entrenched in eastern Jordan, the Israelis might become as attached to it as they were to the west bank. He wanted a swift, surgical Israeli air strike against the Syrian tanks at Irbid; but when his own air force accomplished that (without encountering General Assad's) on September 22, he had no need of the Israelis. Hastily Nixon and Kissinger told the Israelis to desist. Thus the singular spectacle of an Arab king being rescued by Israeli Phantoms never came to pass. Nixon and Kissinger risked the adventure, not out of love for Jordan, but because Syria was a Soviet client, Jordan an American client, and (their chronic obsession asserting itself) the President and his counsellor were as resolved as always to prevent Russian guns from vanquishing American guns. Kissinger thereupon lavished new guns upon the Hashemite army, though only of the caliber to kill *fedayin*, not challenge Israel.

Jordan is a patched-up sort of place. Before World War I it was an undefined desert, part of the hinterland of greater Syria where Bedouins wandered, governed after a fashion by the Sublime Porte of Istanbul. The Arab Revolt—the participation of the Hashemites of Mecca and their armies in Britain's war to expel the Turks from greater Syria—obliged the British to redeem their promises to the Hashemite princes on the morrow of the conflict. The British had promised to create Prince Faisal (the

Sherif of Mecca's son) King of Damascus—but with predictable perfidy they gave Syria to the French and took Palestine for themselves. They fobbed off Faisal with Mesopotamia, proclaiming him King of Iraq. That left them with the Emir (Prince) Abdullah, Faisal's younger brother, who craved a kingdom of his own. Winston Churchill, then colonial secretary, at a conference in Cairo in 1921, unrolled a map of the Middle East, drew some angles and straight lines upon it, and created the Emirate of Transjordan (in his own words) "one Sunday afternoon." A few years later, the Saud family chased the Hashemites from the Holy Hejaz (which they had governed since the twelfth century), leaving Iraq and Transjordan as their only possessions. In 1958, the Hashemites of Baghdad were butchered in a revolution, leaving Amman the sole surviving seat of this dynasty which claimed direct descent from the Prophet Mohammed.

Under the Emir Abdullah, Transjordan remained after 1921 an impoverished backwater protected by the British crown, its Arab Legion commanded by a British officer, Sir John Bagot Glubb ("Glubb Pasha"). Amman remained a village where Bedouins repaired from time to time to trade, to arrange tribal marriages, to seek favors from Abdullah. The Arab-Israeli war of 1948 changed all of that. Though they had inhabited Palestine for more than a millennium, and though they still outnumbered the Jews and legally owned most of the land, the Arabs west of the River Jordan—taking flight from fear or indeed physically expelled by the Zionist armies—stampeded by the hundreds of thousands into the rump of Palestine that remained to them or across the river to Amman. Transjordan has never been the same since.

Glubb Pasha's Legion was the only Arab army that fought creditably in 1948. The Jews substantially expanded that part of Palestine assigned to them by the United Nations partition plan, but the Arab Legion managed to retain the west bank of the river and East Jerusalem—which Abdullah soon absorbed into the Hashemite Kingdom of Jordan. Most of the Palestinian refugees were sheltered in wretched camps that languished on the west bank or encircled Amman itself. More sophisticated, better educated, vastly more resourceful than the Transjordanian Bedu, the Palestinians asserted themselves at once in the politics of the new kingdom—not always pacifically. Many Palestinians considered Abdullah a traitor who, in clandestine meetings with the Israelis, had resolved to fashion a *modus vivendi* between Israel and Jordan that would liquidate the claim of the refugees to recover all of their country. One such Palestinian murdered Abdullah in 1951, as he penetrated Al Aqsa mosque in Jerusalem to perform his Friday prayers. Abdullah's grandson Hussein, then a youth of fifteen, was with the King; a bit of Abdullah's blood splattered Hussein's tunic, and a bullet bounced from one of his buttons.

Hussein's father, Talal, ascended the throne, but was soon deposed for insanity and dispatched to an asylum in Istanbul. At seventeen, a callow and unfinished product of Harrow and Sandhurst, Hussein became the boy-king of Jordan. He was shy, fun-loving, fond of women, confused by his advisers. Nasser's star was rising; the boy's kingdom throbbed with restive Palestinians feeding on the fantasies of Nasser's speeches, delirious with the slogans of pan-Arabism. Hussein dismissed Glubb Pasha from command of the Arab Legion, replacing him with an incompetent Jordanian who proceeded to plot the deposition of the King.

I first met Hussein at about this time, in 1956, not long before the Suez War. His Sandhurst English was impeccable, but his diffidence was embarrassing. He sat chain-smoking in his cabinet at Basman Palace, a small, full-lipped, deep-voiced youth, clad in a pin-striped blue suit, telling me over and over how welcome I was in Jordan and that I must consider his palace my home. My political questions confounded him. "Is it true that Your Majesty has assumed direct control of the government?" I asked. He pondered this, then brightened. *"We do what we can,"* he declared deeply. Later, he took me for a spin in his new sports car (a Ferrari, I think). We raced over desert roads in excess of 100 miles per hour, and as we careened, he turned to me and laughed (deeply), "We enjoy applying our foot to the accelerator."

I assumed that he would be assassinated soon or that at best the cabals that festered round him would chase him from his throne. I was wrong, though the assassins failed not for want of trying—nearly a dozen attempts to date. Callow as he may have been, conspiracy and counterconspiracy oozed from his Hashemite veins. In 1957 his commander of the Arab Legion nearly overthrew him, but Hussein foiled the plot with the assistance of a C.I.A. agent he had sneaked into Basman Palace. The King turned thereafter more and more away from Britain toward the United States for subsidies and weapons. He developed by degrees into a strong ruler, not too diffident to be cruel, devoted above everything to an obsessive vision that his dynasty would prevail. A strong ruler, and (by degrees) a shrewd politician, too—a master of revolving-door cabinets, of juggling this venal minister against that ambitious general, of seducing contentious Bedouin tribes with gifts of wheat and gold watches and commissions in his army.

As the King developed, so did his kingdom. Amman, once a village, began to assume the dimensions of a metropolis. The more industrious of his Palestinians emerged from the camps and flourished as merchants and bankers. Hussein filled his cabinets with Palestinians, and in greater and greater measure they administered the kingdom. What a remarkable people they were, pining for Palestine more than ever, making education in the meanwhile their ancillary obsession, the most unlettered of the fathers and their spouses tongue-lashing the sons and daughters to excel, just as the Jews of the Diaspora did decades earlier. For as a people the Palestinians were as gifted as the Jews, save for some flaw in their character that cheated them of the Jewish genius to transform fantasy into political fact—the Zionist triumph in Palestine exposed the flaw. But with Palestinian energy Jordan grew, however modestly, so that by 1967 the kingdom had ceased to be a debtor and boasted not only its self-respect but a surplus of £100 million in its treasury.

In June of 1967, Hussein committed his most egregious mistake. Eager to appear as militant against Israel as Nasser, persuaded that, despite his fulminations, Nasser did not intend war, the King hastened into Nasser's arms in common cause against the Zionist nation. A command uniting the Egyptian and Jordanian armies was proclaimed on paper, and on June 5, when Israel attacked Egypt, Jordan joined the war. Unlike 1948, the Jordanian army's performance in the battle was disgraceful. Nominally an Egyptian general commanded the Jordanian front, but the disparities of Egyptian (Soviet) equipment and Jordanian (Western) equipment were so vast that Jordanian and Egyptian aircraft could not even communicate. The Jordanian army hardly defended Jerusalem; throughout the west bank, their performance was not much better. The Israelis dashed to the River Jordan within a few days, and deprived Hussein of the most fertile fifth of his kingdom. Throughout the rest of that summer, several hundred thousand new Palestinian refugees descended upon Amman.

Out of that defeat—the most ignoble of modern Arab history—emerged something that, to Arabs at least, seemed splendid: the Palestinian resistance. For a while the *fedayin* launched courageous expeditions from the east bank of the River Jordan into the territory the Israelis had snatched away, most of them militarily insubstantial but enough to exasperate the conquerors. When the Israelis intensified their countermeasures, the *fedayin* turned inward—against Hussein, the "reactionary American stooge" who stood ready to negotiate with Israel. By September of 1970, the *fedayin* and Hussein's (partly) Bedouin army seemed predestined for civil war.

Early that September, commandos of the (Marxist-Leninist) Popular Front for the Liberation of Palestine hijacked three international airliners and flew them full of passengers to a disused airstrip deep in the Jordanian desert. I arrived in Amman next morning. *Fedayin* of Fatah and the Popular Front and the Popular Democratic Front and still other factions, many of them mere thugs, laden with hand grenades and automatic weapons, roamed arrogantly and at will through the streets of the capital, halting traffic to search for arms, commandeering automobiles and cameras and transistor radios, taking potshots at embassies and at the police and at army posts whenever the spirit moved them. In the night there was constant shooting and the shedding of blood; electricity was cut; tracer bullets and mortar fire illumined the black valleys.

At dawn the shooting stopped, began again, died down. I drove out of Amman, through Zerqa into the desert, to visit "Revolution Airport" and the hijacked planes. The road was strewn with barricades, heaped rocks and rubber tires. Dozens of commando roadblocks stood between me and my destination. Clearly, King Hussein no longer controlled his own capital, Zerqa, or its environs. Outside Amman we passed mile upon mile of refugee shelters—ragged tents, hideous one-room concrete block huts and corrugated tin shanties, baking in the sun. My driver, a refugee himself, remarked, "America sends Phantoms to Israel, and tents and blankets to the Palestinians, then wonders why we are not grateful."

The scene at Revolution Airport was unforgettable. The Royal Jordanian Army had encircled the hijacked airplanes with dozens of Centurion tanks, armored cars, anti-aircraft guns, jeeps, and fire trucks, none of them daring to approach the planes for fear that the commandos might kill the hostages. This modern armor and a passing caravan of camels shimmered together in a glassy mirage, as though swimming in some distant sea. At the center of that ocean—marooned on an island of flat salt—gleamed the three airplanes. Army officers and Bedouin troops in *kaffiyehs* and khaki shirts mingled with the unshaven *fedayin*, and a Jordanian colonel said, "These hostages are very happy. It is like a lovely picnic for them. They come out of the plane and go for walks, and their children play games in the sand." A few days later, the Popular Front evacuated the planes, then blew them up.

The King, meanwhile, brooded in Hommar Palace, his limestone villa outside Amman, tinkering with his ham radio, raging now and then against the anarchy, still undecided what to do. He was, as earlier in his reign, the victim of contradictory advisers. His "doves" were urging him to conciliate the *fedayin* so as to avoid the sea of blood his "hawks" exhorted as the only means to reassert royal legitimacy and rescue his tumbling throne. Israel and America, who hardly yearned for a revolutionary Palestinian state along the River Jordan, likewise favored a showdown. "Lucky the man," said a Jordanian proverb, "who speaks last to the King. His Majesty will sleep with his dream." Evidently at bedtime a hawk had the King's ear. In mid-September, Hussein appointed a military government, civil war ensued, and perhaps 2,000 or 3,000 *fedayin* were slaughtered.

The survivors—several thousand—fled to the forest of Ajlun, not far from the Roman ruins of Jerash, in the northwestern corner of the kingdom. Throughout the harsh winter they camped in makeshift shelters and in mountain caves beneath the pines, grizzled, ill-clad, doomed young men—starved, whenever the Bedouins severed their supplies, of ammunition and even food. In spring and early summer the Bedouins—equipped with new weapons from Washington—moved in and began to shoot everybody. Several hundred *fedayin* were killed; others fled to Syria; some swam the River Jordan and surrendered to the Israelis. Others still, so claim some Palestinians, surrendered to the Bedu and were shot in cold blood.

From the nightmare of Ajlun forest emerged a new phenomenon—*Ayloul al Aswad,* Black September, the most notorious of the Palestinian terror squads. As the desparate *fedayin* endured that fierce winter of 1971, hovering over their meager fires, venturing out of their caves only to be picked off by the King's men, they brooded upon the blunders of their absent leaders and upon the disaster of the previous September in Amman. It was there, in the forest, so Palestinian legend asserts, that Abu Ali Iyyad—the Arab Che Guevara—raged to his comrades, "Our leadership is bankrupt and we're getting nowhere. Are we one inch closer to reconquering Palestine? We must go underground—we must kill Hussein and [Prime Minister] Wasfi Tell and wage war against every reactionary Arab government, we must bring the battle to the heart of Europe and to the shores of America itself, we must sow terror far and wide. Remember Algeria: the world won't respond to any other kind of protest. Only in violence and horror will Palestine be reborn."

Abu Ali was killed by the Bedu soon thereafter. Perhaps a thousand survivors of Ajlun, most of them disaffected soldiers of Fatah, descended upon Beirut. Some few of these formed the nucleus of Black September, bound by a bond of secrecy as sacred as a Trappist vow. There ensued the murder of Wasfi Tell in Cairo that November; of five Jordanians in Germany the following February; of 11 Israeli Olympic athletes at Munich in September. The Israeli air force mounted reprisals against Palestinian camps in Lebanon and Syria; scores, possibly hundreds, of people perished.*

*Israeli reprisals against the Palestinians have been pitiless and horrible. In an address to the United States Senate on August 22, 1974, J. William Fulbright, then the chairman of the Foreign Relations Committee, deplored the indifference of the American press to the routine savagery of Israeli attacks upon southern Lebanon. Recalling General Dayan's threat to make southern Lebanon "unlivable" if Palestinian guerrillas did not desist from attacks on Israeli villages, Senator Fulbright pointed out that the toll of life from Israeli reprisals was far greater than from Palestinian raids. "One suspects," the Senator declared, "that these events would not have been treated quite so routinely by these two great journals of record [The New York Times and The Washington Post]—they surely would have been front-page news—if the attacks had been mounted against Israeli civilians by Palestinian guerrillas."

Following the massacre of 16 Israeli adolescents at Maalot on May 15, 1974 (another six eventually died from wounds), Israeli aircraft bombed and strafed several Lebanese towns and Palestinian refugee camps, killing at least 50 civilians and wounding 200 others, including many women and children. On June 21, 1974, Jim Hoagland reported in The Washington Post that further Israeli raids that month revealed "sophisticated phosphorous bombs that have set extensive fires in Lebanese olive groves and wheat fields, seriously damaging the harvest in progress. Fragments of American-made anti-personnel bombs were also recovered."

Senator Fulbright declared that "the Palestinian guerrillas bear a heavy responsibility for provoking the Israeli retaliatory attacks by their acts of terrorism within Israel. . . . But Israel must bear the final responsibility for the indiscriminate retaliation. . . . Never to be forgotten either is the American

Ironically, the methods and organization of Black September were partially modeled upon the Irgun Zvai Leumi and the Stern Gang—the Jewish terrorist groups of the 1940s. In 1944, the Stern Gang assassinated Lord Moyne, the British administrator for the Middle East, in Cario. In 1946, the Irgun blew up the wing of Jerusalem's King David Hotel housing the British high command and killed nearly 100 Britons and Arabs. When the British retaliated with arrests and hangings, the Irgun seized hostages, hanged some of them, and—exporting its terrorism to Europe—bombed the British embassy in Rome. In 1948, the Stern Gang assassinated the United Nations mediator in Palestine, Count Folke Bernadotte. In 1948, the Irgun and the Stern massacred 254 Arabs at Deir Yassin, provoking (deliberately) the flight of Arabs from the rest of Palestine. The link between the Haganah (the regular Jewish army) and the terrorist groups was kept obscure, as was the later link between Fatah and Black September. What can be safely said is that every national movement, despite its disavowals, appears to possess a terror wing. Everybody deplores terrorism except when it serves his own purpose—and that includes the terror war the United States waged in Indochina.

The Jordanian intelligence services collaborated with the C.I.A. (and even to an extent with Israeli intelligence) in endeavoring to crush Black September. This was of course in Jordan's interest, but it was also an earnest of King Hussein's quest for peace with Israel. In expelling the *fedayin,* the King

---

role, which amounts to complicity, in Israel's attacks upon Lebanon. The war planes used by the Israelis are American planes, sold or given by the United States, and so are some, if not most or all, of the bombs. But so far the State Department has registered no more than feeble protests against Israel's campaign to make southern Lebanon 'unlivable.' "

On December 2, 1975—apparently in reprisal for an invitation to the P.L.O. to participate in a debate on the Middle East in the Security Council—Israeli jets attacked Palestinian camps in northern and southern Lebanon, killing and wounding 200 people. The raids were widely condemned within Israel itself. Israel has mounted scores of such attacks over the years, providing substance to the charge that terrorism can be waged officially, by an established state, even more barbarously than by bands of desperadoes.

pacified the east bank and tendered the hand of peace—*de facto* if not *de jure*—across the River Jordan. The Israelis did not reciprocate with any serious offer to return territory. Nevertheless, when the October war erupted in 1973, Hussein—who had learned his lesson six years earlier and whose air force was too feeble anyway—kept his kingdom out of it.

For this and his previous good behavior, the King expected Dr. Kissinger to redeem Nixon's promises of Israeli withdrawal and to include Jordan in his new diplomacy. Some members of the royal family did not repine that much, but Hussein yearned once more to be king of Jerusalem.

King of Jerusalem? That dream, and it was Hussein's fondest, has receded farther than ever from fulfillment. Dr. Kissinger's original scheme for the Geneva conference, once Israel and Egypt were disengaged, was to disengage the Syrian and Jordanian fronts, then assemble all of the parties to fashion (ultimately) a final settlement. This scenario was undone by the delays of the Syrian disengagement, by rivalry amongst the Arabs, Israeli obstruction, and Kissinger's own miscalculations.

In January 1974, Hussein and Prime Minister Rifai presented Kissinger with a map proposing an Israeli withdrawal from the Jordan River eight to ten kilometers into the west bank; the King was prepared for a phased retreat, demilitarization of the zone, inspection by the United Nations. Kissinger passed the map to the Israelis, who rejected it. In July Israel proposed instead, not military disengagement, but a final political settlement with Jordan. The proposition was humiliating, not even serious. Israel would retain Arab Jerusalem, important portions of the west bank, a defensive frontier along the river—and return the remaining balloons, sausages, and corridors to Jordan, intermeshing them with the Israeli army. It would have been an Arab Lesotho. Hussein refused it.

Following the Syrian disengagement, the Jordanians warned Kissinger that either they rapidly regain the west bank or the P.L.O.—Hussein's archenemy—would preempt their claim. Kissinger agreed with this assessment, and on several occasions warned the Israelis accordingly. However, he was distracted by the war in Cyprus and the dénouement of Watergate; with Nixon paralyzed, he was unable to apply effective pressure upon Israel.

On August 9, Richard Nixon relinquished the presidency. Shortly thereafter, Hussein visited Washington, where Kissinger and President Ford assured him that disengagement in the Jordan valley was their next priority. The King was elated, but from past experience he should have known better; moreover, he did not reckon upon the intrigues of his Egyptian cousins. Ismail Fahmy was in Washington, too. The Egyptians coveted a second Israeli withdrawal in Sinai, and they pleaded their preeminence over the Hashemites.

By October, the growing international prominence of the P.L.O. aroused Kissinger's alarm. He was not innately hostile to Palestinian aspirations, but he had little sympathy for their liberation movement. He considered the P.L.O. a pot of contradictions, its moderates immobilized by radicals, its policies the hostage of rhetoric and illusion. Its leader, Yasir Arafat, was like a cyclist atop a tightrope, yearning perhaps to descend to earth but urged by his disciples to pedal up to heaven—to the unattainable secular. Palestine. Granted that in negotiations Arafat might accept a smaller part of paradise—the west bank and the Gaza Strip—but until he put his house in order, why should Kissinger do him favors? Besides, even supposing a rump Palestine was possible, the notion did not enchant Kissinger. His history books had taught him that such miniature principalities breed irredentist passions, cause subsequent explosions, provoke dangerous quarrels between great powers. The Palestinians might have their state, but only as part of Jordan—the very goal that Kissinger had failed to advance.

Kissinger flew to Cairo on October 9, not only to discuss new Sinai negotiations with Sadat but to solicit his support for Jordan at the imminent Arab summit conference. Sadat promised to try, but in the event he did not try hard. At Rabat, a fortnight later, the Arab kings and presidents questioned Hussein about commitments from Kissinger and prospects of Israeli withdrawal from the River Jordan. Hussein held up his empty hands.

With that admission, his case collapsed. Led by Syria, the other Arab governments anointed the P.L.O. as the new sovereign of the west bank, conferring upon the Palestinians the metaphysical right to resolve their own future. In fact, this suited Egypt, for it protected Sadat on his Palestinian flank as he pursued his own national interest and maneuvered to negotiate again with Israel. Secretly (so Sadat informed Kissinger afterwards) the summit approved a resolution recommending a Palestinian state in Gaza and the west bank, along the borders of 1967; the P.L.O. acquiesced. As did Hussein, so long reviled by his brother Arabs, but reinstated now to their good graces; King Faisal soothed his sacrifice with a gift of $300 million. But with Jordan out of the running, and with no prospect in the near future of Israel sitting with the P.L.O., Kissinger perforce would favor Sinai as the site of his next miracle.

"I was distressed," King Hussein told me recently, "by the decision at Rabat. I thought it would weaken the Arab position for implementing Resolution 242. But I accepted it, and now Jordan cannot negotiate for the west bank unless authorized by the Arab leadership in council, including the P.L.O." Rabat was the first major defeat for Kissinger since the October war—and a major brake on interim diplomacy. On subsequent visits to Amman he lamented to the King and Zeid Rifai his own failure, whilst there was still time, to restore the west bank to Jordan.

"So you made a mistake," Rifai said.

"We miscalculated," Kissinger replied, "our manipulative capabilities." (That is the Jordanian version. In the American version Kissinger tells Rifai, "*You* miscalculated our manipulative capabilities.")

On the morrow of Rabat, Dr. Kissinger returned to Cairo. Sadat was ill with influenza, and received his guest clad in a dressing gown in the bedroom of his residence at Giza. Gone was the *bonhomie* of previous visitations, the gracious exchange of flattery ("We could never have come this far, Mr. President,

without your statesmanship"... "Dr. Henry, you are my favorite magician"), for now both men were embarrassed. Sadat
had failed to repulse the P.L.O.'s claim to the west bank; Kissinger's diplomacy was bogged down and his credibility was
beginning to vanish. At Rabat the other Arabs, in Cairo some of
his own advisers, kept warning Sadat that "Kissinger is playing
games with you." Increasingly Sadat was gnawed by doubt, by
suspicion of Kissinger's intentions. Kissinger had no mind to lose
the anchor of his Arab policy, and after ritual pleas for confidence he promised to pursue another Israeli retreat in Sinai.
Sadat sought the Mitla and Gidi passes, his oil fields on the
Gulf of Suez, and he would accept nothing less.

# 11

# Masada

That, Dr. Kissinger knew, would not be easy to achieve. The catastrophe of Watergate, the disgrace of Richard Nixon, the troubled transition to the presidency of Gerald Ford, had impaired America's power in the world and inflicted severe wounds upon Kissinger's own capacity to conduct foreign policy. One of Watergate's chief casualties was the momentum of step-by-step diplomacy, since that diplomacy presupposed a strong and popular president fully prepared to impose his will upon the obstinacy of either party—particularly the Israelis. A paralyzed Nixon was unwilling; an uncertain Ford did not know how. Ford's first 100 days were doomed to beget confusion, not vigor.

Moreover, Rabat and its repercussions—Yasir Arafat in *kaffiyeh* and pistol holster before the plenary General Assembly of the United Nations in November (1974), for example— outraged the Israelis. Privately P.L.O. luminaries had suggested that, in return for recognition of Palestinian rights and a partnership for the Palestinians in peace negotiations, the P.L.O. was prepared eventually to compromise with Israel. Arafat's address, however, though it contained some nuances, was aimed essentially at his militant constituency in Araby, and beyond that to the emotions of the Third World, not to the editorial board of *The New York Times*. "I am a rebel, and freedom is my cause," he proclaimed. "If we turn now to the historical roots of our cause, we do so because at this very moment in our midst are those who, while they occupy our homes, as their cattle graze in our pastures and as their hands pluck the fruit from our trees, claim at the same time that we are disembodied spirits, fictions without presence, without traditions or future."

Should I not dream and hope? For is not revolution the making real of dreams and hopes? So let us work together that my dream may be fulfilled, that I should return with my people out of exile, there in Palestine to live in justice, equality and fraternity . . . in one democratic state [with] Christian, Jew and Moslem. . . . Is this not a noble dream worthy of my struggle alongside all lovers of freedom everywhere? . . .

Let us remember, Mr. President, that the Jews of Europe and the United States have been known to lead the struggles for secularism and the separation of church and state; they have also been known to fight against discrimination on religious grounds. How then do they refuse this humane paradigm for the Holy Land? How then do they continue to support the most fanatic, discriminatory and closed of nations in its policy? How?

In my formal capacity as Chairman of the Palestine Liberation Organization and as leader of the Palestinian Revolution, I proclaim before you that when we speak of our common hopes for the Palestine of tomorrow we include in our perspective all Jews now living in Palestine who choose to live with us there in peace and without discrimination.

In my formal capacity as Chairman of the Palestine Liberation Organization and leader of the Palestinian Revolution, I call upon Jews one by one to turn away from the illusory promises made to them by Zionist ideology and the Israeli leadership. Those offer Jews perpetual bloodshed, endless war and continuous thralldom. We invite them to emerge from their moral isolation into a more open realm of free choice, far from their present leadership's effort to implant in them a Masada complex. We offer them the most generous solution, that we might live together in a framework of just peace in our democratic Palestine. In my formal capacity as Chairman of the Palestine Liberation Organization, I announce here that we do not wish the shedding of one drop of either Arab or Jewish blood; neither do we delight in the continuation of killing, which would end once a just peace, based on our people's rights, hopes and aspirations is finally established.

In my formal capacity as Chairman of the Palestine Liberation Organization and leader of the Palestinian Revolution, I appeal to you to accompany our people in its struggle to attain its right to self-determination. . . . I appeal to you further to aid our people's return to its homeland from an involuntary exile imposed upon it by force of arms, by tyranny, by oppression, so that we might regain our property, our land, thereafter to live in our national homeland, free and sovereign, enjoying all the privileges of nationhood. . . .

Today, Mr. President, I have come bearing an olive branch and a freedom fighter's gun. Do not let the olive branch fall from my hand. Do not let the olive branch fall from my hand.

Arafat might just as well have asked, not only for all of Palestine but for Jupiter, Neptune, and Pluto, too. His "dream" could not be consummated during this generation, nor probably during the next, and he knew it. For this generation, his "dream" was a cloud to climb down from—toward the *terra firma* of serious negotiations to establish that Palestinian state in the west bank and in Gaza which he knew to be feasible.

Not surprisingly, however, Yosef Tekoah, the Israeli delegate to the United Nations, chose to take Arafat literally. Tekoah accused the United Nations of having "prostrated itself before the P.L.O., which stands for the premeditated murder of innocent civilians, denies to the Jewish people its right to live, and seeks to destroy the Jewish state by armed force." There was no need for a separate Palestinian state anywhere. "What is Jordan if not a Palestinian Arab state? . . . Israel will not permit the establishment of P.L.O. authority in any part of Palestine. The P.L.O. will not be forced on the Palestinian Arabs. It will not be tolerated by the Jews of Israel." The previous July,

General Aharon Yariv, in his short-lived capacity as Israel's
minister of information, had declared that Israel might negotiate
with the P.L.O. if it renounced terrorism and accepted Israel's
right to exist. He was disavowed by his government, and now
with Arafat astride the rostrum of Turtle Bay, Israel became
more adamant than ever.

Israel's misgivings applied, it soon appeared, to a resumption
of step-by-step negotiations with Egypt. For another withdrawal
from the Sinai, Prime Minister Rabin required a pact of
nonbelligerency from Anwar Sadat. Israeli strategists talked
openly of separating Egypt from Syria, and of removing Egypt
from the Arab-Israeli conflict. Even for nonbelligerency, Rabin
seemed to be in no hurry. Kissinger and his aides recognized
now that tactically the paramount Israeli purpose was to delay
and prolong whatever negotiation he might favor.

Certainly the clocks of Tel Aviv ticked more slowly than those
of Washington. Ambassador Simcha Dinitz was fond of telling a
fable about a poor rabbi in Czarist Russia of the last century. The
reigning Czar was half mad, and determined that his dog should
learn to talk. He summoned several sorcerers and witches; when
each of them failed to teach the dog to talk, he had their heads
chopped off. Hearing that the rabbi possessed miraculous
powers, the Czar summoned him to court. "Rabbi," said he,
"you will teach this dog to talk—or off with your head."

"*Oy!*" cried the rabbi. But he was a resourceful fellow, and
after reflecting for a moment he said to the Czar, "Sire, I shall
teach your dog to talk—but it will take a little time."

"How long?" asked the Czar.

"Fifteen years."

"Fifteen years!"

"Yes," said the rabbi, "—but in fifteen years Your Majesty's
dog will be a chatterbox."

"Very well," said the Czar, "but if not—off with your head."

The rabbi took the dog home to the ghetto, and his wife said,
"*Oy!* How could you make such a promise? You'll never teach
that dog to talk."

"I know," said the rabbi. "But in fifteen years, the Czar will be dead . . . or I will be dead . . . or the dog will be dead."

Ambassador Dinitz compared the conclusion of Dr. Kissinger's step-by-step diplomacy—a final settlement in the Middle East, with final frontiers and the rest—to the Czar's talking dog. In his own fashion, so did Prime Minister Rabin.

In a revealing interview with the Israeli journal *Haaretz* on December 3, 1974, Rabin stated that "the central aim of Israel should be to gain time"—up to seven years, the period essential to Europe and the United States to free themselves from dependency on Arab oil. During that interval Israel would continue to seek partial agreements, but he implied it would avoid a total settlement until the United States was no longer constrained by the need for oil to impose conditions that Israel found unpalatable. In this interview Rabin did not insist upon Egyptian nonbelligerency; as the winter progressed, however, right-wing pressure intensified in the Knesset and nonbelligerency became his *sine qua non*.

Kissinger, in the meanwhile, juggled several strategic balls at once; in January 1975 he warned the Arabs publicly that invasion of their oil fields was not unthinkable should they attempt to strangle the United States with exorbitant prices or a new embargo. In February, he returned to the Middle East, where he found the Egyptian and Israeli positions still irreconcilable. In Jerusalem, and in Washington for the next three weeks, he exhorted the Israelis again and again to recognize the constraints upon Sadat—that Sadat could not risk a rupture with the other Arabs, that nonbelligerency could only come with formal peace and was unattainable at this stage. Security for Israel, Kissinger contended, had to be a process—not a precondition. The Israelis were either unconvinced or prepared, for the purpose of gaining time, to hazard an abortive negotiation.

An eminent Israeli official ·told me that shortly before the March shuttle he took Kissinger aside and said, "Henry, you must be under no illusions. Israel will never withdraw from the Sinai passes for anything less than full nonbelligerency from

Egypt." Kissinger assumed this was a negotiating position; subsequently he said that the Israelis softened on nonbelligerency, then hardened again when he reached Jerusalem—that they brought him back to the Middle East with premeditated deception.

In Jerusalem on March 9, Rabin began the new negotiation by outlining to Kissinger seven points as the basis of the Israeli position; two days later he presented the points in a formal document, "Proposed Main Elements of Agreement Between Israel and Egypt." Briefly, the document demanded a separate self-contained agreement with Egypt, though Israel remained "ready to negotiate with each of its neighbors"; the agreement had to be "a step toward peace in some practical measure"; it had to terminate the use of force "whatever the legal formula"—nonaggression, nonbelligerency, or whatever; it had to contain "practical arrangements to assure a real buffer zone"; it had to last long enough to solve the "dilemma of vagueness about duration"; it had to define the link between this interim measure and subsequent negotiations at Geneva; and finally it precluded discussion of the new Israeli line in Sinai until Egypt had responded to the first six points.

Dr. Kissinger was dismayed, for it was obvious at once that the Israelis were demanding nonbelligerency. Under point two—practical steps toward peace—they sought (amongst other benefits) Egypt's disavowal of the Arab boycott, and the free movement of peoples between the two nations. Under point three—the "nonuse of force"—they sought a formal "renunciation of belligerency clearly and in its appropriate legal wording." They required many features of a final peace, though after their withdrawal they would remain in possession of most of Sinai. "You're being unrealistic," Kissinger protested. "I'll see what I can do on the nonuse of force."

In the ensuing days, at Aswan, Kissinger persuaded Sadat to offer Israel the "functional equivalent" of nonbelligerency in the military sense—no resort to force until the agreement, renewable annually, was superseded by another. On the political level, Sadat agreed to diminish the boycott and hostile propaganda, and to permit a limited communion of peoples—"maybe some students, and family reunions, but no tourist aircraft flying back and forth," he said—though this dimension would be *de facto,* not a promise he could commit to paper. Kissinger and his aides drew up a working document—a "Main Points Paper"—which endeavored to refine the Egyptian and Israeli positions. They revised it constantly, but—as they shuttled back and forth between Jerusalem and Aswan—Kissinger could not reconcile the contradictions. On March 17, the Israelis insisted still upon formal nonbelligerency.

"Who will be at the eastern end of the Mitla and Gidi passes?" Sadat asked Kissinger the same day.

"The closer the Egyptians are to the western end," said Kissinger, "the closer the Israelis will be to the eastern end. The Israelis haven't yet drawn a line."

Sadat was visibly disturbed. "The Israelis," he said, "should be under no illusion that they will remain in the passes."

His frustration rising, Kissinger flew to Israel, then back to Aswan on March 18. He told Sadat, "I can add little to yesterday. I expected your reaction. I had to present the Israeli paper lest I be accused of compromising my impartiality. If you will give me the final Egyptian position, I'll take it to Israel. Should this fail, we should consult on a common strategy to cope with the situation."

"After our last talk," Sadat replied, "I was about to say that there was nothing new in the Israeli position to warrant carrying on. But I didn't react that way. Better you have another try." Sadat insisted on a total Israeli retreat from the passes, and upon free access to the oil fields farther south at Abu Rudeis and its environs—his final word.

Like Rabin, Sadat was under constraints—not quite so free to negotiate in isolation with Kissinger as he had done during the first disengagement in the Sinai. He had confined Foreign Minister Fahmy and General Gamasy to the periphery of that negotiation; he could not now. The Egyptian generals resented

the first disengagement as enfeebling their war option for the
great future should diplomacy fail to recover all of the "homeland." Sadat's power base was the army, and he dared not risk its
disenchantment another time.

The Gidi and Mitla passes, which reposed respectively about
15 and 20 miles from the southern end of the Suez Canal, were
long and desolate granite corridors surrounded by monotonous
desert strewn with rocks. Strategically the passes were not (as
several Israeli generals would subsequently concede) so important as either Israelis or Egyptians pretended, but symbolically
their possession was paramount. To Israeli public opinion, the
Mitla and the Gidi constituted an invaluable defense border
more than a hundred miles distant from Israel itself. Accordingly
the Israelis had festooned the high ground with radar and listening equipment that could monitor Egyptian MIGs on the other
side of Suez. They had spent $250 million burrowing shelters to
conceal battalions of armor, honeycombing the contiguous
mountains with miniature forts and electronic snooping
stations—most of that equipment provided by the United
States.

Toward the end of the negotiation, in exchange for Sadat's
"nonrecourse to force," the Israelis offered to withdraw halfway
into the passes and to restore the oil fields in an enclave reach-
able by an Israeli road with United Nations checkpoints. Even for
this half loaf, Sadat never saw an Israeli map—and neither did
Kissinger, until the Israelis leaked it later to *The New York
Times*. No matter; Sadat refused. He did not demand that his
army occupy the passes—only that the Israelis relinquish them.
He was anxious but calm.

"I can't think of anything further to ask Egypt," Kissinger
sighed.

"I wanted to defuse this time bomb," Sadat said. "If the Israelis persist in this position, there is no point in carrying on."

"If they do persist," Kissinger asked, "shall I return to
Aswan—or break off the negotiations?"

"If they do not change," Sadat responded, bluntly but politely, "it is best that you leave the area and not come back to Egypt."

Throughout the negotiation, Kissinger complained bitterly to Sadat, and to Assad and Hussein in side trips to their capitals, about the intransigence of the Israelis. "You can't believe what I'm going through," he said. Perhaps in speaking thus Kissinger sought also to ingratiate himself with the Arabs, but his aides insist he was "at his wit's end." At that moment Indochina was collapsing; détente was tenuous; American power was waning in Turkey, in Portugal, and elsewhere in the West. Now the Israelis, vexed with his pressure to make concessions, were taking aim at Kissinger himself—or so he was convinced. "They're trying," he told the Arab leaders, "to bring me down."

On Friday, March 21, Dr. Kissinger returned to Jerusalem. Whilst he was en route to meet Rabin, an urgent message for the Prime Minister arrived from President Ford. "I am disappointed to learn," the President wrote, "that Israel has not moved as far as it might." The United States, he warned, would not finance a state of deadlock that would damage its political interests; if Israel were not more flexible, the United States would drastically reassess its policy in the Middle East—"including our policy towards Israel." This was an obvious threat to suspend American economic and military aid, and it represented the severest American reprimand to the Israelis since President Eisenhower prevailed upon them to stop the Suez War.

The threat backfired, as Kissinger soon recognized, for it simply hardened the Israeli refusal to accept Sadat's terms. Coldly Rabin accused Kissinger of composing the President's ultimatum. Kissinger denied this—but that he inspired the message there could be no doubt.

"I'll tell the cabinet," Rabin said grimly, "that our negotiating team will stick to its proposals. Anything less cannot be done. To ask us to do what Sadat has proposed—I see no justification, including our relationship with the United States."

"I can suspend my mission," Kissinger replied angrily. "You can have your cabinet meeting afterwards."

"No," said Rabin, retreating slightly. "First there must be a cabinet meeting. I'm not empowered to say that this is our final position."

They parted glacially—these two men who, only several years before, had been so close. The next day, the sabbath, at Rabin's request, Kissinger visited Masada. Masada—the fortress atop a desolate mountain where nearly a thousand Jews, besieged by the Romans during the first century, refused to surrender and slaughtered themselves instead.

After sunset of that sabbath—March 22—Dr. Kissinger conferred with the Israelis in two final, dramatic meetings: from 6:30 to 8:15, and from 10:35 to five minutes past midnight. Rabin, Allon, Gur, Dinitz, and Minister of Defense Shimon Peres faced Kissinger, Sisco, Atherton, Saunders, and Ambassador Keating.

ALLON: We'd still like to negotiate an interim or overall agreement... but not on the basis of an ultimatum from the other side.

KISSINGER: There was no ultimatum. . . . In the absence of new Israeli ideas, we received no new Egyptian ideas. We have no illusions. . . . The Arab leaders who banked on the United States will be discredited. . . . Step-by-step has been throttled, first for Jordan, then for Egypt. We're losing control. We'll now see the Arabs working on a united front. There will be more emphasis on the Palestinians, and there will be a linkage between moves in the Sinai and on Golan. The Soviets will step back onto the stage. The United States is losing control over events, and we'd all better adjust ourselves to that reality. The Europeans will have to accelerate their relations with the Arabs. If the interim agreement in 1971 had succeeded, there would have been no war in October of 1973. The same process is at work here. We just don't have a strategy for the situation ahead. Our past strategy was worked out carefully, and now we don't know what to do. There will be pressures to drive a wedge between Israel and the United States, not because we want that but because it will be the dynamic of the situation. Let's not kid ourselves. We've failed.

ALLON: Why not start it up again in a few weeks?

KISSINGER: Things aren't going to be the same again. The Arabs won't trust us as they have in the past. We look weak—in Vietnam,

Turkey, Portugal, in a whole range of things. Don't misunderstand me. I'm analyzing this situation with friends. One reason I and my colleagues are so exasperated is that we see a friend damaging himself for reasons which will seem trivial five years from now—like seven hundred Egyptian soldiers across the canal in 1971. . . .* Events will tend to drive us apart. . . . I don't see how there can be another American initiative in the near future. We may have to go to Geneva for a multilateral effort with the Soviets—something which for five years we've felt did not offer the best hope for success. I had assumed that when Geneva [reconvened] everybody would look to us to propose the way of success. But that won't be so now.

ALLON: The Egyptians really didn't give very much.

KISSINGER: . . . An agreement would have enabled the United States to remain in control of the diplomatic process. Compared to that, the location of the line eight kilometers one way or the other frankly does not seem very important. And you got all the military elements of nonbelligerency. You got the "nonuse of force." The elements you didn't get—movement of peoples, ending of the boycott—are *unrelated* to your line. What you didn't get has nothing to do with where your line is. . . .

PERES: . . . It is a question not just of the passes, but of our military [intelligence] installations that have no offensive purpose and are necessary. The previous government couldn't overcome the psychological blow—that the Syrians and Egyptians launched a surprise attack. We need an early warning system. We need twelve hours of warning. Under the proposed arrangement, we'd only have six. . . . If there had been any Egyptian [concessions] regarding the duration of the agreement and the warning system—then what you've said would be very. . . touching. But then we would have faced new negotiations with Syria. . . .

KISSINGER: . . . This is a real tragedy. . . . We've attempted to reconcile our support for you with our other interests in the Middle East, so that you wouldn't have to make your decisions all at once. . . . Our strategy was to save you from dealing with all those pressures all at

---

*Dr. Kissinger was referring to the collapse of the Israeli-Egyptian negotiations in 1971, under the aegis of Secretary Rogers and Undersecretary Sisco, when Israel refused a token force of Egyptian troops on the east bank of the Suez Canal as part of an interim agreement.

once. If that was salami tactics—if we wanted the 1967 borders, we could do it with all of world opinion and considerable domestic opinion behind us. The strategy was designed to protect you from this. We've avoided drawing up an overall plan for a global settlement.... I see pressure building up to force you back to the 1967 borders—compared to that, ten kilometers is trivial. I'm not angry at you, and I'm not asking you to change your position. It's tragic to see people dooming themselves to a course of unbelievable peril.

RABIN *wryly*: This is the day you visited Masada.

Other Americans at the meeting described the atmosphere as "eerie." The Israelis were passive as Kissinger spoke; now they did not quibble. It was almost as though, from the very first, they wanted no agreement, as though they had determined to demolish—for a time—step-by-step diplomacy. The Israelis were disturbed by the Arabs' riches and by their rising power. The United States was weak; Ford was weak; so was Kissinger. In its weakness America might even sacrifice Israel to satisfy the Arabs. American weakness was one thing, Israeli resolution quite another, and now Israel intended to be strong.

Israel's perception was one thing, Kissinger's quite another. Rabin was not strong, he was clumsy, indecisive, and incompetent. Before the negotiation he had discarded nonbelligerency, but then the Likud challenged him in the Knesset, and he embraced it again. Perhaps Rabin agreed with Kissinger, but it was Rabin's rival, the Minister of Defense, who dominated this negotiation. Ambitious, dogmatic, rather superficial, Peres was the strong man, ready to risk the disasters Kissinger conjured up. Peres was vastly more popular in Israel than Rabin and Allon together, and beneath his shadow their misgivings could not prevail.

Individually several ministers seemed to agree with Kissinger, but they were all feuding with each other, and collectively a positive consensus lay beyond their grasp. Kissinger longed for Golda Meir; for, had he convinced her, the cabinet would have bowed. He missed Dayan, too, for his imagination might have found a way.

Afterwards, to an acquaintance, Dr. Kissinger ruminated on his defeat. "Israel has no foreign policy," he said, "only domestic politics. . . . The Jews in history are generally intellectuals, cosmopolitans, people of long vision. But in Israel the ideal is that of the soldier-peasant. Generally the soldier is not intellectual, and few soldiers have vision. The peasant is known for his recalcitrance and excessive caution. It is the recalcitrance, the excessive caution, the lack of vision, that have caused the Israelis to refuse this agreement. . . . They're so legalistic, so Talmudic."

# 12

# The Spirit of 76

Shortly before the collapse of the negotiation Dr. Kissinger visited King Faisal at Riyadh. Their rapport had never been easy, but now Kissinger's travail with the Israelis provoked the King's compassion and his pledge to persevere in support of Kissinger's diplomacy; it was of their encounters the warmest and most satisfactory. A week later, Faisal was murdered by a mad nephew. The conjunction of that event with the failure in Sinai appeared to render the more probable all of the disasters Kissinger prophesied at Jerusalem. He was furious with the Israelis, and he took their refusal very personally—as directed not only at the United States but, above all, at himself.

For weeks after his return to Washington, Kissinger sulked and raged, castigating Israeli blindness to aides and visitors alike, compulsively telephoning distinguished Jews all over the country to complain of Israel's intransigence. His dismay was echoed by editorial voices in America and even by some within Israel itself. Writing in *The Washington Post*, the eminent political analyst Milton Viorst observed that "what Sadat offered Is-

164

rael was, in effect, his body. Through Kissinger, he was telling Rabin, as he tried to tell Mrs. Meir in late 1973, that he would act as Israel's broker in the Arab world if he could get some visible help from the Israelis. Whatever Israelis may say about him, Sadat clearly considers it more important to get on with Egypt's economic development than to keep on waging futile wars." Yoel Markus, the editor of *Haaretz*, wrote that "if Israel sought to prove to the United States that Egypt is not interested in a peace agreement, it achieved the opposite. . . . Egypt proved that it is ready to accept risks. . . . If Israel sought a limited agreement to 'win time' (obviously) it recoiled at the last moment and achieved nothing. . . . This should teach . . . Israel [to] coordinate its moves with the United States."

Kissinger's much-trumpeted "reassessment" of American policy in the Middle East was his revenge on Israeli recalcitrance, a euphemism for the selective embargo of military equipment that he imposed forthwith upon the Zionist nation. An Israeli request for more than $2.5 billion in new military and financial assistance had been pending for several months; Kissinger suggested that Shimon Peres, Yigal Allon, and Minister of Finance Yehoshua Rabinowitz—all were scheduled to visit Washington—stay home till the reassessment was completed. He suspended negotiations on new F-15 fighter planes for Israel, and delayed the delivery of already committed Lance ground-to-ground missiles.

Moreover, he summoned Dean Rusk, George Ball, David Rockefeller, Robert McNamara, McGeorge Bundy, William Scranton, John J. McCloy, C. Douglas Dillon, David K. E. Bruce, W. Averell Harriman—and several other dignitaries of the foreign policy establishment—plus all of the important American ambassadors in the Middle East (two of them career Arabists) to contribute to this elaborate enterprise. Most of these the Israelis considered unsympathetic—indeed, a "stacked deck." Many of the establishment dignitaries were critical of Kissinger's step-by-step method because in practice it excluded the Soviet Union and the European powers; without Soviet participation particularly, a final Arab-Israeli settlement could never be accomplished. George Ball, above all, advocated a return to Geneva and Soviet-American collaboration for fashioning a solution which, in the last resort—as General de Gaulle had prophesied—might have to be imposed upon the parties.

Dr. Kissinger conferred as well with senators and congressmen, Jewish leaders, and eminent academics. The prospect of reassessment made marvelous theater, but what did it produce?

Three options soon emerged:

1. The United States should announce its conception of a final settlement in the Middle East, based upon the 1967 frontiers of Israel with minor modifications, and containing strong guarantees for Israel's security. The Geneva conference should be reconvened; the Soviet Union should be encouraged to cooperate in this quest to resolve all outstanding questions (including the status of Jerusalem), which should be defined in appropriate components and addressed in separate subcommittees.

2. Failing the first option, the United States should seek a quasi-total settlement, for the near future, with Egypt the beneficiary. Israel should withdraw from most of Sinai in return for political nonbelligerency, her final frontiers with Egypt to be determined at a later stage.

3. Failing the first and second options, the United States should endeavor to revive step-by-step diplomacy.

Most of the dignitaries and academics summoned by Dr. Kissinger favored the first option. On May 1 (1975) I attended a meeting of a dozen academics—Professor Zbigniew Brzezinski of Columbia, Professor Malcolm Kerr of U.C.L.A., Professors Stanley Hoffmann and Nadav Safran of Harvard, former Ambassador to the United Nations Charles Yost, amongst others—who gathered in the Secretary's conference room on the seventh floor of the State Department. Dr. Kissinger seemed cheerful. "We've reached no conclusions on our Middle East strategy," he began, "partly because of *other* preoccupations in recent weeks." He was referring to the fall of Saigon a day or two before, to

the collapse of the peace settlement he had negotiated so
laboriously—for four years, as he often told the Arabs—in Indochina. The Middle East was calm at the moment, he continued, because the Arabs and the Russians "think we're coming
up with something. Otherwise, there is great danger in a stalemate. We have about two months."

A consensus of the academics soon emerged, roughly in favor
of the first option. Without committing himself, Kissinger said,
"Once the President and I decide the right thing to do, we'll do
it. The American political situation is so fluid at this moment, we
can afford to do the right thing." He meant, evidently, that if the
President and he decided to reconvene the Geneva conference
with an American plan based upon the 1967 frontiers, not even
strong opposition from Israel's supporters would stop them.
Brave words. I asked him what plans he had for dealing with the
Palestinians. "Mr. Sheehan," he rejoined, "do you want to start
a revolution in the United States?" Then what of the Russians, at
least—couldn't we include them more significantly in the
negotiating process? His answer, in retrospect, was very revealing.

The Arabs themselves didn't like the Russian negotiating
style, Dr. Kissinger said. The Arabs considered the Russians too
legalistic. The Russians complicated any negotiation. They came
to negotiations with long checklists, eager to mark off every
point. Gromyko had been in Washington recently; Kissinger
brought him to see President Ford. He had a long list about
strategic arms limitation, and he indicated that each of the items
was universally applicable but not universally valid, or universally valid but not universally applicable—Kissinger couldn't
remember which. The President turned to Kissinger and whispered, "What the hell is he talking about?"

Everybody laughed, but I left the meeting slightly confused.
If the Russians and the Palestinians were to be excluded from
the American plan for peace, what, I wondered, was the point in
having one? What was the purpose of reassessment—or were all
these consultations essentially decorative, a melodrama to be

acted out until Dr. Kissinger devised his own solution in isolation?

Certainly, in the beginning, from the end of March till early May, the first option seemed to have a chance. Dr. Kissinger's key ambassadors—Hermann Eilts (Egypt), Richard Murphy (Syria), and Thomas Pickering (Jordan)—all contributed to a long position paper urging this course; Kenneth Keating, his ambassador to Israel, concurred with reservations, then died shortly thereafter. Again, though resolution of the Palestinian problem was implied in the first option, the question was otherwise deferred in the secret position paper and in the numerous discussions Kissinger undertook. That the United States should abandon Kissingerian ambiguity and publicly proclaim its concept of a global settlement based upon total or near-total Israeli withdrawal was the supreme Arab wish; to the Israelis, it had always been the supreme abomination. Non-Zionists such as former Senator J. William Fulbright had been urging it on Kissinger and President Ford as the best means to achieve a settlement, but till now both had demurred for fear of the repercussions amongst Israel's American constituency.

Also contributing to the reassessment were, of course, Dr. Kissinger's principal aides for the Middle East—Undersecretary Sisco, Assistant Secretary Atherton, Deputy Assistant Secretary Saunders, and Robert Oakley, of the National Security Council staff—all of them accomplished technicians, and (save for Sisco) completely self-effacing.

Sisco was the favored target of Kissinger's cruelest jests, but valued, too, because he was a past master of tactics, of concoctions to buy time and carry American policy through a week from Thursday. For many years he was basically pro-Israeli; the domestic dimensions of policy for the Middle East—what American Jews would or would not accept—were his special province. Sisco worked out with the Syrians the formula for the United Nations Disengagement Observer Force on the Golan Heights, a marvel of face-saving semantics and preventive policing arrangements—a good example of his gifts. "Joe," says one of his former colleagues, "is a genius of postponing catastrophe. If the dike is bursting, Joe will dash around, then plug it with a promise or a piece of paper. He'll tell anybody what he wants to hear—he did that with the Egyptians and the Israelis before 1973, and it worked for a while. But *strategy?*—that's long-range, beyond Joe's depth."

Saunders and Oakley compiled many of the staff papers that developed the options for major problems before Kissinger considered them. During the negotiations of March and August 1975, Saunders and Oakley (with Atherton) would draft formulations of points agreed or still to be agreed, and Kissinger would carry on, working over the drafts as the negotiations proceeded and new elements or obstacles were introduced; whereupon these aides consumed more midnight oil, and refined their formulations.

Harold Saunders was a Princetonian, an analyst (briefly) for the Central Intelligence Agency before joining the staff of the National Security Council in 1961. By 1967, two years before Kissinger became his chief, he assumed the senior post on the N.S.C. staff for Middle East affairs. Laconic, cautious, bland of aspect, Saunders was very competent and shrewd. He was renowned in the department for the tightness and lucidity of his prose, for his cogency of analysis in strategic papers. But he contributed to the conventional strategic wisdom prior to the October war—arms for Israel to increase its confidence to negotiate, etc.—and if he entertained more Promethean notions he failed to inflict them upon his superiors. Kissinger took Saunders out of the White House and into the State Department ten months after becoming Secretary.*

Robert Oakley succeeded Saunders on the National Security Council staff. Unlike Saunders and Sisco, who had never served in the Middle East, Oakley knew the region well. Though not an Arabist, he had been until his return to Washington political

*In late 1975 Saunders became director of the department's Bureau of Intelligence and Research. Sisco recently resigned to assume a college presidency.

officer at the American embassy in Beirut, where—amongst
other assignments—he had over several years maintained informal contact with eminent Palestinians. A contemporary of
Saunders at Princeton, a gaunt Southerner too unpretentious to
discard his drawl, Oakley possessed a sharp analytical mind and
considerable independence of perception. Like Saunders, he
was indefatigable in his endeavors to add flesh and bone to
Kissinger's abstractions, but he was too honest (even with Kissinger) to pretend that he agreed with all of them. He was too
much a new boy to command Kissinger's confidence as Atherton
and Saunders did. Oakley was a type as well—the technician
who helps to formulate a policy, sees it diluted on a higher level,
sighs, then supports it out of loyalty. On the Palestinian question, for example, he preferred a less pusillanimous American
policy, but he recognized the domestic pressures that besieged
the Secretary.

Perhaps the most interesting of Dr. Kissinger's aides, however, was his assistant secretary for Near Eastern and South
Asian affairs, Alfred "Roy" Atherton. A product of Pittsburgh
and Springfield, Massachusetts, a son of Harvard, an artillery
officer during World War II, Atherton had been a diplomat for
nearly 30 years, and had reached the rank of career minister. He
had served abroad in Bonn and Stuttgart as well as in Damascus,
Aleppo, and Calcutta, but for a decade he had been based in
Washington. During the October war, he was deputy assistant
secretary of state, then succeeded Sisco (in 1974) as head of the
bureau when Sisco was promoted to the eminence of undersecretary.

Atherton was the incarnation of the Christian work ethic—or
rather, the Unitarian work ethic, since he was an ardent
member of that communion, and loved to devote his leisure (not
that he had much) to the causes of his church. He and his wife,
Betty, now that their sons and daughter had grown up, housed
homeless youths at their residence near the Sheraton Park Hotel
in northwest Washington. (Betty also helped to run a school of
remedial reading for dyslexic children.) Atherton rose at six,

arrived at his office generally by eight in the morning. At ten or eleven in the night he was often still there, given the propensity of the Middle East (not to mention India, Pakistan, North Africa, also within his purview) for chronic crisis. He worked Saturdays, and—whenever Kissinger wanted him or a new crisis erupted—on Sundays, too. Kissinger fetched him from the barber shop, though not from church.

Atherton was a servant of the sleepless night—a not uncommon necessity whenever he flew to the Middle East with Dr. Kissinger. He was in bondage to the button on his telephone that connected him to the Secretary's office on the floor above—another telegram to be drafted for Cairo or Damascus, another memorandum to be negotiated with the Israelis, another pronouncement to be prepared for some congressional committee. Kissinger and Sisco often lost their tempers, but Atherton never did. He rarely even raised his voice. Whenever I visited his office I was struck by his stoic calm, by his capacity to remain serene no matter how harassed or exhausted. Only when the Secretary buzzed him did he betray anxiety. He would leap up, dash for the door. "I'm sorry, Edward," he would say, "but I've got to draft an urgent cable." Or simply: "I'm sorry—the Secretary needs me." More than once I wanted to protest, "Must you run when he calls, Roy? Couldn't you *walk* to him just once? Will the man die—will the world collapse—if you keep Kissinger waiting for five minutes?"

I am overstating Roy Atherton's fleetness of foot, and perhaps exaggerating his dedication. I know that he yearns to escape Washington, to win a quiet embassy where he can glimpse the Mediterranean, take naps in the afternoon, enjoy the laughter of his wife. And I know he has made his measure of mistakes, not the least of them his share in the myopia of American policy before the October war; since then, if he perceived the inadequacies of Kissinger's strategy, he remained silent or was ineffectual in his dissent. As with so many career diplomats, one seldom knew what Atherton *thought* or where he *stood*. Nevertheless, he is my paradigm of the selfless, uncelebrated public servant, superior in his technical capacities, consumed by a need to prove anew each day that he is worthy of his master's confidence.

Dr. Kissinger is a Moloch who demands such sacrifice and devours all who render it. He is often savage and rarely thankful. He stretches his subordinates' minds to the limits of their endurance, flays them further for unattainable perfection, assimilates the best of their ideas to his own purpose, then comes to his decision—alone. When the policy succeeds, *he* receives the acclamation—alone.

This process was repeated roughly during the reassessment, but despite the extraordinary intellectual gymnastics, and despite his apocalyptic warnings to the Israelis on March 22, Kissinger never really refined the first option. For as the weeks passed his emotions cooled, his capacity for cold analysis prevailed, and his plunge into the metaphysics of reassessment was negated by other forces.

The Arabs had no common strategy nor consensus about the concessions they should render Israel should Geneva be revived; the Russians had hesitations about Geneva without a common strategy and no Arab consensus; they were in no hurry to sponsor a fiasco. Sadat coveted territory quickly, but he feared further Israeli procrastination at Geneva, and he could not risk the second option—a quasi-total settlement—because without similar progress on all fronts he would become a leper to his brother Arabs. Besides, Sadat was anxious to assuage his diseased economy; sterile polemics at Geneva might frighten off foreign investors. Kissinger's peroration to the Israelis on March 22 was brilliantly contrived, but their flair for *realpolitik* was as keen as his, and he did not deceive them. Sadat possessed no serious war option—Kissinger's own benefactions of guns and aircraft to Tel Aviv had seen to that—and the Israelis knew it. Sadat's relations with the Russians could hardly have been worse; he had chosen the Americans exclusively and now he was stuck with them. The radicals of Araby roared with impotence; Sadat reaffirmed his faith in Kissinger, renewed the U.N.E.F.

mandate in the Sinai, and, in early June, reopened the Suez Canal. All of these factors coalesced to belie Kissinger's apocalypse—or at least to postpone it—but it was the Israeli lobby that dealt reassessment its *coup de grâce.*

Dr. Kissinger's interaction with American Jews played a crucial and tempestuous part in the fashioning of his policy on the Middle East. If he could not convince American Jews, how could he move Israel? From the morrow of the October war he conferred regularly with Jewish leaders and intellectuals, explaining the motives of his diplomacy and appealing for their support. His basic message never changed—the war created new realities; the moderate Arabs are ready for peace; Israel, for its own survival, must respond whilst America can influence the Arabs; peace can never come unless Israel makes concessions. For a time Kissinger seemed to make some impression with this argument, but by the end of 1974 he was regarded by many American Jews as a foe of Israel and by some as a traitor to his race. It became a truism in the State Department that Kissinger's Jewishness helped him with the Arabs, harmed him with the Israelis. In the summer of 1975, a luminary of the lobby in Washington echoed a sentiment I had heard elsewhere. "I approached Kissinger once at Harvard," he told me, "and I used a Yiddish phrase. He *cringed.* He's the same today—a self-hating Jew."

I cannot penetrate Dr. Kissinger's heart, but his closest aides observed that nothing caused him greater anguish than accusations such as that. "He's objective about Israel," said one, "but not detached. How could he be? He has a strong sense of 'these are my people.' He's immensely proud to be a Jew. When he pleads for changes in Israeli policy, it's precisely because he wants Israel and Jewry to prosper. It tears his guts out to be accused of treachery to his own." During those impassioned weeks following the abortive negotiation, Kissinger asked several of his Jewish visitors, "How could I, as a Jew, do anything to betray my people?" More than once, he came close to tears.

During April (1975) the interminable corridors of the State

Department resounded with brave resolve for the pursuit of the first option. "We've got to save the Israelis from themselves. . . . Congress is fed up, too, and whatever we decide, Congress will go along." There was indeed much general speculation that spring about erosion of pro-Israeli sentiment in Congress; instinctively the lobby recognized that, if Kissinger was to be stopped, he would have to be stopped on Capitol Hill. The American Israel Public Affairs Committee (AIPAC), the vanguard of the lobby in Washington, was intensely active during that period, assailing not only Kissinger's person but his policies in the Middle East, in Cyprus, in Turkey, and far beyond; militants of the lobby canvassed the House and Senate, exhorting the members to even greater moral and military support of Israel. Simultaneously Israeli "truth squads"—composed of such as Eban, Allon, Dayan—dispersed throughout the republic, rebutting Kissinger's version of the March negotiation and struggling to sustain Israel's image as a beleaguered democracy still ardent in the quest of peace.

Whatever resentment many congressmen may inwardly entertain about the unrelenting pressures of the lobby, the American system itself predestines them to yield. Israel possesses a powerful American constituency; the Arabs do not, and despite their wealth, the oil companies as well are unequal to the impact of ethnic politics. In formulating the first option, Dr. Kissinger's advisers envisioned President Ford going to the American people, explaining lucidly and at length on television the issues of war and peace in the Middle East, pleading the necessity of Israeli withdrawal in exchange for the strongest guarantees. The President, too, was angry at Israel, and for a time he toyed with this notion of appealing over the heads of the lobby and of Congress directly to the people. He hesitated. "How will it play in Peoria?" he asked. "You'll never know until you do it," J. William Fulbright urged him. "Do it first—then Peoria will follow." But Ford was afraid of the political repercussions, and so was Kissinger. A senior diplomat who visited Washington frequently during this period told me, "Each time that I returned, I remarked the further erosion of the first option."

On May 21, 1975, 76 United States Senators wrote collectively to the President to endorse Israel's demand for "defensible" frontiers and massive economic and military assistance:

Dear Mr. President:

... Since 1967, it has been American policy that the Arab-Israeli conflict should be settled on the basis of secure and recognized boundaries that are defensible, and direct negotiations between the nations involved. We believe that this approach continues to offer the best hope for a just and lasting peace. While the suspension of the second-stage negotiations is regrettable, the history of the Arab-Israeli conflict demonstrates that any Israeli withdrawal must be accompanied by meaningful steps toward peace by its Arab neighbors.

Recent events underscore America's need for reliable allies and the desirability of greater participation by the Congress in the formulation of American foreign policy. Cooperation between the Congress and the President is essential for America's effectiveness in the world. ... We believe that the special relationship between our country and Israel does not prejudice improved relations with other nations in the region. We believe that a strong Israel constitutes a most reliable barrier to domination of the area by outside parties. Given the recent heavy flow of Soviet weaponry to Arab states, it is imperative that we not permit the military balance to shift against Israel.

We believe that preserving the peace requires that Israel obtain a level of military and economic support adequate to deter a renewal of war by Israel's neighbors. Withholding military equipment from Israel would be dangerous, discouraging accommodation by Israel's neighbors and encouraging a resort to force. Within the next several weeks, the Congress expects to receive your foreign aid requests for fiscal year 1976. We trust that your recommendations will be responsive to Israel's urgent military and economic needs. We urge you to make it clear, as we do, that the United States acting in its own national interests stands firmly with Israel in the search for peace in future negotiations, and that this premise is the basis of the current reassessment of U.S. policy in the Middle East.

The letter was affixed with the Senate's most famous names—save for such as Charles Percy, Mike Mansfield, Mark Hatfield. George McGovern, one of the signatories, confused everybody afterwards when he explained that "it would be folly for Israel to assume that American support means approval of the existing boundaries in the Middle East. The present boundaries are not defensible; they are a virtual assurance of continued conflict. . . . In return for . . . recognition, Israel must agree to return the occupied territories and must accept Palestinian self-determination, including the right to a political entity of their own."

Tom Braden, writing in *The Washington Post*, was less ambivalent:

The Senatorial letter makes Kissinger nothing more than an errand boy and assures the Arab states that he is powerless to arrange a deal. It is conceivable that Israel's leaders have determined on further concessions and regarded the Senate letter only as a means to let Kissinger know who was boss. In that event the step-by-step approach may yet yield results. But unless this is so, the game is over. Kissinger might as well stay home. Under the terms the Senate has laid down, it could send one of its own pages to handle negotiations.

Obviously, the letter was a stunning triumph for the lobby, a capital rebuke for Kissinger in Congress. (The lobby reaffirmed its strength in summer, humiliating Kissinger and King Hussein by obstructing in the Senate the sale of defensive Hawk missiles to Jordan.) The senatorial epistle was Israel's riposte to reassessment; it helped to kill the reassessment, notwithstanding later pretenses that the corpse lived on. At about this time, Sisco, Atherton, Saunders, and Oakley unanimously advised Kissinger that the first option had no hope of surviving the counterattacks of the lobby—that now the administration had no choice but to resume step-by-step diplomacy. Kissinger concurred, and reserved a new option—that at some future date, when the President was stronger, when his prospects were more auspicious, he might go to the people with an American plan for peace based upon the first option.

Thus when Ford met Sadat in the ancient palace of the prince-archbishops at Salzburg in early June, he repulsed Sadat's plea for a public commitment to the 1967 borders, and soothed him instead with a restatement of Nixon's secret promise. Reluctantly Sadat had already reached Kissinger's conclusion—that for the near future no choice existed save to resume interim negotiations, but he stood on his insistence that Israel disgorge the passes and the oil fields. They explored what new concessions Egypt might render; for the first time Sadat volunteered that he could countenance American (but not Israeli) technicians in the buffer zone of Sinai.

Sadat and Ford warmed at once to one another. Unlike Nixon, Ford chattered constantly—of pipes, tobacco, and other trifles that he knew would set Sadat at ease. Nixon had hinted he would install a "hot line" for emergencies between Washington and Cairo, and that eventually Egypt could count on American weapons. Ford has yet to establish the direct telephone, but with Kissinger he suggested to Sadat that the American embargo on arms to Egypt would be terminated soon, however modestly at first.

When Rabin visited Washington a week later, Kissinger and Ford were extremely stern. Again they endorsed the Egyptian demands, stressing that Israel could not count on substantial American aid until she negotiated a new settlement in Sinai. With unwonted adroitness Ford dangled the first option before Rabin's wary eye—if Israel did not negotiate more generously, the President warned, then he would revive Geneva. There, he implied, the United States would favor restitution of the 1967 frontiers. Kissinger, in fact, protested the continuing entrenchment of Israeli settlements in occupied Arab territory, and bluntly told Rabin that eventually Israel must abandon the settlements and retreat substantially to the boundaries of 1967.

Rabin got the message. Like Sadat, the Israeli cabinet had already decided that Israel had no choice but to resume interim negotiations. Nevertheless, Rabin knew that to sustain its Arab policy the United States needed the agreement desperately, and for that he intended to extract a very high price. Thus the Israelis resumed their tested posture—playing for time—whilst the price was worked out. At Jerusalem, cabinet meetings were postponed, "clarifications" were requested, "elucidations" were demanded of Kissinger and Sadat. The Israelis aspired to retain at least a foothold in the passes; the rest of June, all of July, much of August was consumed as they haggled with Kissinger over the locus of the new line.

Kissinger promised about $1.8 billion in new arms and economic aid; the Israeli request for $2.5 billion was still pending, but by mid-August the demand had mounted to nearly $3.5 billion. At that point Mordechai Gazit, the director general of Rabin's office, arrived in Washington with the Israeli drafts of the secret memoranda of understanding that Israel expected the United States to append to the new agreement. The drafts, says one of Kissinger's senior aides, "were simply incredible. They amounted to a formal political and military alliance between Israel and the United States. They would have granted Israel an outright veto over future American policy in the Middle East."

Dr. Kissinger, in the meanwhile, was distressed by the Israeli maps. He had to be certain the Israelis would leave the passes, so he sent a senior C.I.A. official to authenticate their line *sur place*. On August 11 the official strolled through Gidi with Mordechai Gur. "General," he said, "you're still inside the pass."

# 13

# Cornucopia

Nevertheless, Dr. Kissinger resumed his shuttle on August 20, 1975, flying from Andrews Air Force Base at nearly midnight—his twelfth major mission to the Middle East. The next evening, at Jerusalem, Prime Minister Rabin entertained the Secretary and his party at dinner at the Knesset. Kissinger was late; his motorcade could not reach that futuristic structure but by circuitous dirt paths, for the streets teemed with rightist youths accusing him of perfidy. The dinner, when we got there, was a dazzling event. Much of the buffet (beef, carp, fresh fruit) had already been consumed, but in compensation we had the company of the entire Israeli cabinet and many other eminences of Zionism.

As we passed into that vast room I was greeted by Yitzhak Rabin. He grasped my hand, and I gazed for an instant into his brown eyes. He was, by profession, a soldier—he had fought bravely with the Allies in Syria during World War II, commanded a brigade that broke the Arab siege of Jerusalem in 1948, and served as chief of staff during the Six-Day War. But to me he seemed soft, almost irresolute. A few moments later, I found myself beside a good-looking man with receding silver hair, who exuded strength, even—somehow—raw force. "Are you Mr. Peres?" I asked.

"I believe so," said the Minister of Defense.

I wondered if part of Peres' force had been borrowed from David Ben-Gurion, whose protégé he had been. Peres was of the Jews of Byelorussia—a robust race. I assumed, I told him, that during this shuttle Dr. Kissinger would conclude a new agreement between Israel and Egypt—but what would follow? Would Israel move toward general peace, or sit for several years upon the remainder of her conquests?

PERES: After the agreement with Egypt, we should try to conclude a new agreement with Syria as quickly as possible. It will be—ah—cosmetic.

AUTHOR: But the Syrians say they will not accept an Israeli withdrawal on the Golan of only five to ten kilometers.

PERES: Who said anything about five to ten kilometers? That's far too much.

AUTHOR: The Syrians will reject a "cosmetic" withdrawal on the Golan.

PERES: Then let them. *We* don't care. . . . Dr. Kissinger can talk to Assad. He's Assad's great friend. . . .

AUTHOR: What of an overall settlement?

PERES: That's far away.

AUTHOR: Is there any chance of establishing a separate state for the Palestinians?

PERES: None whatever. The Palestinians are dispersed in Israel and on the west bank, intermixed with Jews. They can't be disentangled and given a separate state. The best hope is a confederation between Israel and the west bank, but that is for the distant future.

AUTHOR: Such a confederation, it seems to me, would be dominated by Israel.

PERES: Of course.

I drifted back to Prime Minister Rabin. Three years before, when I interviewed Golda Meir, I had offered her a Jordanian cigarette ("Why not?" she grimaced, then smoked it) and now I hoped that her successor might spare me one of his. He gave me a Kent. Bernard Gwertzman drifted over. "I don't like what you've been writing in *The New York Times*," the Prime Minister said. "This new agreement will *not* be essentially the same as the one we rejected in March. There are *significant* differences."

Others pressed in. Amidst the confusion Rabin did not pursue his point. What of an overall settlement? I wondered again.

"We're going to wait to see how the agreement with the Egyptians works out," the Prime Minister said.

What if the Arabs refused to wait?

"Then there will be another war," Rabin responded.

I withdrew. Dr. Kissinger was conversing with a man in a yarmulke, encircled by ministers and other members of the Israeli establishment—no penetrating that phalanx, I decided. I chatted for a few minutes with Foreign Minister Allon—a short, square man, another old soldier, a veteran of the Haganah and the Palmach, commander of Upper Galilee, central Palestine, the Jerusalem corridor, the Negev desert during the war of 1948. He was known now as a "dove," in the Israeli definition. I probed for his opinion of a Palestinian state.

"We could reunite the populations of the east and west banks," he said.

But the Israeli government had been saying the same before the October war, I observed, and the proposal was hampered by a hundred restrictions—not the least of them the permanent entrenchment of the Israeli army along the length of the River Jordan. Had there been no evolution in Israeli thinking since the war—or since the summer of 1974, when King Hussein had refused this very proposition? Couldn't the Israeli army remain upon the Jordan for a fixed period, and then—as Hussein had once suggested—be gradually withdrawn as peace progressed?

"This is a problem for generations," the Foreign Minister responded. "Our security belt on the Jordan must remain, but there could be breaks in it to reunite the populations and allow for trade. The natural home of the Palestinians is Jordan."

The Palestinians might beg to differ with the Foreign Minister.

"Transjordan was part of Palestine until Winston Churchill chopped it off in 1922," Allon insisted.

The Palestinians might question that as well. At best this was a legalism, since the immense majority of the Palestinians—perhaps 98 or 99 percent—lived west of the River Jordan prior to the creation of Israel.

"This is a complicated question," Allon rejoined. "You must come to see me at the Foreign Ministry." He turned to someone else.

Nearby, Roy Atherton was conversing with Schlomo Hillel, the small, gray-maned minister of police, and with General Mordechai Gur, the lithe, bespectacled chief of staff, clad in sleeveless khaki.

"There was great bitterness in Israel over your *reassessment,*" Hillel said intensely. "It was aimed at us. It was pressure on Israel."

"Anxiety . . . ," Atherton replied pleasantly.

"No—deep bitterness," the Minister of Police insisted.

"I was with the army yesterday," General Gur interjected, "—and 98 percent of the regulars and the reserves are against this new agreement."

I drifted again, amongst those clusters of Americans and the Israeli establishment, digesting fragments of their discourse: ". . . significant differences between now and March . . . the Secretary made a good statement at the airport . . . we're not giving in to American pressure . . . this shuttle has been better prepared . . . Kissinger put so much pressure on Israel . . . the carrot and the stick . . . *significant* differences." It seemed almost as though this party were a play, as though each Israeli luminary had been assigned a speaking part. The theme of the play, the sum of the parts, was that Israel was enduring deep sacrifice in consenting to negotiate at all, that Israel would give nothing in exchange for nothing, that Israel had received some concessions from the Egyptians but expected more, that Israel would not be pushed around by Dr. Kissinger or by anybody, and that—again—Israel would haggle hard.

The hour by now was nearly midnight. Undersecretary Sisco said, "When can we get out of here? I want to go to bed." The Secretary and his wife sat at a table with Mrs. Toon and Mrs. Dinitz, tiredly making small talk. I went out onto the terrace of the Knesset and looked down to the streets where the youths were massed, squadrons of police and soldiers straining to contain them with tear gas and water cannon. It occurred to me then that we were trapped, that neither Dr. Kissinger nor the rest of us could take our leave till the way was rendered safe. Finally we departed, but Atherton's limousine was beaten on, and our press bus also was assailed by epithets and the banging fists of mobs. Thousands of young men and women had surrounded the Knesset and the streets beyond. *"Kissinger go home!"* The government subsequently denounced them, but their disenchantment was another proof of how deeply unpopular Dr. Kissinger and his diplomacy had become in Israel—another justification for haggling in the negotiation to unfold upon the morrow.

When the Secretary regained the King David, the youths gave him no repose. My room was situated a few floors below his, and toward four o'clock in the morning I was awakened by a chorus of loudspeakers. "Kissinger go home! Kiss-in-ger! Kiss-in-ger go! Kiss-in-ger go go! Kiss-in-ger go go home home! Jew boy! Jew boy, go home! Jew boy, go! Jew boy, go go home home! Jew boy, Jew boy, Jew boy!" I got up from bed and opened the shutters. The youths were concealed in the darkness of the old no-man's-land; beyond them the ancient walls of the Arab city and the Mount of Olives loomed in a soft light. *"Jew boy, go home!"* They were the Gush Emunim—Front of the Faithful—and every time the police suppressed one loudspeaker, another erupted somewhere else. In the morning, Kissinger was beside himself. "They kept me awake all night!" he raged to his entourage. "We're moving to the Hilton!" But the King David was a transplanted State Department—a hive of electronics, a cocoon of functionaries, a fortress of security—and could not be abandoned.

Later, at Rabin's residence (secretly, so as to elude the Front of the Faithful) Kissinger embarked upon the negotiation. During summer the bones of the agreement had been assembled, but now they needed flesh and blood. The Israelis had acquiesced in principle to withdraw from the passes and from the oil fields, but their line was a contradiction. The Egyptians had to define the "nonuse of force" and its longevity as well. "We've discussed with the Egyptians our understanding that you will be out of the passes," Kissinger told the Israeli negotiators. "I'm concerned that your line is still *not* out of the passes." Sadat had agreed at Salzburg to American monitoring stations—but not to stations manned by Israelis—in the Mitla and in the Gidi. Would Sadat agree to stations manned separately by Americans, Israelis, and Egyptians? Kissinger focused first upon the American presence.

KISSINGER: I'm not sure the Egyptians will accept that idea. I don't think an American presence is a good idea. I think it's a mistake.

PERES: It has a logic and a purpose. The aerial reconnaissance the United States provided after the first disengagement—mere American involvement—reduced tension and helped stabilize a nervous situation. To that aerial reconnaissance we're now adding [an American] land reconnaissance role in the most sensitive part of the Sinai. . . . The passes are both a symbol and a strategic location. The mere presence of even a symbolical group of American technicians would serve as a [deterrent] for either side in considering any attack. Israel has not had an entirely satisfactory experience with international forces. That's why we have a special feeling about an American presence. . . . I know that Americans might say, "This is the way things began in Vietnam." I see no comparison. A buffer zone is a buffer zone. It's extraterritorial.

KISSINGER: . . . It's a mistake. There will be a reaction in the United States to this kind of thing. There will be real questions in the United States—if this is a wise thing to do. . . . How will it appear to the American people . . . Americans there against a surprise attack?

At Alexandria, President Sadat seemed strangely resigned to whatever Dr. Henry might do for him. Sadat could not accept less than the passes and the oil fields, but otherwise he accommodated most Israeli conditions. Kissinger spent comparatively little time in Egypt. Sadat was simply not a quibbler; he guided the negotiation, but left the details to Foreign Minister Fahmy and General Gamasy. Whilst Sadat napped in the afternoons, Kissinger repaired to Fahmy's beach house on the Mediterranean, in the shadow of Montaza Palace, King Farouk's old fantasy of Kubla Khan. There, sometimes as they waded in the sea, Kissinger resolved with the two ministers such complexities as United Nations checkpoints, early warning systems, the limitation of SCUD missiles. Once, Sadat joined them, for luncheon and a swim.

Kissinger astonished the spare, punctilious Gamasy with his mastery of military detail—the ranges of SCUDs and Lances, the precise dispositions of the armies in the Sinai. Not that Gamasy was much happier with this new negotiation than he had been with the others—the territorial yield was too meager, nor would Kissinger allow sufficient time, as he did in Israel, for full discussion of details. Fahmy felt likewise, and he was at pains to tell Kissinger. Fahmy was a quibbler, too, in his own fashion—not legalistic like the Israelis, but full of fire and thunder in disputing technical details. Sparks flew constantly when he conversed with Kissinger; often he was brutally blunt: "What you're doing is stupid! . . . Your arguments are no good!" Usually, Kissinger rebutted him with humor, and whenever necessary appealed over his head directly to Sadat.

After a week in Israel, eager to follow the negotiation from the Egyptian side, I flew in the Secretary's Boeing back to Alexandria. The mood, the environment of Alexandria, were utterly unlike Jerusalem. The negotiation invariably began on the velvet lawn of Sadat's villa at Maamura just outside the city. The President and his negotiating team—Fahmy, Gamasy, Vice-President Husni al-Mubarak (representing not only the military establishment, as Gamasy did, but the Egyptian technocracy and other elements of Sadat's constituency)—sat waiting for Kissinger in a circle of garden chairs, sipping from great glasses of orange (or was it mango?) juice. The villa itself was a modernistic yellow-buff building that reminded me of an American motel. A French journalist asked me what I thought ot it. *"C'est un petit peu nouveau riche, n'est-ce pas?"* I replied. *"Ah! Voilà!"* he laughed. *"C'est le style parvenu."*

The villa was surrounded by a vast park, which led in the front to a long boardwalk, the turquoise Mediterranean, and the President's motorboats. Police and security men were everywhere, even behind the bushes. Maamura was but one of the nine or ten villas and palaces that Sadat maintained throughout Egypt. Odd, I remarked to a friend of his, this love of opulence—in such a poor country. His friend's reply was incomparably Egyptian, worth a thousand lectures in social anthropology. "President Sadat," he said, "wants every Egyptian to be rich. He wants every Egyptian to own a palace and a Mercedes. But if that's impossible for every Egyptian, he'll take them for himself."

We were standing, as he said this, on the periphery of the garden circle, watching Sadat and his subordinates sip their mango juice. It was midafternoon, near the end of August. At last we heard a chopping of the air, and just above the palms and eucalyptus trees a great brown helicopter hove into view. It alighted at the far end of the park. Dr. Kissinger descended, Sisco and his other subordinates in train, followed in running strides by the Washington correspondents, who had landed in a second helicopter. Sadat rose from his chair, extracting a white handkerchief from his pin-striped lounge suit, and dabbed his sweating brow. He advanced, followed by Fahmy, Gamasy, and Mubarak, to greet the Secretary of State. Near the gravel path they came together, where, amongst the pushing journalists and the whirring television cameras, they embraced mechanically. They proceeded to the garden chairs, sat down beside each other, and—mobbed by journalists and photographers—began their customary press conference.

MISS BERGER: Mr. President, there was a report before we started coming here today that Egypt has requested a larger number of troops in the limited forces zone—numbering twelve thousand. Is that correct?

KISSINGER *laughing, to Sadat*: I don't know why you give her a visa.

SADAT: I do not know where you got this information.

KISSINGER: She tried it already on me, Mr. President.

SADAT: I shall be discussing this with Dr. Kissinger.

Q: Is that report incorrect, Sir?

SADAT: I cannot say yes or no.

Q: Mr. President, is there one particular issue that is sort of slowing down the pace at this point?

SADAT: What?

Q: Is there one particular problem that is causing this slight delay in wrapping up the agreement?

SADAT: From my side?

Q: No, no, generally, from your side and the Israeli side?

SADAT: From my side, no.

Q: Is there one from the Israeli side?

SADAT: Maybe. . . .

Q: Are there any difficulties, Dr. Kissinger, you feel that you are facing?

KISSINGER: I think we are now dealing with very technical, very complicated subjects. And when you get to the last phase, those are the issues that usually remain. I do not find any deadlock or any problems that cannot be solved. We have worked in a very good atmosphere here yesterday and overnight on the other side, in Israel. . . .

Q: Mr. President, could these technical issues that are now remaining be resolved with someone other than Dr. Kissinger? Is it really necessary for him to come back and forth, to follow this rather tiring pace? Could it be done by phone or emissary?

SADAT: How could it be done?

Q: Through an emissary or ambassadors. Is that possible?

SADAT: Well, the whole thing has been handled since the beginning by Dr. Kissinger. He should end it. He should finish it.

Q: Mr. President, do you feel that Israel has raised some unexpected demands in the course of this week?

SADAT: They are always raising hell, as you say in America.

Q: Mr. President, can you imagine, having come this far, that failure is still possible?

SADAT: Believe me, as I have seen and as happened during the March mission, it may come to this. But not from the Egyptian side. We are quite ready and we are quite understanding. But I do not know what goes there on the Israeli side.

Q: Well, the only conclusion we can draw then, Sir, since you say
you are ready for an agreement and no difficulties are being raised from
your side—the only conclusion we can draw is your suggestion that
there are difficulties being raised by the Israeli side?

KISSINGER: Unless they are raised by my side. (*Laughter*.)

So much for the public spectacle. A rectangular table, covered
with green velvet, reposed on the lawn near a high hedge; when
the press withdrew, Kissinger, Sisco, and Ambassador Eilts
would seat themselves on one side, opposite Sadat, Fahmy,
Gamasy, and Mubarak. They would consider the outstanding
problems of the negotiation, then adjourn so that Fahmy and
Gamasy could resolve the particulars with Kissinger. During
these visits to Alexandria, Kissinger complained again to the
Egyptians of Israeli excess. "It's unbelievable what they're demanding," he said. "Rabin, Peres, Allon—they're not negotiating as a team, they're each pursuing personal ambitions." Or
were they, he asked, deliberately endeavoring again to destroy
the negotiation and to bring him down?

Until very late in the negotiation, the great issue remained
the passes. The Israelis claimed their line took them out, but
Kissinger examined aerial photographs and told them it did not.
By August 26, the Egyptians had agreed to Israeli and American
monitoring stations, but the Israeli maps were unsatisfactory and
their line was still in doubt. At the eleventh hour, the Israelis
capitulated—though not completely. In the Mitla, it was difficult to define where the eastern entrance was, but essentially
they were out of that pass. In the Gidi, they relinquished the
road, but clung to some high ground on the northern perimeter,
and bent their line westward slightly between the passes to
retain some hills. Sadat was bemused that Kissinger could not
push them further, but acquiesced.

Whilst Kissinger was resolving the line, the depth of the buffer zones, the limitations of troops and weaponry—reserving till
propitious moments the respective "fallback" positions of Israel
and Egypt, then revealing them to extract ultimate
concessions—Atherton remained in Jerusalem negotiating

American commitments to Israel. That was a task equally tortuous, for it involved appeasing the demands that Kissinger had complained of to Sadat. The Israeli drafts, which they had insisted be renamed "Memoranda of Agreement" to render them more binding, were phrased in absolute language which Atherton kept watering down. When Kissinger returned each night to Jerusalem, he diluted them further still. For example, the Israelis wanted an absolute American commitment to intervene if the Soviet Union threatend to attack Israel; Kissinger promised only to consult Israel. They wished the United States to assure them of oil supplies under all conceivable conditions; Kissinger inserted escape clauses. They wished the United States to finance almost half of Israel's $4 billion-per-annum military modernization program over the next decade; Kissinger said, "Impossible."

The flood of detail immersed the mind. Sisco crawled over maps upon the floor to verify particulars of the Israeli line in the region of Abu Rudeis. Sometimes the memoranda of conversation for a single session at Jerusalem consumed 60 pages, single-spaced. The discarded drafts of the agreement—going back to March, through Salzburg and the summer—rivaled the dimensions of the Washington telephone directory. At the end of the negotiation, Atherton went two nights without sleep as the Israelis kept demanding word changes in the main agreement and military annex. Peres did not wish the Egyptians to renew the U.N.E.F. mandate "annually" but "for a year every year." The quibbling continued till the moment the Israelis initialed the agreement and Kissinger took his last leave for Alexandria on September 1. "What you must understand," an Israeli leader told me, "is that for Israel every detail is vital. We're not negotiating with the Americans. We're negotiating with the Arabs."

The Egyptians initialed the agreement in a ceremony upon the lawn at Maamura, in the presence of President Sadat and Dr. Kissinger, during the night of September 1. Essentially, the Israelis consented to withdraw to a new line fluctuating 20 to 40 miles from the Suez Canal; they rendered the passes to the United Nations, and—within a sliver of sand along the Gulf of Suez—the oil fields to the Egyptians. They remained in possession of nearly nine-tenths of the Sinai.

The Egyptian forces were permitted to advance to the eastern perimeter of what had been, since the disengagement of 1974, the United Nations buffer zone. Between the new Israeli and Egyptian lines, a new U.N. buffer zone was established, varying in depth between eight and 35 miles. The Israelis were allowed to keep a monitoring post at Umm Khisheib, just inside the buffer northwest of the Gidi pass, and their military air base at Refidim nearly 20 miles northeast of that.

Inside the passes, Israel and Egypt were allowed surveillance stations, with 200 American civilian technicians assigned to them and to six stations of their own—a guarantee against surprise attack from either side, making the United States a "witness" (Sadat's word) of the accord and thus consecrating the American commitment to more substantial peace in future. In the oil fields to the south, only Egyptian civilians were granted access, along a road to be shared with the Israelis and controlled by U.N. checkpoints.

In exchange for the passes and Abu Rudeis, Egypt agreed that the conflict in the Middle East should be settled by peaceful means, eschewing armed force and naval blockades, publicly sanctioning nonmilitary Israeli cargoes to transit the canal, and declaring that the pact would remain binding till superseded by another. The mandate of U.N.E.F. was to be renewed annually, in effect for a total of three years. In the meanwhile, within the limited-forces zones on either side of the U.N. buffer, each party was publicly confined to 8,000 troops, 75 tanks, and 60 pieces of heavy artillery.

More intriguing, from the American point of view, were Dr. Kissinger's secret commitments to Israel which soon emerged in *The New York Times*. Even as modified by the Secretary of State, the final American-Israeli Memoranda of Agreement were—as his own aides admitted—"mind-boggling." For example:

The United States Government and the Government of Israel
will... conclude a contingency plan for a military supply operation to
Israel in an emergency situation.... The United States Government... will seek to prevent... proposals which it and Israel agree
are detrimental to the interests of Israel.... The United States is
resolved... to maintain Israel's defensive strength through the supply
of advanced types of equipment, such as the F-16 aircraft [and] to
undertake a joint study of high technology and sophisticated items, including the Pershing ground-to-ground missiles with conventional
warheads, with the view to giving a positive response.... The United
States... will not recognize or negotiate with the Palestine Liberation
Organization so long as the Palestine Liberation Organization does not
recognize Israel's right to exist and does not accept Security Council
Resolutions 242 and 338. The United States Government will consult
fully and seek to concert its position and strategy at the Geneva peace
conference on this issue with the Government of Israel.*

In the shadow of such promises, Dr. Kissinger's commitment
of 200 American technicians in the Sinai seemed suddenly in-
consequential.

The memoranda, however qualified and despite Kissinger's
and Ford's denials, amounted almost to a marriage contract. If
America must pay a dowry so large for a small fraction of the
Sinai, what must it pay for real peace? Such were the alarums of
the United States Congress, whose letter of the 76 had helped to
kill Kissinger's first option, and whose members were themselves at fault. I have no evidence of this, but I suspect that
lurking in Dr. Kissinger's Medicean mind was at least half the
wish that the Israelis would overreach their American constituency and embarrass their power base in Congress. If that was his
trap, the Israelis stepped into it. Demanding the Pershing

*The full text of the "Agreement Between Egypt and Israel" initialed on Sep-
tember 1, 1975, and signed several weeks subsequently; together with the
Annex, and the American Proposal for the Early Warning System; the secret
Memoranda of Agreement and Addendum on arms assistance to Israel; and the
Memorandum of Assurances to Egypt, will be found in Appendix Eight.

Maps of the Middle East—including the areas of disengagement negotiated
in the Sinai during January 1974 and August/September 1975, and on the
Golan Heights in May 1974—will be found in Appendix Nine.

missile—with its capacity to carry atomic warheads from Tel Aviv to Aswan—was a terrible mistake, and it is not astonishing that later the Israelis demurred.*

Nevertheless, the second Sinai agreement was a major tactical triumph for Israel. She relinquished little (by the admission of several Israeli generals) of strategic value in the passes and wrested from the United States a moral, monetary, and military cornucopia unattained by any other foreign power. Above all, the pact partially fulfilled Rabin's central purpose. As a senior Israeli official told *Time* magazine:

Given non-acceptance of Israel by the Arabs, we have been maneuvering since 1967 to gain time and to return as little as possible. The predominant Government view has been that stalemates are to our advantage. Our great threat has been the Rogers plan—and American policy to move us back to the [1967] lines. The... Agreement with Egypt is another nail in the coffin of that policy. We realize that the entire world is against us on the issue of borders and that we are terribly dependent on one nation for sophisticated arms. Nevertheless, we have been successful for the past... eight years, and we may have to go on maneuvering for another ten. If the... interim Agreement [gave] us only six months rather than three years, we would buy it because the alternative is Geneva and... more pressure to go back to the 1967 borders. The... Agreement has delayed Geneva, while... assuring us arms, money, a coordinated policy with Washington and quiet in Sinai.... We gave up a little for a lot.

Moreover, even though the agreement may not assure Israel a stalemate of several years, it seemed doubtful she would move an inch before the American presidential election of 1976. The pause was more than ample to enable the Israeli government to pursue the second level of its policy—entrenchment in the occupied territories. In Gaza and all over Golan; at Yamit and Sharm el Sheikh in Sinai; at Jerusalem and near Jericho, near Hebron, Nablus, Bethlehem, and Ramallah on the west bank— thousands of acres have been expropriated, thousands of Arabs

*In March 1976, the Israelis again requested the Pershing.

have been evicted, thousands of Israelis have taken root in farms, industries, apartment complexes. The entrenchment continues with deliberate speed.

On the Golan plateau the government has inexorably implanted more and more settlements, populating them with members of the militant parties, the better to prevent itself or any future government from relinquishing that territory. The hills of Biblical Jerusalem have been irremediably profaned by high apartment blocks, homes for hundreds of Israeli families, which make Brooklyn Heights seem aesthetic by comparison. The great settlement at Hebron, erected largely upon Arab farmland, is surrounded by a high steel fence, and with its block buildings, narrow windows, and observation towers it looks like an armed fortress.

"I don't see those installations," Kissinger has remarked privately. "They're transparent. I look right through them. When the time comes for me to open my dossiers on Golan and the west bank, I shan't let them impede a settlement. When the time comes, the President will prevail on the Israelis to withdraw." I wonder.*

*Dr. Kissinger's private sentiments were echoed publicly—and more forcefully—in the Security Council by William W. Scranton, the United States Ambassador to the United Nations, on March 23, 1976. Reiterating the American position on the status of Jerusalem, Ambassador Scranton emphasized "that as far as the United States is concerned . . . unilateral measures, including expropriation of land or other administrative action taken by the Government of Israel, cannot be considered other than interim and provisional and cannot affect the present international status nor prejudge the final and permanent status of Jerusalem. . . . The future of Jerusalem will be determined only through the instruments and process of negotiation, agreement and accommodation. Unilateral attempts to predetermine that future have no standing."

Ambassador Scranton then turned to "the question of Israeli settlements [throughout] the occupied territories. Again, my Government believes that international law sets the appropriate standards. An occupier must maintain the occupied areas as intact as possible, without interfering with the customary life of the area. . . . The Fourth Geneva Convention speaks directly to the issue of population transfer in Article 49: 'The occupying power shall not deport or transfer parts of its own civilian population into the territory it occupies.'

"Clearly then substantial resettlement of the Israeli civilian population in

As for Egypt, Sadat gave Israel nonbelligerency in all but name. Secretly he promised Kissinger to abstain from battle should Syria attack Israel. Kissinger briefed him about the American-Israeli memoranda, but not about the super-weapons. In another secret memorandum, Kissinger promised Sadat that the "United States intends to make a serious effort to help bring about further negotiations between Syria and Israel [on the Golan Heights]." Informally the Secretary also transmitted to Sadat Israel's pledge not to attack Syria, and promised that the United States would honestly endeavor to insure Palestinian participation in a peace settlement.

Sadat disliked the agreement, but he had no choice. Egypt's economy was desperate; it would collapse without foreign investment. The army, bereft of weapons to match Israel's, could not resume war for several years. No choice?—nonsense, said Mohammed Hassanein Heikal, Sadat's disaffected strategist. "Kissinger is destroying his own investment in Sadat," Heikal told me in Cairo after the agreement. "He's isolated him from the rest of the Arab world, and in that isolation Sadat will fail to find the oil money he needs for Egypt. Kissinger has no strategy, except to reduce the Arab-Israeli conflict into fragments. Egypt alone will not be worth much to the United States, and powerless to cope with its own poverty."

Heikal feared that the cornucopia of weapons Kissinger had promised Israel would provoke Sadat to waste whatever oil

---

occupied territories, including in East Jerusalem, is illegal under the Convention and cannot be considered to have prejudged the outcome of future negotiations between the parties on the location of the borders of states of the Middle East. Indeed, the presence of these settlements is seen by my Government as an obstacle to the success of the negotiations for a just and final peace between Israel and its neighbors."

Nevertheless, following severe Israeli protests, the United States vetoed a moderate resolution in the Security Council deploring Israeli policies in the occupied territories. Ambassador Scranton's address denouncing the settlements pleased the Arabs. It was a perfect example of the verbal reassurance to the Arabs that Dr. Kissinger produced, at various intervals, as a substitute for physical progress toward further Israeli withdrawal prior to the presidential election.

money he possessed in quest of compensatory arms for Egypt. Furthermore, he said, Sadat's regime, Egyptian society itself, was plagued with profiteers and parasites so avaricious they might push the masses to insurrection. The social gains of Nasserism were being junked in the name of economic liberalization; the poor were wretched in their want. He recalled the food riots in Cairo the previous winter. "O Hero of the Crossing!" the mob shouted to Sadat. "Where is our breakfast?"

Indeed, I recognized that for all his stature as a world statesman, Sadat knew little of managing an economy, and parts of his government were dank with corruption. The Saudis, upon whom Sadat was so dependent, kept him on a short leash and made him beg each time he needed money. Shortly before King Fuisul died, he visited Egypt; Sadat's exchequer was almost barren, and he could not repay his short-term borrowings of Eurodollars. The King wrote out a check for $125 million, but then it went untouched for weeks, since Sadat is above details and none of his subordinates had authority to cash it.

Wretched Egypt! Stand on the Nile corniche, not far from the Hilton, and watch the mob beneath the noon sun, waiting for a bus. At last the bus comes; a hundred people stampede to climb aboard, though there is no place for ten, not even on the roof. A woman emerges from the mob inside the bus, with a baby and a milk bottle; she drops the bottle upon the pavement, and flails her way free. Abandoned, the mob waits beneath the sun for the next bursting bus. A Mercedes speeds by, bearing a Kuwaiti or a bureaucrat, alone or with his chauffeur.

Or drive up the Pyramid Road, to that gallery of garish nightclubs—the Café Ramses, the Café Arizona, the Café Parisiana, the Café Kuka Abdo. Behind that facade of pleasure domes looms the quarter called Bebsi Cola (Pepsi Cola), a name only Egyptians could have thought up. It is primeval, Pharaonic, in its squalor. The paths are of dust, moistend by piss and piles of garbage. The plaster hovels are squeezed together, but not so squeezed as the people who live inside them—five, six, 15 to a room, without water, toilets, electric light. Shriveled men and

young men, grandmothers and wives in black—they pop from
the rooms like peas from a pod, frail infants in their arms. Children numerous as flies splash in mud puddles or taunt each
other by tossing donkey buns. These people are as "poor as the
needle which clothes the rich but which itself remains unclad."
Is Egypt the Bangladesh of Araby? Will Saudi and Kuwaiti gold,
will sixpence of the $700 million Dr. Kissinger promised to
Sadat ever touch the multitude of Bebsi Cola?

Egypt's military expenditure exceeds 30 percent of its national
product (whilst Israel's exceeds 40 percent); Egypt's trade deficit
exceeds $3 billion, and its debt to the Soviet Union may amount
to $6 billion. Egypt in isolation cannot cope with such burdens,
but Sadat's acceptance of the second Sinai agreement—the appearance that he had sued for a separate peace with Israel—
fractured whatever remained of Arab unity. Just as the Rogers
initiative helped to provoke the civil war in Jordan five years
before, Kissinger's diplomacy in Sinai severed Syria from Egypt.

Dr. Kissinger visited President Assad in early September, en
route home from Alexandria. For 15 months, since the Golan
disengagement, Kissinger had struggled to sustain the confidence of the Syrians whilst he focused on the Sinai. He respected Assad's gift for making mischief, and he was resolved
that Syria should not obstruct peace for other parties. "War is
not our hobby—killing is not our sport," Assad repeated
whenever Kissinger visited Damascus. "But I warn you, if there
is not equal progress on all fronts—and for the Palestinians—
then we shall not endorse what you do in Egypt."

Now, after the second Sinai agreement, Assad informed Kissinger that he had no interest in a "cosmetic," miniscule Israeli
withdrawal on the Golan Heights. He accused Kissinger of dividing "the Arab nation," a foreshadowing of his furious attacks
upon Sadat. The second Sinai agreement, Assad said, removed
Egypt from the Arab-Israeli conflict and left Syria an orphan.
Already, reacting to Egypt's self-centered policy, Assad had
forged a new alliance in northern Araby—with Syria's chronic
enemy, the King of Jordan.

Indeed, during an angry meeting with Dr. Kissinger at

Amman the day before, Prime Minister Zeid Rifai had assailed
the Sinai agreement and refused to support it publicly. King
Hussein was more cordial, though equally distressed.

I saw both Assad and Hussein in late September. President
Assad received me in his palace (beneath Saladin's great conquest of the Crusaders) not long before midnight; we conversed
until nearly five in the morning. He wore a blue suit and un-
shined black shoes; near the side of his mouth I remarked a dull
gold tooth. Constant coffee, constant tea, constant rattling of his
worry beads.

ASSAD: When I first met Dr. Kissinger, he did not wish to dwell on
trifles, but conceived of peace in large steps. It seems to us now that
the United States has three goals—to strengthen Israel, to weaken the
Arab nation, and to eliminate Soviet influence in the Middle East. The
pursuit of these goals makes it impossible to achieve peace. The goals
explain why so little has been accomplished.

AUTHOR: The Israelis think Dr. Kissinger is pro-Syrian.

ASSAD: He's intelligent, but his policies contradict his intelligence.
His intelligence contradicts his enthusiasm for Israel. I submit that
enthusiasm for Israel contradicts the interest of the United States. Is it
in the interest of the United States to give Israel billions of dollars in
weapons, financed by the American taxpayer, while American citizens
are out of work?

AUTHOR: I suppose some might say it's madness.

ASSAD: *Al junun funun!*—madness is many arts! Or so we say. But
the United States will not support Israel when it recognizes that the
Arabs have caught up with Israel. Too costly. Believe me, *then* the
United States and the Arabs will come to terms.

At Amman a few days later, in the library of his villa near
Basman Palace, King Hussein chain-smoked Marlboro cigarettes
and suggested (in his deep, understated British way) that he had
despaired of the United States. He was shocked and insulted by
the obstructions of the Israeli lobby in Congress against his purchase of defensive Hawk batteries, but he had other complaints
as well.*

*As of early May 1976, it was still uncertain whether Jordan would receive the
Hawk batteries.

HUSSEIN: Sir, we've often heard in this part of the world of a balance of power between the Arabs and Israel, but we believe it never existed. Even if Israel does not use the Pershing missile with nuclear warheads—even if Israel does not get that missile at all—the rest of the Israeli arms list would be enough to destroy any semblance of balance, not only between Israel and her immediate neighbors but between Israel and the entire Arab world.

AUTHOR: Does Your Majesty believe that Israel has developed an atomic bomb?

HUSSEIN: Sir, it is my impression that Israel has had the atomic bomb—with the capacity to produce several nuclear warheads—for a long period of time. Israel has had the capacity to produce annually, since quite a few years ago, bombs of the potency used in Hiroshima and Nagasaki. This, sir, is definite information that I possess.

AUTHOR: From Jordanian intelligence?

HUSSEIN: Not Jordanian intelligence alone, but from the observations of many throughout the world, sir. I have the feeling that the Israelis might drop the bomb under certain circumstances. But whether they use it or not, sir, in my opinion their possession of it [would provoke] the Arabs to do everything possible to acquire a similar capability.

AUTHOR: Your Majesty seems pessimistic.

HUSSEIN: After all I've lived through, my optimism has diminished. The prognosis for peace is poor, sir. The point of no return would be reached when the Arabs lose hope in any possibility of progress toward the implementation of Resolutions 242 and 338. Then, sir, the scene will be set for new disasters. That psychological moment may not be far away. Sometimes, sir, in the middle of the night, I wake up and think about this problem.

Assad and Hussein were no more vexed about the Israeli weapons than were numerous officials of the United States government. Led by Secretary of Defense James Schlesinger, most of the Pentagon, the C.I.A., the Treasury, the Office of Management and Budget, many officials of the State Department, strongly opposed substantial quantities of new arms for Israel. If Kissinger's current commitments are sustained for the next four years, Israel will have received between $10 billion and $12 billion in arms during this decade, many of them outright gifts. Does Israel truly require hundreds of F-15 and F-16 aircraft, Hawk missles, Lance missiles (which can be converted to carry atomic warheads), M60 A3 tanks, laser-guided "smart" bombs, to maintain an effective deterrent against the Arabs? "Israel wants one thousand percent security," says a Pentagon official, "and she's getting it. She can decisively defeat any combination of Arab armies at least through 1980."

Since the October war, the United States has provided Israel with more than $3 billion worth of precision-guided munitions, cluster-bomb units, tanks, armored personnel carriers, self-propelled artillery, cargo trucks, cargo aircraft, rifles, helicopters, anti-tank guided rockets, electronic counter-radar boxes, Phantoms, Skyhawks. Before October 1973 the Israelis relied excessively upon their air force, but now the United States has rectified their failings in infantry and artillery and instilled in them the science of coordinated warfare. General Electric, Rockwell, and other American firms are transferring to Israel the technology to construct ever more cunning electronic weapons. Israel is developing as well its own missile, the Jericho, with a range of 250 miles.

"In quality, and even quantitatively in some respects," says the Pentagon official, "Egypt, Syria, and Jordan together cannot match the force of Israel, nor shall they for the next decade. Their MIGs cannot compare with the F-15s and F-16s, and besides, their pilots lack skill. Their SCUDs? If they fired a dozen at Tel Aviv, half might hit Beirut."

Any arms race, no matter who provokes it, becomes in time a self-fulfilling prophecy of blood. Several ministers in Rabin's own government dissent from his and Peres' arms policy, protesting that, if Israel continues thus, she may—at the very least—perish from insolvency. Early in 1975 Dr. Kissinger complained to friends, "I ask Rabin to make concessions, and he says he can't because Israel is weak. So I give him more arms, and he says he doesn't need to make concessions because Israel is strong." During the abortive negotiation of March 1975 Kissinger lamented his failure to extract concessions first; immense arms shipments to Israel "was naïve—my biggest mistake." Following the second Sinai agreement, Kissinger argued that the new arms would encourage Israeli flexibility. He had said the same five years before, when he assumed concessions would result once Israel was invincible. Dr. Kissinger had come full circle.

CHAPTER

# 14

# Futurology

We have witnessed in Dr. Kissinger's journeys through Israel and Araby a diplomatic Odyssey unequaled in our time. But the works of peace he undertook in October of 1973 seem suspended in a limbo—eight months after the second Sinai agreement, as I finish this book—between incertitude and stalemate. In late 1975 I confronted Kissinger in Washington with some of the reservations about his policies that I have recorded upon these pages. He appeared harassed and exhausted, but emphatically he justified his policies with the philosophy of what is, not of what might have been. "What were the alternatives?" he asked. "The conflict in the Middle East has a history of decades. Only during the last two years have we produced progress. It's easy to say that what we've done is not enough, but the steps we've taken are the biggest steps so far. They were *the attainable*— given our prevailing domestic situation."

"Our prevailing domestic situation"—he meant, it seemed, the pressures of the Israeli lobby. His maxim, "Israel has no foreign policy, only domestic politics," he might have uttered of the United States—especially as it involves the Middle East. When I observed once to an aide of Kissinger's that Israel's American constituency is the greatest constraint upon our policy, he replied, "Of course. And the constraint becomes the determinant." Within and sometimes against those constraints, despite his errors, Kissinger often behaved heroically. He pursued the interest—not of Israel or of the Arabs—but of the United States as he conceived its interest within the perimeters of the possible, and for that he deserves the gratitude of the republic.

Moreover, the second level of his policy—promoting American technology amongst the Arabs whilst he coped with the Arab-Israeli conflict—has proven a considerable success. In Saudi Arabia (despite disputes about the Arab boycott), in Egypt, Jordan, Algeria, Abu Dhabi, even in Syria and Iraq, American trade and technology have surpassed all previous reckoning. For this Kissinger must share his laurels with several agencies of the government and with American technology at large, but he encouraged the phenomenon and helped it prosper. Paradoxically, despite her tactical victory in the second Sinai agreement, Israel may ultimately be the most to suffer from Kissinger's parallel policy if she does not conclude a final peace before the Arabs master all the marvels of American technology.

Kissinger's Arab policy—still anchored on Sadat—remains intact, though it is buffeted by angry winds. Kissinger erred in supposing that Sadat could control the rest of Araby. Assad's acrimonious rupture with Egypt in September 1975 was the direct consequence of Kissinger's diplomacy; Kissinger should have foreseen the impact of the second Sinai agreement upon Syria, Jordan, and the Palestinians. The fault was Sadat's as well. Had Sadat been less ardent in pressing Kissinger to favor the Egyptian interest and more loyal to the Arab unity he achieved for the October war, the Arab world might be more confident today to make concessions and closer to peace with Israel.

A questionable hypothesis, perhaps—but strategy is based upon hypothesis and we must wonder about Kissinger's. Did Kissinger ever conceive a coherent strategy for concluding the

Arab-Israeli conflict? President Assad, had he eavesdropped on that dramatic meeting at Jerusalem on March 22, 1975, might have confirmed his fear that Kissinger's strategy was simply to protect Israel from having to retreat to her old borders. I feel that Kissinger planned to nudge the Israelis back toward those very boundaries, and much more quickly, but was obstructed by circumstances he himself helped to bring about. I agree with Professor Stanley Hoffmann of Harvard, who observed to me that Kissinger was caught in the dilemma of "playing several roles at once. He's a conceptualist, a negotiator, and a day-to-day manager. The conceptualist begins by defining his goal, then recognizes obstacles en route, and tries to reduce them. The negotiator is caught up in the complications of the day, no longer defines the goal for its own sake, and makes the goal whatever remains after allowing for all the obstacles. Henry has done this in Vietnam and in the Middle East. He favors the short-run over the long-run. Curious, because he's equally gifted in either direction. He'll produce a brilliant conceptual analysis of a problem, then a set of proposals that are almost completely tactical."

Thus tactical success became a goal of itself. If Arafat was like a cyclist atop a tightrope, Kissinger was like a lumberjack leaping from log to log, wishing that the river would lead him somewhere else. Henry Brandon has written that "Kissinger has been accused of displaying an arrogance of power, but if anything his fault is an arrogance of intellect which makes him believe that he can control and manage reality." During his first audience with King Faisal, Dr. Kissinger pronounced words to this effect: "I arranged détente with Russia. I opened the door to China. I brought peace to Vietnam. I want to bring peace to the Middle East. I hate failure. I have not failed. I shall not fail." If we juxtapose the immense egoism of this pronouncement, this conviction of Kissinger's that he could manage reality, with the veracity of Professor Hoffmann's diagnosis, we may glimpse the essence of Kissinger's method in the Middle East. He set very severe limits on the reality he wished to manage, for he suffered, by his own admission, from the syndrome of success. He wanted peace, but he would not seek total peace too quickly if in doing so he should risk failure. Though his tactics of partial peace were brilliant and his techniques, too, strategically he sinned on the side of caution.

Perhaps Dr. Kissinger's greatest achievement is to have bought time, to have prevented war, to have erected the foundation for the pursuit of real peace. But the method he chose was simply too slow, and if clung to may imperil peace for the great future. Interim diplomacy could conceivably conclude another minor Israeli withdrawal on the Golan Heights, but it cannot address the central issues of the Arab-Israeli conflict such as the future of the Palestinian people, and those issues cannot be postponed much longer.

Having said all this, I recognize that I must reserve a measure of my judgment regarding the future impact of Kissinger's policies. Not all of the results have been reckoned yet—but when they are, perhaps in a year or two, possibly he will have accomplished more than any of us may imagine at this moment; for example, through his alliance, or quasi-alliance, with Egypt.

Sadat's strategic divorce from the Soviet Union may produce historic consequences for the Middle East, for American policy, and for the Arab-Israeli conflict. To an extent, it already has—in fact, the divorce involves a caravan of events that began with Sadat's expulsion of the Soviet technicians in the summer of 1972. Since then, motivated partly by Moscow's parsimony in replenishing the Egyptian arsenal, Sadat's hostility to the Soviet Union has grown ever more dramatic. In March 1976, provoked as well by the Kremlin's refusal to reschedule Egypt's $6 billion debt, convinced that the Russians were still scheming to overthrow him in revenge for favoring the Americans, Sadat staged another *coup de théâtre*. Declaring to the People's Assembly that "the Soviet Union is trying to bring us to our knees" and that "I will kneel to nobody but God," Sadat formally and unilaterally abrogated Egypt's Treaty of Friendship and Cooperation with the Soviet Union.

The treaty, which Sadat signed in 1971 and which was supposed to have lasted for 15 years, had solemnly proclaimed "indissoluble bonds of firm friendship" between Egypt and the Soviet Union, and had committed Egypt to a "Socialist transformation" based upon intimate contact between the Soviet Communist party and the Arab Socialist Union. (Sadat's promise of a "Socialist transformation" was never serious, and in truth was eventually negated by his policy of economic liberalization.) Moreover, in tandem with the abrogation, Sadat closed Egyptian seaports to vessels of the Soviet navy.

The pattern of Sadat's strategy had long since become clear. Professor William E. Griffith of the Massachusetts Institute of Technology, a specialist on Soviet affairs, has written that "until August 1972 the Soviet Union had air and naval bases in Egypt and was the most important foreign power in Syria and Iraq, while U.S. influence was largely confined to Israel. Today Soviet influence is still primary only in South Yemen and important in Libya and Somalia, while American influence in the Arab world has grown greatly, notably in Egypt, largely because Washington has become the active, 'evenhanded' mediator between Israelis and Arabs. This diplomatic revolution, even if perhaps only temporary, was as of November 1975 Moscow's greatest political defeat and Washington's greatest political victory since the Sino-Soviet split."

To this we might add that, more recently, Saudi Arabia has mounted a major diplomatic and financial penetration of South Yemen to wean it away from Soviet tutelage. Nevertheless, Professor Griffith's analysis should not inspire premature euphoria. Syria and Iraq, though they too have rejected the Russian model of development, still depend on Moscow for their weapons. Lebanon seethes with leftist militias. The strategic realignment Professor Griffith describes will prove of permanent benefit to the United States only if Washington reinforces it with drastic measures to conclude the Arab-Israeli conflict.

As we observed in Chapter 6, Sadat from the beginning of his friendship with Kissinger urged the United States to pursue with him a "common strategy" for removing Soviet influence from the Middle East. Kissinger certainly wished to reduce Soviet influence, but it is doubtful that he ever conceived of Egypt as a strategic ally to expunge the area of the Soviet presence—that would be too crude, too risky, too perilous to détente. Sadat, however, having burned his bridges to the Soviet Union, seemed all the more resolved to turn Egypt—the keystone of the eastern Mediterranean, the heart of Araby and Islam, the crossroads of two continents, the gateway to Africa and the Indian Ocean—into a strategic ally of the United States. For with such an ally, so felicitously placed, America's need of Israel would diminish accordingly, and in its wish to retain Egypt's friendship Washington would be compelled to press Israel the more to relinquish her conquests.

Dr. Kissinger and President Ford recognized the need to reward Egypt for choosing the United States, to manifest to the world at large and to the other Arabs in particular that Sadat's fidelity would be returned in coin. This explains Ford's decision to sell military cargo aircraft to Sadat, surely but a forerunner of more important quantities of arms to come. But Egypt's acquisition of weaponry in future, no matter how vital from her point of view, will perforce be wasteful of her substance. Furthermore, that Sadat can rely on Washington and Western Europe to fortify his defenses is no substitute for a strategy of peace. It buys more time for Washington, and for Sadat, but it solves nothing.

Only by pursuing a clearly defined final settlement can the United States redeem Egypt's act of faith and preserve its own strategic interest in the Middle East. Interim diplomacy has served its purpose. *La paix générale s'impose.* The "first option"—proposed in the spring of 1975 by most American officials involved with the Middle East—should be revived. The President should go to the American people, announce that the United States favors the frontiers of 1967, and face the consequences.

Under that American plan for peace, Israel would withdraw to the old frontiers insubstantially rectified in her favor—such rectifications to be negotiated. The settlement would perforce include the demilitarization of the Golan Heights; most of the Sinai with Sharm el-Sheikh; much or all of the west bank and the Gaza Strip; the stationing in the demilitarized zones of United Nations forces which could not be removed save with the consent of both sides; and great-power guarantees deposited with the Security Council. Jerusalem would remain a united city, possibly to be governed by a municipal council with Israeli and Arab members, but basic sovereignty in East Jerusalem would be restored to the Arabs. Should Israel so wish, the United States could seal her security with a formal defense treaty as well.

Save for the Israeli government, there exists an international consensus for a settlement of such a nature. It has been endorsed implicitly by the principal Arab parties and by the Russians. Foreign Minister Gromyko declared on April 23, 1975, that "Israel may get, if she desires, the strictest guarantees with the participation—under an appropriate agreement—of the Soviet Union." Moreover, Israel would not be asked to withdraw at once. She would simply accept the principle, then negotiate a timetable tied to concessions from the Arabs. For each new Arab commitment to peace—nonbelligerency, an end to boycotts and economic warfare, postal agreements, the free passage of goods and peoples, etc.—Israel would retreat further to her old frontiers until the process is consummated: final peace and formal Arab recognition of Israel's legitimacy.

The entire process might consume several years, but it must not be dragged out indefinitely. Of paramount importance and urgency is Israel's consent in principle to total (or practically total) withdrawal in exchange for contractual peace.

This is an outline, not a blueprint. A hundred arguments could be hurled against it, and it conjures up a thousand risks— for the Arab moderates no less than for the Israelis. But the alternatives are either too slow, or too uncertain, or completely sterile, and they conjure risks that are greater still.

Most guarantees for Israel's security have been conceived as negative deterrents—demilitarized zones, buffer forces, defense treaties, and the rest. The Egyptian leftist intellectual Mohammed Sid Ahmed, in an astonishing, futurological book called *After the Guns Fall Silent* (in Arabic, 1975) has suggested some positive incentives for both Arabs and Israelis—if they ever conclude a peace—to refrain from resuming war and to cooperate with one another. Should the religious, national, and "colonial" causes of the Arab-Israeli conflict ever be disposed of, Sid Ahmed argues, there would remain only one obstacle to the achievement of Arab-Israeli "complementarity." That is the Arabs' phobia of technological domination by Israel. And yet, with peace, even that obstacle could be removed. The October war itself reassured the Arabs that Israeli quality need not always vanquish Arab quantity, and that eventually Arab quality could equal Israel's.

"In the light of such new realities," Sid Ahmed asks, "is it impossible to imagine some Arab quarters coming to see Israeli technological skills as a factor that could promote, rather than hinder, development of the [region]?" Might they not consider a commingling of Arab money and Israeli technological prowess to pursue that purpose?

All the aspects of this "complementarity"—if it is to come about—will definitely not be realized at a stroke. "Security needs" might be the key to a take-off of this process [i.e.] demilitarized zones or UN Emergency Forces. [As for] "positive incentives" [as against] "negative sanctions" . . . certain circles consider that one of the main incentives could be, for instance, a "belt" of heavy industry on either side of the confrontation lines in the hope of dissuading all parties from exposing a lucrative industrial build-up to destruction.

Industrial projects could conceivably be set up in Sinai, in the Negev, the Gaza Strip, the West Bank, in various parts of the Palestinian state to come and even on the borders separating Israel from Syria and South Lebanon. Possibly petrochemical plants could be erected in some of these regions and more and more of the crude oil that now goes to the West could be retained to feed these petrochemical complexes. This Arab asset could be exported not in the form of crude oil alone but also in the form of finished or semi-finished products.

Setting up projects like this in these regions is tempting for more than one reason. They respond to the "security requirements" of the various parties. The quest to reinforce security can attract the necessary capital for these sophisticated industries, which would in any case be less costly than present arms expenditures. This last consideration would overcome the reluctance of business circles to furnish huge sums just for development, or to help the Arab countries in their drive to enter the domain of modern industries which has hitherto been confined to the developed nations.

Enlarging this vision, Sid Ahmed argues that such developed industries (not necessarily confined to petrochemicals) could also assist the nations of the region—particularly Egypt—to dilute the density of their populations and to reclaim their deserts. Nuclear plants to desalinate sea water for irrigating deserts and increasing food supply could eventually be built. "Furthermore, industrial projects erected inside the Palestinian state will invalidate the argument that this state is not viable. It is to the advantage of the Arabs to prove that it is. Even today the Palestinians enjoy the highest per capita ratio of experts and intelligentsia in the Arab world. This is bound to increase once opportunities are available to develop their capacities."

Sid Ahmed sees the initial "negative" security arrangements between Israel and the Arabs as the "springboard for complementarity and cooperation" across the borders in the future. Moreover, such cooperation could become contagious.

It could extend to a wider area of the Arab world. Once it is accepted in principle, certain Arab parties could go so far as to contemplate two distinct phases after the settlement: a first phase in which they would seek the help of the international community to "tame" Israel and to absorb it into the region; a second phase in which they would "resort" to Israel, using its human and technological assets to strengthen the Arab community vis-à-vis the international community and the map of the world expected—at the turn of the century—to be composed of great geographical conglomerates, leaving no room for splinter units.

Sid Ahmed's futurology is exceedingly Utopian and full of caveats—not the least of them the drastic changes he insists are essential in Israeli thinking. Nevertheless, his visions reflect remarkably one of the fervent dreams of the idealists of Zionism—Arabs and Israelis working together to enrich the region for both of the Semitic peoples.

Such fantasies, should they ever come to life, are for the great future. For the near future, to be relevant, to be realistic, and finally to be just, any settlement based upon the boundaries of 1967 must accommodate, somehow, the Palestinian people.

As adamant as the Rabin government has been in refusing to contemplate a separate Palestinian state—composed of the west bank and of Gaza, influenced or dominated by the Palestine Liberation Organization—it does not speak for all Israelis. Numerous reports from correspondents inside Israel (some of them Israelis) indicate that at least eight ministers of Rabin's own cabinet—including the ministers of Foreign Affairs, Finance, Housing, and Justice—privately oppose Rabin's and Peres' barren policy. The dissident ministers are known to feel that Israel should volunteer to negotiate with any Palestinian group that acknowledges Israel's right to exist and renounces terrorism. They feel that Israel should be ready to recognize a Palestinian state upon the west bank and in Gaza—provided that the Palestinians sign a final peace agreement and abandon all other claims to pre-1967 Israeli territory.

Another, more liberal group, the Israeli Council for Israeli-Palestinian Peace—composed of such as former Major General Mattityahu Peled; Arieh Eliav, a former Secretary-General of the Labor party, and Meir Pail, the leader of the leftist Moked party, both members of the Knesset; Uri Avnery and Amos Kenan, both prominent political journalists—are more emphatic. They are campaigning openly for an Israeli withdrawal to the 1967 borders ("except for changes agreed on by the parties"), for a joint Israeli-Arab municipal administration of Jerusalem, and for the establishment through negotiations of an independent Palestinian state that would include the P.L.O. The group's impact upon Israeli opinion at large has so far been marginal, though parts of their program evoke the longing of many Israelis to make peace with the Palestinians.

General Peled, a professor of Arabic at Tel Aviv University, has courageously and indefatigably endeavored to seek paths to that purpose. Following the collapse of Dr. Kissinger's negotiation in March 1975, he and Dr. Elias H. Tuma, a Palestinian and a professor of economics at the University of California, issued a joint statement:

We are fully aware of the complexity of reaching reconciliation. In order to facilitate the process of negotiation in the spirit of reconciliation, we propose a four-step sequence of action and reactions, and call upon the Government of Israel and the Palestine Liberation Organization to implement them, prior to the Geneva Conference, in the following order:

*First,* the Government of Israel and the PLO should issue declarations by which they denounce war and territorial expansionism and commit themselves to the principle that *all territorial war gains are returnable.*

*Second,* the Government of Israel should issue a declaration by which it recognizes the right of the Palestinians to form a state of their own west of the River Jordan within the internationally recognized boundaries.

*Third,* the PLO should reciprocate by issuing a declaration recognizing the right of the Israeli people to live in their own state peacefully and securely.

*Fourth,* the Government of Israel should declare itself ready to negotiate with the PLO, directly, as the representative of the Palestinian people, on all future relationships between their two states.

The rub, of course, is the task of persuading both Israel and the P.L.O. to recognize each other. Privately Yasir Arafat has assured Senators Adlai Stevenson and Charles Percy of Illinois, plus numerous other congressmen and eminent Americans over a span of several years, that he will recognize Israel under certain conditions. Significantly, the joint communiqué from Arafat's visit to Moscow in November 1975 eschewed the P.L.O.'s customary call for a "secular, democratic Palestine" and stated that a "settlement could be reached if Israel withdrew from all occupied Arab territories" taken in 1967 and if "the Palestinians were allowed to establish their own national state on

Palestinian territory." This was a clear public hint, but most probably Arafat will not go further until he knows in advance what sort of settlement he is likely to get. Most probably, he will not publicly deal his most potent card—explicit recognition of Israel's right to exist—until he is explicitly assured by the United States that it will work for the creation of a Palestinian state on the west bank and in Gaza.

Despite American denials, secret contacts between the United States and the P.L.O. have been maintained sporadically for several years—at the United Nations, at Beirut, and (sometimes through the C.I.A.) elsewhere in the Middle East and North Africa. However, as of early 1976 no negotiations of substance had resulted. Dr. Kissinger authorized American officials to exchange views with the Palestinians, and little else. On more than one occasion, through a number of intermediaries, the Palestinians indicated they wished to negotiate substantively with the United States—in the hope that this would produce a secret Israeli acceptance of the P.L.O., prior to the possible elaboration of a formula for mutual public accommodation. The Palestinians were persuaded that, for a while at least, Dr. Kissinger was interested—but then nothing happened.

I have, earlier in this book, stated my belief that Dr. Kissinger, in his dealings with Arabs and Israelis, was not culpable of duplicity regarding final frontiers. The accusation of duplicity comes closer to the truth when we consider his assurances to the Arab chiefs of state regarding a role for the Palestinians in a peace settlement. On several occasions he assured Presidents Sadat and Assad and other Arab leaders that he would seek a way to include the Palestinians in the negotiations, but upon the basis of results he simply was not serious. He capitulated to the Israelis each time they voiced their protestations.

Until late 1975, at least. After that, murky signals began to emerge from Washington that Dr. Kissinger—eager to satisfy Sadat and to revive the confidence of Assad—was softening his attitude toward the Palestinians. For example, the declaration of former Deputy Assistant Secretary Saunders defining the Palestinian dimension as the "heart" of the Arab-Israeli conflict, and Kissinger's acquiescence to the participation of the P.L.O. in a debate on the Palestinian question in the Security Council in January 1976.

In his statement to a congressional subcommittee on November 12, 1975, Saunders declared:

What is needed as a first step is a diplomatic process which will help bring forth a reasonable definition of Palestinian interests—a position from which negotiations on a solution of the Palestinian aspects of the problem might begin. The issue is not whether Palestinian interests should be expressed in a final settlement, but how. There will be no peace unless an answer is found. . . . We are prepared to consider any reasonable proposal from any quarter, and we will expect other parties to the negotiation to be equally broadminded.

This last was a hint to the Israeli government that it had best reconsider its intractable attitude to the P.L.O. The Saunders document was largely a compendium of previous American statements on the Palestinian question, but it brought the United States government—for the first time—into a public exposition of the political aspects of the problem. It suggested certain conditions—acceptance of Israel, disavowal of terrorism—under which the P.L.O. might qualify in the American view as a negotiating partner.

The Israeli government was indignant. At Jerusalem the cabinet examined the declaration with an intense textual analysis, then protested to Dr. Kissinger. The Secretary dismissed the document as an "academic and theoretical exercise" and denied—to Ambassador Dinitz—that he had anything to do with it. In fact, Kissinger had carefully edited the declaration, investing it with his own co-authorship. The affair represented the first stumbling step toward eventual American recognition of the P.L.O.

Diplomacy, it has been said, is the art of postponing the inevitable as long as possible. The great question, it seems to me, is not whether we shall see a Palestinian state, but how soon. That

state—confined to Gaza and the west bank, largely demilitarized, totally autonomous or confederated with Hashemite
Jordan—will confront immense obstacles before it can be
achieved, but the alternative to its achievement will be unend-
ing disorder in the Middle East. The modalities of its creation,
once all parties agree upon the goal, should be comparatively
easy to devise.

For example, King Hussein might be authorized by an Arab
"summit" to hold the west bank in trust until its final destiny is
decided. Or the United Nations might administer the west bank
and Gaza for an interregnum of two, three, or five years whilst
the Palestinians consider the composition of their leadership in
future. The Security Council might empower a commission to
poll the Palestinians throughout the Middle East, to consult
with the P.L.O. and local leaders in Gaza and the west bank,
and eventually to sponsor elections and establish a provisional
government. In fact, the riddle of mutual recognition by Israel
and the P.L.O. might—in the beginning—be mastered by the
Security Council itself. The Security Council would initiate the
process of creating a Palestinian state; Israel and the P.L.O.
would acquiesce, then eventually negotiate with one another—
perhaps under the aegis of the United Nations—to fashion the
phases that should follow.

*Phases* and *stages*—words that wave red flags. Many Palestinians might be content with half a loaf—part of Palestine, not all
of it—but it would be dishonest to deny that others would see
this rump Palestine as simply a *phase* for reconquering the remainder of their fatherland. No settlement will satisfy everybody; no settlement can be wrapped in a perfect package; the
fact must be confronted. Just as the Irish Republican Army refused the Ulster partition following World War I, factions of the
*fedayin* will refuse a rump Palestine. They will raise arms
against a rump Palestine or endeavor to use it as a base for
continuing attacks against Israel. The task of the peacemakers
will be to isolate these "rejectionists," to confine their outbursts
to the category of marginal annoyance—without, one hopes,
causing great bloodshed within the Palestinian family itself.

The rejectionists will be isolated or dissuaded to the extent that the new Palestinian state is rendered attractive to the greatest number of Palestinians. The state, it seems to me, once it has its autonomy, will wish to establish some sort of confederal bond with Jordan—for defense and viability. It need not be a radical leftist state. No less than Israel, royalist Jordan and Saudi Arabia will not tolerate a regime of radicals upon their borders. The Saudis' wishes should carry weight, for they will be called upon to subsidize the new Palestine. Nor should the Syrians covet a radical republic on the west bank—they proved, during the civil war, that they did not covet one in Lebanon.

"The Palestinian republic," says a prominent Palestinian intellectual, "must be a state that Israel will live with without watchtowers, without searchlights, without police dogs, without minefields." Perhaps such Israeli confidence could only come with time, but the mind of Israel and of the Palestinians must evolve after the settlement itself. The Palestinians, in order to have their state, will be obliged to disavow violence forever. But Palestinians and Jews will perforce proceed from there to a permanent, pacific dialogue about their common destiny in the land of Palestine. The Palestinians will perforce dilute their dream of a secular state embracing all of Palestine, but they will never abandon it completely. The Jews reject that vision out of hand—today. But is it heretical to suggest that—five or 15 years hence—Israel might readjust its reliance on the United States, revise its role in the international system, and begin to swim in the mainstream of the Middle East? Is it outrageous to suggest that—20, 30, 50 years hence—Jews and Arabs together might accomplish some new reality that permits both peoples to share the government and the earth of all of Palestine?

Again, that is futurology. For the here and now, the task of American diplomacy is to pursue a general settlement with stamina and speed. The United States has perhaps until the middle or the end of 1977 to deliver to President Sadat the tangible assurance of a general settlement and the restitution of his territory. Otherwise, Sadat will finally be discredited in Egypt and throughout Araby—and if *he* does not collapse, then

America's Arab policy surely shall. The consensus that prevails amongst most levels of the United States government—in the State Department, in the C.I.A., in the Pentagon, and elsewhere—favoring a settlement based upon the 1967 boundaries, a state for the Palestinians, strong guarantees for Israel, must be translated into the imperatives of high policy.*

The United States and Israel have no other choice. The October war and the oil embargo cost the United States (so the National Petroleum Council estimated) between $30 and $60 billion in lost Gross National Product. The next war in the Middle East, should it be waged, will cost the United States and Western Europe considerably more. Well into the 1980s, America will remain dependent upon Arab oil—Israel cannot kill time for another decade. Nor can Israel, even assuming she wins the next war, pay for the war from her own pocket.

Even today, Israel teeters at the abyss of bankruptcy. She has devalued her currency ten times in 18 months. Her deficit for

---

*Mr. Mark Bruzonsky, analyzing my article in Foreign Policy, asserts that the "first option" I have described in Chapter 12 is already being implemented. In Interchange (April 1976), a publication of Breira (Alternative), a most enlightened Jewish group, Mr. Bruzonsky wrote that "the 1975 'reassessment' was, in fact, the starting point for expression of this [chronic crisis between Israel and the United States described by Mr. Sheehan]. It began with President Ford's blunt letter to . . . Rabin in . . . March [1975] insisting that Israel show more flexibility. It continued with Saunders' statement on the Palestinians in November [1975. In March 1976] there was Ford's rebuff of Jewish leaders over the sale of C-130s for Egypt, the reduction in military aid for Israel for fiscal 1977, and most recently, William Scranton's calculated attack on Israeli settlements in the occupied territories as violations of the Geneva Convention. . . .

"The letter from the seventy-six Senators [in May 1975] . . . stopped the verbal articulation of America's conception of a Middle East peace [but] it did not stop its implementation. In fact, the letter may have made it easier for Kissinger since it prevents Israeli supporters from challenging the fundamentals of American policy, forcing them to focus on the slow and subtle manifestations of pressure which have been growing since March 1975. In effect, Israel is getting all the pressure implicit in option No. 1, without the benefit of an articulated overall policy to challenge."

I find Mr. Bruzonsky's analysis a trifle too neat. I do not agree that Israel is already "getting all the pressure implicit in option No. 1." As for the trend of policy Mr. Bruzonsky describes, I very much agree.

1976 exceeds $4 billion; her national debt surpasses $7 billion. Her own economists protest that this small nation, with such a narrow fiscal base and a population of little more than three million, cannot afford to go on spending like a major military power. Israel's next war can only be paid for by the United States—and the United States cannot afford it, either. The United States is, in effect, partially financing Israel's present occupation of the Sinai, the Golan, the Gaza Strip, and the west bank. It can hardly contemplate financing an Israeli thrust to the gates of Cairo and Damascus.*

Dr. Kissinger has forged the Middle East's first small steps to peace, but it is doubtful he will remain in power to consummate the grander task. That will fall to the next president, whoever he may be, and to the next secretary of state. For essentially peace in the Middle East will be a presidential problem. Peace will require a resolute president ready to undertake arduous decisions, prepared to encourage the forces of conciliation in both Israel and Araby—and resolved, when necessary, to apply strong pressure upon Israel for the sake of concessions that will produce peace. It will all be very difficult, but the alternatives of war and radical upheaval will be much worse.

Or is real peace a pure illusion? Ironically the sort of settlement I have urged in these pages might have been possible on the morrow of the October war had Henry Kissinger truly seized the opportunities of that period. But he feared then that to seek so much so soon was doomed to fail. We shall never know. We must render him respect for what he managed to accomplish. Alas, what he accomplished, as I suggested at the beginning of this book, resembles the reconciliation between T. S. Eliot's Archbishop and the King—"Peace, but not the kiss of peace, a patched-up affair, if you ask my opinion." I pray that the next president and his secretary of state will make an act of faith in failure, and in the end help Arabs and Jews to fashion something more substantial than interim solutions.

*For a fascinating—and far more frightening—scenario of the future, by former Senator J. William Fulbright, see Appendix Ten.

# Appendix One
# United Nations Security Council
# Resolution 242 (1967)

*Adopted by the Security Council at its 1382nd meeting,*
*on 22 November 1967*

*The Security Council,*

*Expressing* its continuing concern with the grave situation in the Middle East,

*Emphasizing* the inadmissibility of the acquisition of territory by war and the need to work for a just and lasting peace in which every State in the area can live in security,

*Emphasizing further* that all Member States in their acceptance of the Charter of the United Nations have undertaken a commitment to act in accordance with Article 2 of the Charter,

1. *Affirms* that the fulfilment of Charter principles requires the establishment of a just and lasting peace in the Middle East which should include the application of both the following principles:

   (i) Withdrawal of Israeli armed forces from territories occupied in the recent conflict;

   (ii) Termination of all claims or states of belligerency and respect for and acknowledgement of the sovereignty, territorial integrity and political independence of every State in the area and their right to live in peace within secure and recognized boundaries free from threats or acts of force;

2. *Affirms further* the necessity
   (a) For guaranteeing freedom of navigation through international waterways in the area;
   (b) For achieving a just settlement of the refugee problem;
   (c) For guaranteeing the territorial inviolability and political independence of every State in the area, through measures including the establishment of demilitarized zones;

3. *Requests* the Secretary-General to designate a Special Representative to proceed to the Middle East to establish and maintain contacts with the States concerned in order to promote agreement and assist efforts to achieve a peaceful and accepted settlement in accordance with the provisions and principles in this resolution;

4. *Requests* the Secretary-General to report to the Security Council on the progress of the efforts of the Special Representative as soon as possible.

# Appendix Two
# A Lasting Peace in the Middle East:
# An American View

*An Address by Secretary of State William P. Rogers,*
*December 9th 1969.*

I am very happy to be with you this evening and be a part of this impressive conference. The Galaxy Conference represents one of the largest and most significant efforts in the Nation's history to further the goals of all phases of adult and continuing education.

The State Department, as you know, has an active interest in this subject. It is our belief that foreign policy issues should be more broadly understood and considered. As you know, we are making a good many efforts toward providing continuing education in the foreign affairs field. I am happy tonight to join so many staunch allies in those endeavors.

In the hope that I may further that cause I want to talk to you tonight about a foreign policy matter which is of great concern to our nation.

## U.S. POLICY IN THE MIDDLE EAST

I am going to speak tonight about the situation in the Middle East. I want to refer to the policy of the United States as it relates to that situation in the hope that there may be a better understanding of that policy and the reasons for it.

Following the third Arab-Israeli war in 20 years, there was an upsurge of hope that a lasting peace could be achieved. That hope has unfortunately not been realized. There is no area of the world today that is more important, because it could easily again be the source of another serious conflagration.

When this administration took office, one of our first actions in foreign affairs was to examine carefully the entire situation in the Middle East. It was obvious that a continuation of the unresolved conflict there would be extremely dangerous, that the parties to the conflict alone would not be able to overcome their legacy of suspicion to achieve a political settlement, and that international efforts to help needed support.

The United States decided it had a responsibility to play a direct role in seeking a solution.

Thus, we accepted a suggestion put forward both by the French Government and the Secretary General of the United Nations. We agreed that the major powers—the United States, the Soviet Union, the United Kingdom, and France—should cooperate to assist the Secretary General's representative, Ambassador Jarring, in working out a settlement in accordance with the resolution of the Security Council of the United Nations of November 1967. We also decided to consult directly with the Soviet Union, hoping to achieve as wide an area of agreement as possible between us.

These decisions were made in full recognition of the following important factors:

*First,* we knew that nations not directly involved could not make a durable peace for the peoples and governments involved. Peace rests with the parties to the conflict. The efforts of major powers can help, they can provide a catalyst, they can stimulate the parties to talk, they can encourage, they can help define a realistic framework for agreement; but an agreement among other powers cannot be a substitute for agreement among the parties themselves.

*Second,* we knew that a durable peace must meet the legitimate concerns of both sides.

*Third,* we were clear that the only framework for a negotiated settlement was one in accordance with the entire text of the U.N. Security Council resolution. That resolution was agreed upon after long and arduous negotiations; it is carefully balanced; it provides the basis for a just and lasting peace—a final settlement—not merely an interlude between wars.

*Fourth,* we believe that a protracted period of no war, no peace, recurrent violence, and spreading chaos would serve the interests of no nation, in or out of the Middle East.

## U.S.-SOVIET DISCUSSIONS

For 8 months we have pursued these consultations in four-power talks at the United Nations and in bilateral discussions with the Soviet Union.

In our talks with the Soviets we have proceeded in the belief that the stakes are so high that we have a responsibility to determine whether we can achieve parallel views which would encourage the parties to work out a stable and equitable solution. We are under no illusions; we are fully conscious of past difficulties and present realities. Our talks with the Soviets have brought a measure of understanding, but very substantial differences remain. We regret that the Soviets have delayed in responding to new formulations submitted to them on October 28. However, we will continue to discuss these problems with the Soviet Union as long as there is any realistic hope that such discussions might further the cause of peace.

The substance of the talks that we have had with the Soviet Union has been conveyed to the interested parties through diplomatic channels. This process has served to highlight the main roadblocks to the initiation of useful negotiations among the parties.

On the one hand, the Arab leaders fear that Israel is not in fact prepared to withdraw from Arab territory occupied in the 1967 war.

On the other hand, Israeli leaders fear that the Arab states are not in fact prepared to live in peace with Israel.

Each side can cite from its viewpoint considerable evidence to support its fears. Each side has permitted its attention to be focused solidly and to some extent solely on these fears.

What can the United States do to help to overcome these roadblocks?

Our policy is and will continue to be a *balanced* one.

We have friendly ties with both Arabs and Israelis. To call for Israeli withdrawal as envisaged in the U.N. resolution without achieving agreement on peace would be partisan toward the Arabs. To call on the Arabs to accept peace without Israeli withdrawal would be partisan toward Israel. Therefore, our policy is to encourage the Arabs to accept a permanent peace based on a binding agreement and to urge the Israelis to withdraw from occupied territory when their territorial integrity is assured as envisaged by the Security Council resolution.

### BASIC ELEMENTS OF U.N. RESOLUTION

In an effort to broaden the scope of discussion we have recently resumed four-power negotiations at the United Nations.

Let me outline our policy on various elements of the Security Council resolution. The basic and related issues might be described as peace, security, withdrawal, and territory.

*Peace Between the Parties.* The resolution of the Security Council makes clear that the goal is the establishment of a state of peace between the parties instead of the state of belligerency which has characterized relations for over 20 years. We believe the conditions and obligations of peace must be defined in specific terms. For example, navigation rights in the Suez Canal and in the Strait of Tiran should be spelled out. Respect for sovereignty and obligations of the parties to each other must be made specific.

But peace, of course, involves much more than this. It is also a matter of the attitudes and intentions of the parties. Are they ready to coexist with one another? Can a live-and-let-live attitude replace suspicion, mistrust, and hate? A peace agreement between the parties must be based on clear and stated intentions and a willingness to bring about basic changes in the attitudes and conditions which are characteristic of the Middle East today.

*Security.* A lasting peace must be sustained by a sense of security on both sides. To this end, as envisaged in the Security Council resolution, there should be demilitarized zones and related security arrangements more reliable than those which existed in the area in the past. The parties themselves, with Ambassador Jarring's help, are in the best position to work out the nature and the details of such security arrangements. It is, after all, their interests which are at stake and their territory which is involved. They must live with the results.

*Withdrawal and Territory.* The Security Council resolution endorses the principle of the nonacquisition of territory by war and calls for withdrawal of Israeli armed forces from territories occupied in the 1967 war. We support this part of the resolution, including withdrawal, just as we do its other elements.

The boundaries from which the 1967 war began were established in the 1949 armistice agreements and have defined the areas of national jurisdiction in the Middle East for 20 years. Those boundaries were armistice lines, not final political borders. The rights, claims, and positions of the parties in an ultimate peaceful settlement were reserved by the armistice agreements.

The Security Council resolution neither endorses nor precludes these armistice lines as the definitive political boundaries. However, it calls for withdrawal from occupied territories, the nonacquisition of territory by war, and the establishment of secure and recognized boundaries.

We believe that while recognized political boundaries must be established and agreed upon by the parties, any changes in the preexisting lines should not reflect the weight of conquest and should be confined to insubstantial alterations required for mutual security. We do not support expansionism. We believe troops must be withdrawn as the resolution provides. We support Israel's security and the security of the Arab states as well. We are for a lasting peace that requires security for both.

## ISSUES OF REFUGEES AND JERUSALEM

By emphasizing the key issues of peace, security, withdrawal, and territory, I do not want to leave the impression that other issues are not equally important. Two in particular deserve special mention: the questions of refugees and of Jerusalem.

There can be no lasting peace without a just settlement of the problem of those Palestinians whom the wars of 1948 and 1967 have made homeless. This human dimension of the Arab-Israeli conflict has been of special concern to the United States for over 20 years. During this period the United States has contributed about $500 million for the support and education of the Palestine refugees. We are prepared to contribute generously along with others to solve this problem. We believe its just settlement must take into account the desires and aspirations of the refugees and the legitimate concerns of the governments in the area.

The problem posed by the refugees will become increasingly serious if their future is not resolved. There is a new consciousness among the young Palestinians who have grown up since 1948 which needs to be channeled away from bitterness and frustration toward hope and justice.

The question of the future status of Jerusalem, because it touches deep emotional, historical, and religious wellsprings, is particularly complicated. We have made clear repeatedly in the past two and a half years that we cannot accept unilateral actions by any party to decide the final status of the city. We believe its status can be determined only through the agreement of the parties concerned, which in practical terms means primarily the Governments of Israel and Jordan, taking into account the interests of other countries in the area and the international community. We do, however, support certain principles which we believe would provide an equitable framework for a Jerusalem settlement.

Specifically, we believe Jerusalem should be a unified city within which there would no longer be restrictions on the movement of persons and goods. There should be open access to the unified city for persons of all faiths and nationalities. Arrangements for the administration of the unified city should take into account the interests of all its inhabitants and of the Jewish, Islamic, and Christian communities. And there should be roles for both Israel and Jordan in the civic, economic, and religious life of the city.

It is our hope that agreement on the key issues of peace, security, withdrawal, and territory will create a climate in which these questions of refugees and of Jerusalem, as well as other aspects of the conflict, can be resolved as part of the overall settlement.

### FORMULAS FOR U.A.R.-ISRAEL ASPECT OF SETTLEMENT

During the first weeks of the current United Nations General Assembly the efforts to move matters toward a settlement entered a particularly intensive phase. Those efforts continue today.

I have already referred to our talks with the Soviet Union. In connection with those talks there have been allegations that we have been seeking to divide the Arab states by urging the U.A.R. to make a separate peace. These allegations are false. It is a fact that we and the Soviets have been concentrating on the questions of a settlement between Israel and the United Arab Republic. We have been doing this in the full understanding on both our parts that, before there can be a settlement of the Arab-Israeli conflict, there must be agreement between the parties on other aspects of the settlement—not only those related to the United Arab Republic but also those related to Jordan and other states which accept the Security Council resolution of November 1967.

We started with the Israeli–United Arab Republic aspect because of its inherent importance for future stability in the area and because one must start somewhere.

We are also ready to pursue the Jordanian aspect of a settlement; in fact the four powers in New York have begun such discussions. Let me make it perfectly clear that the U.S. position is that implementation of the overall settlement would begin only after complete agreement had been reached on related aspects of the problem.

In our recent meetings with the Soviets we have discussed some new formulas in an attempt to find common positions. They consist of three principal elements:

*First,* there should be a binding commitment by Israel and the United Arab Republic to peace with each other, with all the specific obligations of peace spelled out, including the obligation to prevent hostile acts originating from their respective territories.

*Second,* the detailed provisions of peace relating to security safeguards on the ground should be worked out between the parties, under Ambassador Jarring's auspices, utilizing the procedures followed in negotiating the armistice agreements under Ralph Bunche in 1949 at Rhodes. This formula has been previously used with success in negotiations between the parties on Middle Eastern problems. A principal objective of the four-power talks, we believe, should be to help Ambassador Jarring engage the parties in a negotiating process under the Rhodes formula.

So far as a settlement between Israel and the United Arab Republic goes, these safeguards relate primarily to the area of Sharm al-Shaykh controlling access to the Gulf of Aqaba, the need for demilitarized zones as foreseen in the Security Council resolution, and final arrangements in the Gaza Strip.

*Third,* in the context of peace and agreement on specific security safeguards, withdrawal of Israeli forces from Egyptian territory would be required.

Such an approach directly addresses the principal national concerns of both Israel and the U.A.R. It would require the U.A.R. to agree to a binding and specific commitment to peace. It would require withdrawal of Israeli armed forces from U.A.R. territory to the international border between Israel [or Mandated Palestine] and Egypt which has been in existence for over a half century. It would also require the parties themselves to negotiate the practical security arrangements to safeguard the peace.

We believe that this approach is *balanced* and fair.

### U.S. INTERESTS IN THE AREA

We remain interested in good relations with all states in the area. Whenever and wherever Arab states which have broken off diplomatic relations with the United States are prepared to restore them, we shall respond in the same spirit.

Meanwhile, we will not be deterred from continuing to pursue the paths of patient diplomacy in our search for peace in the Middle East. We will not shrink from advocating necessary compromises, even though they may and probably will be unpalatable to both sides. We remain prepared to work with others—in the area and throughout the world—so long as they sincerely seek the end we seek: a just and lasting peace.

# Appendix Three

## Security Council Resolution 338[1]

*The Security Council*

1. *Calls upon* all parties to the present fighting to cease all firing and terminate all military activity immediately, no later than 12 hours after the moment of the adoption of this decision, in the positions they now occupy;

2. *Calls upon* the parties concerned to start immediately after the cease-fire the implementation of Security Council resolution 242 (1967) in all of its parts;

3. *Decides* that, immediately and concurrently with the cease-fire, negotiations start between the parties concerned under appropriate auspices aimed at establishing a just and durable peace in the Middle East.

## Security Council Resolution 339[2]

*The Security Council,*

*Referring to* its resolution 338 (1973) of 22 October 1973,

1. *Confirms* its decision on an immediate cessation of all kinds of firing and of all military action, and urges that the forces of the two sides be returned to the positions they occupied at the moment the cease-fire became effective;

2. *Requests* the Secretary-General to take measures for immediate dispatch of United Nations observers to supervise the observance of

---

[1]Adopted on Oct. 22, 1973, at 12:50 A.M. by a vote of 14 to 0 (China did not participate in the voting).
[2]Adopted on Oct. 23 by a vote of 14 to 0 (China did not participate in the voting).

the cease-fire between the forces of Israel and the Arab Republic of Egypt, using for this purpose the personnel of the United Nations now in the Middle East and first of all the personnel now in Cairo.

### Security Council Resolution 340[3]

*The Security Council,*

*Recalling* its resolutions 338 (1973) of 22 October and 339 (1973) of 23 October 1973,

*Noting with regret* the reported repeated violations of the cease-fire in non-compliance with resolutions 338 (1973) and 339 (1973),

*Noting with concern* from the Secretary-General's report that the United Nations military observers have not yet been enabled to place themselves on both sides of the cease-fire line,

1. *Demands* that immediate and complete cease-fire be observed and that the parties return to the positions occupied by them at 1650 hours GMT on 22 October 1973;

2. *Requests* the Secretary-General, as an immediate step, to increase the number of United Nations military observers on both sides;

3. *Decides* to set up immediately under its authority a United Nations Emergency Force to be composed of personnel drawn from States Members of the United Nations except the permanent members of the Security Council, and requests the Secretary-General to report within 24 hours on the steps taken to this effect;

4. *Requests* the Secretary-General to report to the Council on an urgent and continuing basis on the state of implementation of the present resolution, as well as resolutions 338 (1973) and 339 (1973);

5. *Requests* all Member States to extend their full co-operation to the United Nations in the implementation of the present resolution, as well as resolutions 338 (1973) and 339 (1973).

[3]Adopted on Oct. 25 by a vote of 14 to 0 (China did not participate in the voting).

# Appendix Four
## From *Yediot Aharonot*, (Israel), February 15th, 1974 (Translated from Hebrew)

*Kissinger: Israel Should Get a Settlement*
*While the Arabs Are Still Afraid of Her*

What does Dr. Henry Kissinger think about us? This question is troubling many Israelis. They—like many others the world over—follow the indefatigable Secretary of State, who is of Jewish origin, with wonder. His methods fire the imagination. The impression he creates is one of global authority. But very little is known about his conversations with the policy-makers of the world, and in particular, of Israel. Dr. Kissinger makes it a practice to protect the confidentiality of his conversations—and so do those he talks with.

For once, however, we can penetrate a bit into the realm of the "private talks" of the American Secretary of State. Dr. Kissinger has lately held closed meetings with various groups of intellectuals in the U.S. A full report on one of those meetings has reached the editors, and it follows in its entirety. This discussion took place in Washington on December 6, 1973.

What follows is not a transcript recorded while Kissinger was speaking; rather, it was subsequently reconstructed on the basis of notes taken during his lecture.

Here is the text of the report:

Everybody, including Dr. Kissinger, as well as the Israelis themselves, had assumed (before the Yom Kippur War) that there was no urgency in the situation, and no need to do anything, since the Arabs lacked the power to compel action.

When the war broke out, the assumption prevailed, with Kissinger and among the American military experts, that Israel would win within three or four days. Accordingly, there was no plan for a resupply effort to Israel. The Israelis, too, believed they would win quickly. One of the reasons it took so long to organize delivery of ammunition, spare parts and weapons to Israel was that the Israelis didn't request it in time; they didn't think they would need such a large supply.

When the urgent demand for arms came up, it was necessary to apply pressure on the American bureaucracy—in order to get the airlift going—and also on Portugal, for permission to make landing stops; while the Russians, meanwhile, were flying their own "Air Express" through NATO airspace unimpeded.

Kissinger said that Israel, despite her tactical victory, had lost the war from the strategic standpoint. The fact that the Arab armies were able to fight for 17 days without breaking must be considered a victory—making them the real winners in the war.

The weapons in Arab hands—especially their anti-aircraft and anti-tank missiles—put 400 Israeli tanks and 70 Israeli planes out of action already in the first few days of the war. Israel's ammunition reserve was used up. Planes returning from bombing runs with some bombs still aboard were ordered, in spite of the danger, not to jettison them before landing—as is the usual practice—so grave was the shortage.

Were it not for their mistakes, the Arabs might well have scored even greater achievements. They sent their tanks out to attack beyond the range of their missiles, thus allowing the Israeli air force to strike at them, as in 1967. The Arab armies should instead have advanced more slowly, only after bringing up their anti-aircraft missiles.

Kissinger said he had warned the Israelis from the start that the U.N. would order a cease-fire the moment the tide turned in their favor. Their strategy should therefore have been guided by political considerations: to get the maximum results before the cease-fire.

When the pressure for a cease-fire began, the Secretary of State employed all the delaying tactics at his command. He flew to Moscow to gain time. According to him, he gained an extra 96 hours of fighting time for the Israelis—and they know it. But Israel, he claims, failed to provide the U.S. with exact information about its military plans. He was told, for example, that the Israeli counteroffensive thrust (west of the Suez Canal) would turn north—instead, it turned south.

Before his trip to Moscow, Kissinger revealed, he told Israel that he would consent to stop in Tel Aviv on his way back only if Israel promised to observe the cease-fire. He did not, however, demand (unconditionally) that Israel obey the cease-fire order. While he was in Israel, Golda Meir and Abba Eban told him that Israel would accept the cease-fire; but when he got to London, he was told by the British that there were still problems. He contacted the Soviet ambassador and warned him that it was up to the Soviet Union to keep the Arabs from breaking the agreement. Kissinger asked him how it would look if Gromyko went to Cairo and then, four hours after his departure, Egypt opened an assault. Who would believe that the Russians weren't implicated?

Kissinger said that the last-minute gains scored by Israel on the Egyptian front were not important. She could not have fundamentally altered the situation even in another two days of fighting.

Kissinger then went on to talk about Israel's future vulnerability in the wake of the oil crisis. Support for Israel in Congress was obviously on the way down. He had encountered many difficulties in trying to obtain a guarantee for Israel of the $2.2 billion in aid. The Congressional committee wanted to cut $500 million from that sum, which he was able to prevent only by claiming that the U.S. had already made a commitment for the full sum, and that the arms had already been expended in battle. Thus, if Congress were actually to cut the aid, the administration would have to make a new request for the $500 million, as another item in the budget, which the Arabs would view as a fresh hostile step.

Kissinger expressed deep worry over the consequences of another large-scale war. Israel would require a new airlift, and he was not sure that Congress and the rest of the government apparatus would go along with that request. As a result, Israel was liable, in the event of another war, to be left with no ammunition.

He also indicated that Israel's diplomatic isolation would worsen. He believes Japan will break diplomatic relations with Israel in the next six months, and that other Asian nations will follow suit. Europe will not break relations, but otherwise will do everything to undermine the American and Israeli positions in order to curry favor with the Arabs. He mentioned the Common Market declaration, representing total support of the Arab position, that was made public while he was still in Cairo. This declaration was of concern not only to him but even to Sadat, who had taken a position more moderate than he was invited to do by Europe!

The Secretary of State was very angry with the European states. On several occasions he characterized their behavior as "cowardly," "shameful," or "harmful," and the nations themselves as a "den of crocodiles." He believes they will continue their "sabotage" in the hope of gaining a foothold in the Arab world. For this reason he insisted on their exclusion from the peace conference. The one nation besides the U.S. itself which he characterized as a supporter of Israel—though with "certain reservations"—was Iran.

The efforts to appease the Arabs destroyed the prestige of Europe and its potential for exerting influence in the Middle East. In Kissinger's opinion, the Arabs no longer respect Europe, while they do respect the U.S. for openly supporting Israel. Japan, too, is acting foolishly. She offered King Faisal of Saudi Arabia a billion dollars, even though he has neither the need nor the desire for more money. Nor will Japan be rewarded for her efforts. In the U.S., the energy crisis will intensify in the coming months, and further erode popular support for Israel, according to the Secretary.

Turning to the past, Kissinger criticized both Israel and the U.S., himself included, for not having pressed harder for a peace settlement. In his opinion, Israel's chance came right after the Six-Day War. Had Israel offered then to withdraw from the captured territories, in exchange for their demilitarization, the Arabs would gladly have accepted. Hussein was ready, in 1971–72, to sign a peace agreement with Israel—so he told Kissinger. Kissinger also noted that there were periods when the Egyptians showed a readiness to begin real bargaining. After expelling the Russians, they expected a reciprocal gesture on the part of Israel and the U.S. He blamed himself for being so preoccupied with the problem of Vietnam that he didn't press Israel to take such a step.

Surveying the problems of negotiation, Kissinger said there were five topics: frontiers; security (demilitarized buffer zones); guarantees; the Palestinians; Jerusalem.

In his opinion, it was unwise to try and solve all the problems at once; while promises regarding ultimate goals, like *de jure* recognition, had no power to prevent war. (The proof—India and Pakistan.) One has to deal with these topics one at a time. The most important thing to which efforts should be directed at Geneva is the creation of wide buffer zones between the armies. As an optimal goal—the demilitarization of the entire Sinai peninsula, from which Israel would withdraw. According to him, history shows that the side in possession of Sinai turns out to be militarily the weaker one. A demilitarized Sinai, on the other hand, means that the entry of an army there would constitute a *casus belli* for the opening of full hostilities. The situation in the Golan

Heights is different, but most of it would have to be demilitarized as well. In a war of missiles, borders and even territory are no defense.

Once these withdrawals are agreed upon and accomplished, it will be possible to move on to the other topics. The withdrawal and demilitarization must be arranged as soon as possible, preferably in the next two to four months, at most within a year. Otherwise, another war is to be expected, along with all the problems that limited American aid will bring.

Kissinger said he objects to the idea of a security pact [for Israel] with American guarantees. He sees no substitute for agreed boundaries.

He does not believe that the Palestinian problem can at present be solved. "They would have to be a lot hungrier than they are now" before they will agree to settle and to recognize Israel's status. The problem of Jerusalem must likewise be reserved for later.

King Faisal, whom Kissinger described as a "religious fanatic," is mainly concerned about Jerusalem. The fate of the Palestinians or of Sinai does not interest him. Faisal now finds himself, for the first time, in a position of influence in the Arab world, able to hold back the secularist or radical Arabs. It is therefore not to be expected that he will sponsor a reconciliation with the U.S. His only hold on the Arab world is his (anti-American) oil policy.

Israel must understand that she cannot afford to cause delays in the negotiations. There is no hope that things might change in her favor in the meantime. The Arabs, in fact, did even better than they imagine. They are still afraid of Israel, but if she is not quickly persuaded to withdraw, there is every possibility of renewed fighting with potentially disastrous results for her. Kissinger nevertheless emphasized that he does not mean Israel will have to withdraw to the 1967 borders; he believes rather that a more favorable border will be agreed upon in the negotiations. On the other hand, he stressed again that Israel will have no choice but to withdraw from (some of) the occupied territories, which he hopes will be demilitarized and turned into buffer zones.

Kissinger declared at the start of his remarks, and repeated several times in the course of the discussion, that the U.S. has no advance agreement, with the Soviets or with the Arabs, on either the course or the outcome of negotiations. As he sees it, the parties at Geneva must "write their own script." He opposed the view of those in the State Department or the White House who wanted to design a strategy for a comprehensive agreement in advance.

Israel's public posture should be one of intransigence, but within the Israeli government—so Kissinger believes—there must be an understanding that they be ready to give up substantial territories. However, such a concession must not appear to be a function of weakness, or fear or loss of nerve. It must come about as a natural result of negotiation.

Kissinger showed great sensitivity to possible Israeli reactions. He said that the old generation, those who emigrated to Israel, drained her swamps, and built a new society and a new state there, experienced success against great odds time and time again; now, all of a sudden, they find themselves in a position they thought they had forever left behind: that of a weak Jewish community facing a strong and hostile world. In Kissinger's opinion, this group will have the most trouble adjusting to the new reality.

Kissinger said he had been told that the Israelis suspect his own Jewishness might be a source of weakness for them, by making him "bend over backwards" to favor the Arabs. To this Kissinger responded that while he cannot, of course, analyze all of his own (subconscious) motives, he does not believe his "religion" will weaken his support for Israel. As one whose family was destroyed in concentration camps, he cannot avoid feeling an emotional involvement. Had he known beforehand, when he was appointed Secretary of State, how things would later develop in the Middle East, he might not have accepted that position. But now that he is in it, he will do all he can to secure the best possible peace.

Although in the future it will be harder to obtain American assistance for Israel—especially another airlift—Kissinger said that the present administration would stand behind her. When pressed with questions about what would happen if fighting were renewed, he said that he would take the same position as in October, viz., that Israel should be given all the weapons and other items she needs. (It seems that he takes a substantial part of the credit for the October decision to airlift weapons to Israel.) He estimates the odds of success (in assuring immediate military aid to Israel) at two to one; but he cannot absolutely guarantee it, since opposition to an airlift in Congress and in the bureaucracy will be greater than in the past.

One reason for the lack of time for extended negotiations—and for Israel's need to be ready to reach an agreement quickly—is, in his opinion, that peace is not in the interest of the Arabs, who only stand to gain from another war. At the moment, however, many of them are not so sure about this. They still fear what Israel can do on the battlefield, and, at the same time, they want to get rid of the Russians. American intelligence has reported that in Egypt, Syria and Algeria there is a widespread feeling that the Russians were only lukewarm in their support. As a result, there is still a reasonable chance for a fair agreement on boundaries during the next few months.

Kissinger made known his idea that Israel must terminate the border issue and withdraw—before the conclusion, or even the start, of discussion on the questions of the Palestinians and of *de jure* recognition. Israel erred in the past in insisting on negotiations that would solve all the problems at once; she can no longer afford, now that she has been weakened so, to maintain this position.

In his opinion, had an agreement providing for substantial Israeli withdrawal from and demilitarization of the territories been signed after the 1967 war, the Arabs would have found it difficult to open hostilities by sending tanks into a demilitarized area in their own possession.

The occupation of Sinai is a most significant factor for Sadat and for all Egyptians. Kissinger claimed—according to this report—that for years the Egyptians have been saying so to the U.S. and to Israel as well; and they are ready to compromise on less than the borders of 1967.

Kissinger's long-range goal is to establish peace in the Middle East for another ten years. During that time many factors—such as the oil factor and perhaps the European position as well—will change. He does not believe that the goal should be defined in terms of "true peace." One must aspire to the best that can be achieved, that is, conditions that will prevent the outbreak of another war.

# Appendix Five

*Letter Dated 18 December 1973 from the Secretary-General
to the President of the Security Council*

I have received the attached letters from the Permanent Representatives of the Union of Soviet Socialist Republics and the United States of America concerning the forthcoming Conference on the Middle East. I should be grateful if you would communicate these letters to the members of the Security Council. It is my intention to proceed on the basis of these letters which I consider to be in accordance with Security Council resolution 344 (1973) of 15 December 1973.

*(Signed)* Kurt Waldheim

*Letter Dated 18 December 1973 from the Acting Permanent
Representative of the United States of America
to the United Nations Addressed to the Secretary-General*

I have the honour to transmit to you the following letter from Secretary Kissinger.

[*Author's note:* The letter from the Permanent Representative of the Soviet Union to the Secretary-General of the United Nations was essentially the same.]

"Dear Mr. Secretary-General:

"On October 22, 1973, the Security Council adopted resolution 338 (1973), jointly sponsored by the Soviet Union and the United States, which calls for negotiations to start between the parties concerned under appropriate auspices, aimed at establishing a just and durable peace in the Middle East. The Soviet Union and the United States have now been informed by the parties concerned of their readiness to participate in the Peace Conference which will begin in Geneva on December 21. The Conference should be convened under the auspices of the United Nations.

"The parties have agreed that the Conference should be under the co-chairmanship of the Soviet Union and the United States. The parties have also agreed that the question of other participants from the Middle East area will be discussed during the first stage of the Conference.

"It is our hope that you will find it possible to participate in the opening phase of the Conference at which it is expected that the Governments concerned will be represented by their respective Foreign Ministers and, later, by their specially appointed representatives with ambassadorial rank. We also hope that you can make available a representative who would keep you fully informed as the Conference proceeds. Finally, we would also appreciate it if the United Nations could make appropriate arrangements for the necessary conference facilities.

"If as we hope you find it possible to participate, as co-chairmen the Soviet Union and the United States would appreciate it if you would agree to serve as convener of the Conference and preside in the opening phase.

"We request that you circulate this letter to members of the Security Council for their information. We believe it would be appropriate for the President of the Security Council to consult informally with the membership with a view to securing a favorable consensus of the Council."

(*Signed*) W. Tapley Bennett, Jr.
Acting Permanent Representative
of the United States of America
to the United Nations

# Appendix Six
# Egyptian-Israeli Agreement on Disengagement of Forces in Pursuance of the Geneva Peace Conference

A. Egypt and Israel will scrupulously observe the ceasefire on land, sea, and air called for by the U.N. Security Council and will refrain from the time of the signing of this document from all military or para-military actions against each other.

B. The military forces of Egypt and Israel will be separated in accordance with the following principles:

1. All Egyptian forces on the east side of the Canal will be deployed west of the line designated as Line A on the attached map. All Israeli forces, including those west of the Suez Canal and the Bitter Lakes, will be deployed east of the line designated as Line B on the attached map.

2. The area between the Egyptian and Israeli lines will be a zone of disengagement in which the United Nations Emergency Force (UNEF) will be stationed. The UNEF will continue to consist of units from countries that are not permanent members of the Security Council.

3. The area between the Egyptian line and the Suez Canal will be limited in armament and forces.

4. The area between the Israeli line (Line B on the attached map) and the line designated as Line C on the attached map, which runs along the western base of the mountains where the Gidi and Mitla Passes are located, will be limited in armament and forces.

5. The limitations referred to in paragraphs 3 and 4 will be inspected by UNEF. Existing procedures of the UNEF, including the attaching of Egyptian and Israeli liaison officers to UNEF, will be continued.
6. Air forces of the two sides will be permitted to operate up to their respective lines without interference from the other side.

C. The detailed implementation of the disengagement of forces will be worked out by military representatives of Egypt and Israel, who will agree on the stages of this process. These representatives will meet no later than 48 hours after the signature of this agreement at Kilometer 101 under the aegis of the United Nations for this purpose. They will complete this task within five days. Disengagement will begin within 48 hours after the completion of the work of the military representatives and in no event later than seven days after the signature of this agreement. The process of disengagement will be completed not later than 40 days after it begins.

D. This agreement is not regarded by Egypt and Israel as a final peace agreement. It constitutes a first step toward a final, just and durable peace according to the provisions of Security Council Resolution 338 and within the framework of the Geneva Conference.

For Egypt: Mohammed Abdel Ghani al-Gamasy, Major General,
Chief of Staff of the Egyptian Armed Forces
For Israel: David Elazar, Lieutenant General,
Chief of Staff of the Israel Defence Forces
Witness: Ensio P. H. Siilasvuo, Lieutenant General,
Commander of the United Nations Emergency Force
Kilometer 101, Egypt
January 18, 1974

# Appendix Seven
# Agreement on Disengagement
# Between Israeli and Syrian Forces

A. Israel and Syria will scrupulously observe the ceasefire on land, sea and air and will refrain from all military actions against each other, from the time of the signing of this document, in implementation of United Nations Security Council Resolution 338 dated October 22, 1973.

B. The military forces of Israel and Syria will be separated in accordance with the following principles:

1. All Israeli military forces will be west of the line designated as Line A on the map attached hereto, except in the Quneitra area, where they will be west of Line A-1.
2. All territory east of Line A will be under Syrian administration, and Syrian civilians will return to this territory.
3. The area between Line A and the line designated as Line B on the attached map will be an area of separation. In this area will be stationed the United Nations Disengagement Observer Force established in accordance with the accompanying protocol.
4. All Syrian military forces will be east of the line designated as Line B on the attached map.
5. There will be two equal areas of limitation in armament and forces, one west of Line A and one east of Line B as agreed upon.
6. Air forces of the two sides will be permitted to operate up to their respective lines without interference from the other side.

C. In the area between Line A and Line A-1 on the attached map there shall be no military forces.

D. This agreement and the attached map will be signed by the military representatives of Israel and Syria in Geneva not later than May 31, 1974, in the Egyptian-Israeli Military Working Group of the Geneva Peace Conference under the aegis of the United Nations, after that group has been joined by a Syrian military representative, and with the participation of representatives of the United States and the Soviet Union. The precise delineation of a detailed map and a plan for the implementation of the disengagement of forces will be worked out by military representatives of Israel and Syria in the Egyptian-Israeli Military Working Group who will agree on the stages of this process. The Military Working Group described above will start their work for this purpose in Geneva under the aegis of the United Nations within 24 hours after the signing of this agreement. They will complete this task within five days. Disengagement will begin within 24 hours after the completion of the task of the Military Working Group. The process of disengagement will be completed not later than twenty days after it begins.

E. The provisions of paragraphs A, B and C shall be inspected by personnel of the United Nations comprising the United Nations Disengagement Observer Force under this agreement.

F. Within 24 hours after the signing of this agreement in Geneva all wounded prisoners of war which each side holds of the other as certified by the ICRC will be repatriated. The morning after the completion of the task of the Military Working Group, all remaining prisoners of war will be repatriated.

G. The bodies of all dead soldiers held by either side will be returned for burial in their respective countries within ten days after the signing of this agreement.

H. This agreement is not a peace agreement. It is a step toward a just and durable peace on the basis of Security Council Resolution 338 dated October 22, 1973.

Signed by Israel, Syria,
and a Witness for the United Nations,
at Geneva, May 31, 1974

### Protocol to Agreement on Disengagement
### Between Israeli and Syrian Forces

#### CONCERNING THE UNITED NATIONS
#### DISENGAGEMENT OBSERVER FORCE

Israel and Syria agree that:

The function of the United Nations Disengagement Observer Force (UNDOF) under the Agreement will be to use its best efforts to maintain the ceasefire and to see that it is scrupulously observed. It will supervise the Agreement and protocol thereto with regard to the areas of separation and limitation. In carrying out its mission, it will comply with generally applicable Syrian laws and regulations and will not hamper the functioning of local civil administration. It will enjoy freedom of movement and communication and other facilities that are necessary for its mission. It will be mobile and provided with personal weapons of a defensive character and shall use such weapons only in self-defense. The number of the UNDOF shall be about 1,250, who will be selected by the Secretary-General of the United Nations in consultation with the parties from members of the United Nations who are not permanent members of the Security Council.

The UNDOF will be under the command of the United Nations, vested in the Secretary-General, under the authority of the Security Council.

The UNDOF shall carry out inspections under the Agreement, and report thereon to the parties, on a regular basis, not less often than once every fifteen days, and, in addition, when requested by either party. It shall mark on the ground the respective lines shown on the map attached to the Agreement.

Israel and Syria will support a resolution of the United Nations Security Council which will provide for the UNDOF contemplated by the Agreement. The initial authorization will be for six months subject to renewal by further resolution of the Security Council.

There follows the text of the U.S. position as given to the Israelis: *Begin Text.* The position of the United States with respect to the first paragraph of the Agreement between Israel and Syria on Military Disengagement is as follows:

Raids by armed groups or individuals across the demarcation line are contrary to the ceasefire. Israel in the exercise of its right of self-defense may act to prevent such actions by all available means. The United States will not consider such actions by Israel as violations of the ceasefire and will support them politically. END TEXT.

There follows the text of the pasage concerning terrorism from the Government of Israel's official English-language translation of Prime Minister Meir's address to the Knesset at 1500 May 30 re the Syrian-Israeli Disengagement Agreement:

*Begin Text.* As for the prevention of terrorist activities, the United States has informed us of its position on the first paragraph of the Agreement, and this is: QUOTE raids by armed groups or individuals across the demarcation line are contrary to the ceasefire. Israel, in its exercise of its right of self-defense, may act to prevent such actions by all available means. The United States will not consider such actions by Israel as violations of the ceasefire, and will support them politically. END QUOTE.

I assume that the United States would not have made such a declaration to us had it not had a solid foundation for doing so, and I make this statement public with the knowledge of the United States. END TEXT.

# Appendix Eight
# Agreement Between Egypt and Israel

The Government of the Arab Republic of Egypt and the Government of Israel have agreed that:

### Article I

The conflict between them and in the Middle East shall not be resolved by military force but by peaceful means.

The Agreement concluded by the Parties January 18, 1974, within the framework of the Geneva Peace Conference, constituted a first step towards a just and durable peace according to the provisions of Security Council Resolution 338 of October 22, 1973.

They are determined to reach a final and just peace settlement by means of negotiations called for by Security Council Resolution 338, this Agreement being a significant step towards that end.

### Article II

The Parties hereby undertake not to resort to the threat or use of force or military blockade against each other.

## Article III

The Parties shall continue scrupulously to observe the ceasefire on land, sea and air and to refrain from all military or para-military actions against each other.

The Parties also confirm that the obligations contained in the Annex and, when concluded, the Protocol shall be an integral part of this Agreement.

## Article IV

A. The military forces of the Parties shall be deployed in accordance with the following principles:

(1) All Israeli forces shall be deployed east of the lines designated as Lines J and M on the attached map.

(2) All Egyptian forces shall be deployed west of the line designated as Line E on the attached map.

(3) The area between the lines designated on the attached map as Lines E and F and the area between the lines designated on the attached map as Lines J and K shall be limited in armament and forces.

(4) The limitations on armament and forces in the areas described by paragraph (3) above shall be agreed as described in the attached Annex.

(5) The zone between the lines designated on the attached map as Lines E and J, will be a buffer zone. In this zone the United Nations Emergency Force will continue to perform its functions as under the Egyptian-Israeli Agreement of January 18, 1974.

(6) In the area south from Line E and west from Line M, as defined on the attached map, there will be no military forces, as specified in the attached Annex.

B. The details concerning the new lines, the redeployment of the forces and its timing, the limitation on armaments and forces, aerial reconnaissance, the operation of the early warning and surveillance installations and the use of the roads, the United Nations functions and other arrangements will all be in accordance with the provisions of the Annex and map which are an integral part of this Agreement and of the Protocol which is to result from negotiations pursuant to the Annex and which, when concluded, shall become an integral part of this Agreement.

## Article V

The United Nations Emergency Force is essential and shall continue its functions and its mandate shall be extended annually.

## Article VI

The Parties hereby establish a Joint Commission for the duration of this Agreement. It will function under the aegis of the Chief Coordinator of the United Nations Peacekeeping Missions in the Middle East in order to consider any problem arising from this Agreement and to assist the United Nations Emergency Force in the execution of its mandate. The Joint Commission shall function in accordance with procedures established in the Protocol.

## Article VII

Non-military cargoes destined for or coming from Israel shall be permitted through the Suez Canal.

## Article VIII

This Agreement is regarded by the Parties as a significant step toward a just and lasting peace. It is not a final peace agreement.

The Parties shall continue their efforts to negotiate a final peace agreement within the framework of the Geneva Peace Conference in accordance with Security Council Resolution 338.

## Article IX

This Agreement shall enter into force upon signature of the Protocol and remain in force until superseded by a new agreement.

For the Government
of the Arab Republic of Egypt

For the Government of Israel

[September 1975]

## Annex to Egypt-Israel Agreement

Within 5 days after the signature of the Egypt-Israel Agreement, representatives of the two Parties shall meet in the Military Working Group of the Middle East Peace Conference at Geneva to begin preparation of a detailed Protocol for the implementation of the Agreement. The Working Group will complete the Protocol within 2 weeks. In order to facilitate preparation of the Protocol and implementation of the Agreement, and to assist in maintaining the scrupulous observance of the ceasefire and other elements of the Agreement, the two Parties have agreed on the following principles, which are an integral part of the Agreement, as guidelines for the Working Group.

### I. DEFINITIONS OF LINES AND AREAS

The deployment lines, areas of limited forces and armaments, Buffer Zones, the area south from Line E and west from Line M, other designated areas, road sections for common use and other features referred to in Article IV of the Agreement shall be as indicated on the attached map (1:100,000—U.S. Edition).

### II. BUFFER ZONES

(a) Access to the Buffer Zones will be controlled by the United Nations Emergency Force, according to procedures to be worked out by the Working Group and the United Nations Emergency Force.

(b) Aircraft of either Party will be permitted to fly freely up to the forward line of that Party. Reconnaissance aircraft of either Party may fly up to the middle line of the Buffer Zone between Lines E and J on an agreed schedule.

(c) In the Buffer Zone, between Lines E and J there will be established under Article IV of the Agreement an Early Warning System entrusted to United States civilian personnel as detailed in a separate proposal, which is a part of this Agreement.

(d) Authorized personnel shall have access to the Buffer Zone for transit to and from the Early Warning System; the manner in which this is carried out shall be worked out by the Working Group and the United Nations Emergency Force.

### III. AREA SOUTH OF LINE E AND WEST OF LINE M

(a) In this area, the United Nations Emergency Force will assure that there are no military or para-military forces of any kind, military fortifications and military installations; it will establish checkpoints and have the freedom of movement necessary to perform this function.

(b) Egyptian civilians and third country civilian oil field personnel shall have the right to enter, exit from, work, and live in the above indicated area, except for Buffer Zones 2A, 2B and the United Nations Posts. Egyptian civilian police shall be allowed in the area to perform normal civil police functions among the civilian population in such numbers and with such weapons and equipment as shall be provided for in the Protocol.

(c) Entry to and exit from the area, by land, by air or by sea, shall be only through United Nations Emergency Force checkpoints. The United Nations Emergency Force shall also establish checkpoints along the road, the dividing line and at other points, with the precise locations and number to be included in the Protocol.

(d) Access to the airspace and the coastal area shall be limited to unarmed Egyptian civilian vessels and unarmed civilian helicopters and transport planes involved in the civilian activities of the area as agreed by the Working Group.

(e) Israel undertakes to leave intact all currently existing civilian installations and infrastructures.

(f) Procedures for use of the common sections of the coastal road along the Gulf of Suez shall be determined by the Working Group and detailed in the Protocol.

## IV. AERIAL SURVEILLANCE

There shall be a continuation of aerial reconnaissance missions by the United States over the areas covered by the Agreement (the area between Lines F and K), following the same procedures already in practice. The missions will ordinarily be carried out at a frequency of one mission every 7–10 days, with either Party or the United Nations Emergency Force empowered to request an earlier mission. The United States Government will make the mission results available expeditiously to Israel, Egypt and the Chief Coordinator of the United Nations Peacekeeping Missions in the Middle East.

## V. LIMITATION OF FORCES AND ARMAMENTS

(a) Within the Areas of Limited Forces and Armaments (the areas between Lines J and K and Lines E and F) the major limitations shall be as follows:

(1) Eight (8) standard infantry battalions

(2) Seventy-five (75) tanks

(3) Seventy-two (72) artillery pieces, including heavy mortars (i.e. with caliber larger than 120 mm), whose range shall not exceed twelve (12) km.

(4) The total number of personnel shall not exceed eight thousand (8,000).

(5) Both Parties agree not to station or locate in the area weapons which can reach the line of the other side.

(6) Both Parties agree that in the areas between Lines J and K, and between Line A (of the Disengagement Agreement of January 18, 1974) and Line E, they will construct no new fortifications or installations for forces of a size greater than that agreed herein.

(b) The major limitations beyond the Areas of Limited Forces and Armament will be:

(1) Neither side will station nor locate any weapon in areas from which they can reach the other line.

(2) The Parties will not place anti-aircraft missiles within an area of ten (10) km. east of Line K and west of Line F, respectively.

(c) The United Nations Emergency Force will conduct inspections in order to ensure the maintenance of the agreed limitations within these areas.

### VI. PROCESS OF IMPLEMENTATION

The detailed implementation and timing of the redeployment of forces, turnover of oil fields, and other arrangements called for by the Agreement, Annex and Protocol shall be determined by the Working Group, which will agree on the stages of this process, including the phased movement of Egyptian troops to Line E and Israeli troops to Line J. The first phase will be the transfer of the oil fields and installations to Egypt. This process will begin within two weeks from the signature of the Protocol with the introduction of the necessary technicians, and it will be completed no later than eight weeks after it begins. The details of the phasing will be worked out in the Military Working Group.

Implementation of the redeployment shall be completed within 5 months after signature of the Protocol.

For the Government
of the Arab Republic of Egypt

For the Government of Israel

## Proposal

In connection with the Early Warning System referred to in Article IV of the Agreement between Egypt and Israel concluded on this date and as an integral part of that Agreement, (hereafter referred to as the Basic Agreement), the United States proposes the following:

1. The Early Warning System to be established in accordance with Article IV in the area shown on the map attached to the Basic Agreement will be entrusted to the United States. It shall have the following elements:

   a. There shall be two surveillance stations to provide strategic early warning, one operated by Egyptian and one operated by Israeli personnel. Their locations are shown on the map attached to the Basic Agreement. Each station shall be manned by not more than 250 technical and administrative personnel. They shall perform the functions of visual and electronic surveillance only within their stations.

   b. In support of these stations, to provide tactical early warning and to verify access to them, three watch stations shall be established by the United States in the Mitla and Gidi Passes as will be shown on the map attached to the Basic Agreement. These stations shall be operated by United States civilian personnel. In support of these stations, there shall be established three unmanned electronic sensor fields at both ends of each Pass and in the general vicinity of each station and the roads leading to and from those stations.

2. The United States civilian personnel shall perform the following duties in connection with the operation and maintenance of these stations.

   a. At the two surveillance stations described in paragraph 1 a. above, United States civilian personnel will verify the nature of the operations of the stations and all movement into and out of each station and will immediately report any detected divergency from its authorized role of visual and electronic surveillance to the Parties to the Basic Agreement and to the United Nations Emergency Force.

   b. At each watch station described in paragraph 1 b. above, the United States civilian personnel will immediately report to the Parties to the Basic Agreement and to the United Nations Emergency Force any movement of armed forces, other than the United Nations Emergency Force, into either Pass and any observed preparations for such movement.

c. The total number of United States civilian personnel assigned to functions under this Proposal shall not exceed 200. Only civilian personnel shall be assigned to functions under this Proposal.

3. No arms shall be maintained at the stations and other facilities covered by this Proposal, except for small arms required for their protection.

4. The United States personnel serving the Early Warning System shall be allowed to move freely within the area of the System.

5. The United States and its personnel shall be entitled to have such support facilities as are reasonably necessary to perform their functions.

6. The United States personnel shall be immune from local criminal, civil, tax and customs jurisdiction and may be accorded any other specific privileges and immunities provided for in the United Nations Emergency Force agreement of February 13, 1957.

7. The United States affirms that it will continue to perform the functions described above for the duration of the Basic Agreement.

8. Notwithstanding any other provision of this Proposal, the United States may withdraw its personnel only if it concludes that their safety is jeopardized or that continuation of their role is no longer necessary. In the latter case the Parties to the Basic Agreement will be informed in advance in order to give them the opportunity to make alternative arrangements. If both Parties to the Basic Agreement request the United States to conclude its role under this Proposal, the United States will consider such requests conclusive.

9. Technical problems including the location of the watch stations will be worked out through consultation with the United States.

_____

Henry A. Kissinger
Secretary of State


Accepted by:


_____

Mamdouh Salem
Prime Minister
of the Arab Republic of Egypt

## Text of U.S.-Israeli Memorandum

From The Washington Post, Tuesday, September 16, 1975.
Following is the text of the Memorandum of Agreement between the United States and Israel, which, according to diplomatic sources, was signed by Secretary of State Henry A. Kissinger and Israeli Foreign Minister Yigal Allon on Sept. 1:

The United States recognizes that the Egypt-Israel Agreement initialed on Sept. 1, 1975 (hereinafter referred to as the Agreement), entailing the withdrawal from vital areas in Sinai, constitutes an act of great significance on Israel's part in the pursuit of final peace. That agreement has full United States support.

### UNITED STATES-ISRAELI ASSURANCES

1. The United States government will make every effort to be fully responsive, within the limits of its resources and congressional authorization and appropriation, on an on-going and long-term basis to Israel's military equipment and other defense requirements, to its energy requirements and to its economic needs. The needs specified in Paragraphs 2, 3 and 4 below shall be deemed eligible for inclusion within the annual total to be requested in FY '76 and later fiscal years.

2. Israel's long term military supply needs from the United States shall be the subject of periodic consultations between representatives of the U.S. and Israeli defense establishments, with agreement reached on specific items to be included in a separate U.S.-Israeli memorandum. To this end, a joint study by military experts will be undertaken within three weeks. In conducting this study, which will include Israel's 1976 needs, the United States will view Israel's requests sympathetically, including its request for advanced and sophisticated weapons.

3. Israel will make its own independent arrangements for oil supply to meet its requirements through normal procedures. In the event Israel is unable to secure its needs in this way, the United States government, upon notification of this fact by the government of Israel, will act as follows for five years, at the end of which period either side can terminate this arrangement on one year's notice.

(a) If the oil Israel needs to meet all its normal requirements for domestic consumption is unavailable for purchase in circumstances where no quantitative restrictions exist on the ability of the United States to procure oil to meet its normal requirements, the United States government will promptly make oil available for purchase by Israel to meet all of the aforementioned normal requirements of Israel. If Israel is unable to secure the necessary means to transport such oil to Israel, the United States Government will make every effort to help Israel secure the necessary means of transport.

(b) If the oil Israel needs to meet all of its normal requirements for domestic consumption is unavailable for purchase in circumstances where quantitative restrictions through embargo or otherwise also prevent the United States from procuring oil to meet its normal requirements, the United States government will promptly make oil available for purchase by Israel in accordance with the International Energy Agency conservation and allocation formula as applied by the United States government, in order to meet Israel's essential requirements. If Israel is unable to secure the necessary means to transport such oil to Israel, the United States government will make every effort to help Israel secure the necessary means of transport.

Israeli and U.S. experts will meet annually or more frequently at the request of either party, to review Israel's continuing oil requirement.

4. In order to help Israel meet its energy needs, and as part of the overall annual figure in Paragraph 1 above, the United States agrees:

(a) In determining the overall annual figure which will be requested from Congress, the United States government will give special attention to Israel's oil import requirements and, for a period as determined by Article 3 above, will take into account in calculating that figure Israel's additional expenditures for the import of oil to replace that which would have ordinarily come from Abu Rudeis and Ras Sudar (4.5 million tons in 1975).

(b) To ask Congress to make available funds, the amount to be determined by mutual agreement, to the government of Israel necessary for a project for the construction and stocking of the oil reserves to be stored in Israel, bringing storage reserve capacity and reserve stocks now standing at approximately six months, up to one year's need at the time of the completion of the project. The project will be implemented within four years. The construction, operation and financing and other relevant questions of the project will be the subject of early and detailed talks between the two governments.

5. The United States government will not expect Israel to begin to implement the Agreement before Egypt fulfills its undertaking under

the January, 1974, Disengagement Agreement to permit passage of all Israeli cargoes to and from Israeli ports through the Suez Canal.

6. The United States government agrees with Israel that the next agreement with Egypt should be a final peace agreement.

7. In case of an Egyptian violation of any of the provisions of the Agreement, the United States government is prepared to consult with Israel as to the significance of the violation and possible remedial action by the United States government.

8. The United States government will vote against any Security Council resolution which in its judgment affects or alters adversely the Agreement.

9. The United States government will not join in and will seek to prevent efforts by others to bring about consideration of proposals which it and Israel agree are detrimental to the interests of Israel.

10. In view of the long-standing U. S. commitment to the survival and security of Israel, the United States government will view with particular gravity threats to Israel's security or sovereignty by a world power. In support of this objective, the United States government will in the event of such threat consult promptly with the government of Israel with respect to what support, diplomatic or otherwise, or assistance it can lend to Israel in accordance with its constitutional practices.

11. The United States government and the government of Israel will, at the earliest possible time, and if possible, within two months after the signature of this document, conclude the contingency plan for a military supply operation to Israel in an emergency situation.

12. It is the United States government's position that Egyptian commitments under the Egypt-Israel Agreement, its implementation, validity and duration are not conditional upon any act or developments between the other Arab states and Israel. The United States government regards the Agreement as standing on its own.

13. The United States government shares the Israeli position that under existing political circumstances negotiations with Jordan will be directed toward an overall peace settlement.

14. In accordance with the principle of freedom of navigation on the high seas and free and unimpeded passage through and over straits connecting international waters, the United States government regards the Straits of Bab-el-Mandeb and the Strait of Gibraltar as international waterways. It will support Israel's right to free and unimpeded passage through such straits. Similarly, the United States government recognizes Israel's right to freedom of flights over the Red Sea and such straits and will support diplomatically the exercise of that right.

15. In the event that the United Nations Emergency Force or any other United Nations organ is withdrawn without the prior agreement of both parties to the Egypt-Israel Agreement and the United States before this Agreement is superseded by another agreement, it is the United States view that the Agreement shall remain binding in all its parts.

16. The United States and Israel agree that signature of the Protocol of the Egypt-Israel Agreement and its full entry into effect shall not take place before approval by the United States Congress of the U.S. role in connection with the surveillance and observation functions described in the Agreement and its Annex. The United States has informed the government of Israel that it has obtained the government of Egypt's agreement to the above.

### Secret Addendum
### on Arms Assistance

*Following is the text of the secret addendum to the Memorandum of Agreement between the United States and Israel:*

On the question of military and economic assistance to Israel, the following conveyed by the U.S. to Israel augments what the Memorandum of Agreement states.

The United States is resolved to continue to maintain Israel's defensive strength through the supply of advanced types of equipment, such as the F-16 aircraft. The United States government agrees to an early meeting to undertake a joint study of high technology and sophisticated items, including the Pershing ground-to-ground missiles with conventional warheads, with the view to giving a positive response. The U.S. administration will submit annually for approval by the U.S. Congress a request for military and economic assistance in order to help meet Israel's economic and military needs.

### U.S.-Israel Pact on Geneva

*From* The New York Times, *Thursday, September 18, 1975.*

*Following is the text of a previously unpublished memorandum of agreement between the United States and Israel dealing with the Geneva Conference:*

1. The Geneva peace conference will be reconvened at a time coordinated between the United States and Israel.

2. The United States will continue to adhere to its present policy with respect to the Palestine Liberation Organization, whereby it will not recognize or negotiate with the Palestine Liberation Organization so long as the Palestine Liberation Organization does not recognize Israel's right to exist and does not accept Security Council Resolutions 242 and 338. The United States Government will consult fully and seek to concert its position and strategy at the Geneva peace conference on this issue with the Government of Israel. Similarly, the United States will consult fully and seek to concert its position and strategy with Israel with regard to the participation of any other additional states. It is understood that the participation at a subsequent phase of the conference of any possible additional state, group or organization will require the agreement of all the initial participants.

3. The United States will make every effort to insure at the conference that all the substantive negotiations will be on a bilateral basis.

4. The United States will oppose and, if necessary, vote against any initiative in the Security Council to alter adversely the terms of reference of the Geneva peace conference or to change Resolutions 242 and 338 in ways which are incompatible with their original purpose.

5. The United States will seek to insure that the role of the cosponsors will be consistent with what was agreed in the memorandum of understanding between the United States Government and the Government of Israel of Dec. 20, 1973.

6. The United States and Israel will concert action to assure that the conference will be conducted in a manner consonant with the objectives of this document and with the declared purpose of the conference, namely the advancement of a negotiated peace between Israel and its neighbors.

*Memorandum of Assurances to Egypt*

*From* The New York Times, *Wednesday, September 17, 1975.*

1. The United States intends to make a serious effort to help bring about further negotiations between Syria and Israel, in the first instance through diplomatic channels.

2. In the event of an Israeli violation of the Agreement, the United States is prepared to consult with Egypt as to the significance of the violation and possible remedial action by the United States.

3. The United States will provide technical assistance to Egypt for the Egyptian Early-warning Station in the Sinai.

4. The United States reaffirms its desire to assist the economy of Egypt, subject to the approval of the United States Congress.

# Appendix Nine

*From* The New York Times, *Tuesday, September 2nd 1975*

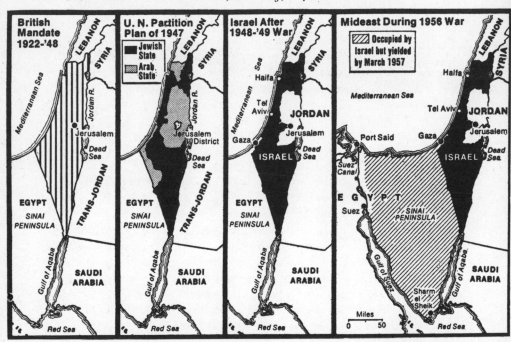

New accord allows Egyptian forces to advance to eastern edge of old U.N. zone set up in 1974, recover oil fields at Abu Rudeis in the far south and establish civilian rule in coastal strip on gulf under U.N. observation. Israelis are to withdraw from Gidi and Mitla Passes, and U.S. is to control early warning systems in them. (The New York Times/Sept. 2, 1975.)

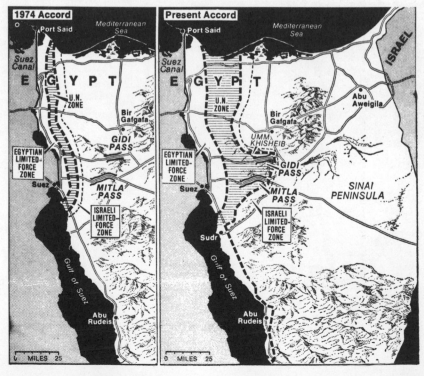

*From* The New York Times, *Sunday, September 7th 1975*

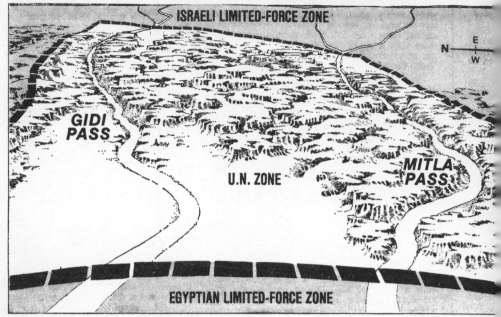

ISRAELI LIMITED-FORCE ZONE

GIDI PASS

U.N. ZONE

MITLA PASS

EGYPTIAN LIMITED-FORCE ZONE

Schematic drawing by Martin A

Map of Middle East as of May 1st 1976.

Israeli-Syrian Disengagement, May 1974.

# Appendix Ten
# Fulbright's 1980 Middle East Scenario

*(By J. William Fulbright)*

From *The Washington Star,* July 13, 1975

One morning in the early summer of 1980 I sat at my desk contemplating an invitation: "Dear Mr. Fulbright: The Young Americans for Peace and Justice in the Middle East invite you to be a featured speaker at their forthcoming rally on the Washington Monument grounds. As you may know, this rally is expected to be the climactic event in the three years' crusade to end American military involvement in the Middle East. An attendance of at least half a million concerned Americans is anticipated.

"In addition to popular folk singers and one of the nation's top rock bands, the program will feature five of the leading candidates for the presidential nomination at next month's Democratic Convention. All five were also candidates in 1976, and each will offer a plan for the extrication of the United States from the military quagmire in the Middle East. One of the candidates, hitherto regarded as an all-out supporter of Israel, will lead a ceremonial burning of the notorious 'letter of the 76' of May 1975, in which 76 senators had called for all-out military support of Israel. Although you are no longer in politics, we believe that your long interest in the Middle East entitles you to participate in an event which we feel sure will rock the White House to its foundation."

Momentarily undecided on whether to accept the invitation, I reflected on the events of the preceding five years:

In the course of the year 1975 and the first half of 1976, most of the Arab leaders stated publicly their willingness to accept Israel as a permanent Jewish state within its borders of 1967. Even the PLO leadership conceded privately that Palestine aspirations would have to be confined to the West Bank and the Gaza strip. Israel, however, with solid backing from the United States Congress, held out for "defensible" borders, the exact extent of which she was unprepared to define but which were generally understood to include the eastern part of Sinai, the Golan Heights, some parts of the West Bank with the right to establish Israeli military installations in the relinquished portion, and east Jerusalem, which was held to be "non-negotiable."

In the fall of 1976, following several abortive renewals of step-by-step diplomacy and the final collapse of the Geneva peace conference, the "Second Yom Kippur War"—or, as it is sometimes called, the "Ten Days' War"—burst upon the Middle East without warning. It is still not known whether the war began with an Arab surprise attack or an Israeli pre-emptive attack, but despite fearful casualties and the havoc wrought by several missile strikes on Tel Aviv and even heavier missile strikes on Cairo and Damascus, the Israeli Army won a stunning victory on all fronts after 10 days of hard fighting. On the tenth day the Soviet-American mediation team commissioned by the United Nations Security Council secured a cease-fire, with Israeli forces positioned just outside of Cairo, Damascus, and Amman.

On the third day of the war the Arab oil-producing states imposed an embargo on all NATO countries. France and Portugal managed to escape the effects of the embargo by promptly denouncing the NATO treaty and withdrawing from the Atlantic alliance. The embargo continued after the cease-fire, and by the third month the affected Western nations were in severe economic crisis. Unemployment in West Germany reached 10 percent, and in Italy, following civil disorders in Rome and Milan, the government resigned and was replaced by a popular front of Communists and left-wing Socialists.

The United States, still producing 60 percent of its own oil requirements, was least affected. Unemployment held steady at 15 percent, but the United States government found it necessary to repudiate previous emergency oil-sharing agreements with its allies.

On the first day of the fifth month of the embargo, the President of the United States went on national television to announce that at that very moment United States marines and paratroopers were landing on the Persian Gulf coast of Saudi Arabia and Kuwait to occupy the coastal oil fields. The action, he said, was being carried out in accordance with a long standing Pentagon contingency plan, and in strict compliance with the emergency procedures of the War Powers Act.

The oil fields, the President emphasized, would be occupied only temporarily—"until the oil producers come to their senses"—and the oil would be extracted and sold by the occupying authority as an "international public trust." Several days later Congress adopted a resolution applauding the President's action. The resolution was carried by a vote of 435 to 0 in the House and by a vote of 98 to 2 in the Senate.

Unfortunately, the landings were not a complete surprise. Through an inexplicable breach of security, the Saudis and Kuwaitis had gained 24 hours' advance notice of the landings, and by the time the marines and paratroopers were on the ground gigantic oil fires were raging across the Ghawar and Burgan fields, and, to the amazement of the occupying force, on the surface of the Persian Gulf as the result of the demolition of sub-surface oil facilities.

Through the skill and heroic efforts of highly trained oil fire-fighting teams flown in from Texas, most of the fires were extinguished within three months and within another month, by mid-1977, production was back to half of its pre-embargo capacity and rapidly increasing.

It was not until the fall of 1977, however, that Persian Gulf oil was again reaching world markets, owing to the blockage of the Strait of Hormuz by two sunken supertankers which had been torpedoed by PT boats manned by Arab terrorists.

The "International Petroleum Authority" which had been set up to run the oil fields—with membership consisting of the United States, Bolivia, Paraguay and the Dominican Republic—announced in January 1978 that, owing to the costs of security, reconstruction, and anti-terrorist operations, it would be necessary to raise the price of oil $1 a barrel above the OPEC price of 1975. This, however, was only a temporary measure, it was announced, and the Authority, as required by its charter, would continue to treat the oil it extracted and sold as an "international public trust."

An Arab summit conference held at Khartoum in the winter of 1978 resulted in a declaration of "jehad"—or holy war—against America and American interests all over the world. The Khartoum declaration also formally revoked previous offers to settle with Israel on the basis of the borders of 1967, insisting instead on the original United Nations partition plan of 1947.

In the months that followed, a series of terrorist attacks against Americans occurred in various parts of the world. Three American embassies were bombed and, despite new security measures, two

American aircraft were hijacked on trans-Atlantic flights. In the spring of 1978 bombings occurred in Chicago, New York, and in National Airport in Washington, D.C., all with substantial loss of life. After each of these outrages, the clandestine radio of the terrorist "Arab Liberation Organization" claimed responsibility.

The United States government responded to these provocations in several ways. After an extended, acrimonious debate, the Congress by narrow majorities authorized the President to send 50,000 additional troops to bolster our security forces in the Persian Gulf, and additional naval units were sent to patrol the Strait of Hormuz.

New measures also were taken to deal with domestic terrorism. Acting on the report of a special study mission which had been sent to Israel to study airport security, the Federal Aviation Agency announced that all passengers on domestic flights would be required to check in two hours ahead of flight time for security checks. Congress also adopted legislation imposing a mandatory death penalty for all persons convicted of acts of terrorism.

Throughout the years 1978 and 1979, despite repeated pleas by the President for "patience" and "fortitude," public support for the administration's Middle East policy waned steadily. In the trail of public opinion, congressional opinion followed. The President's request for an additional 30,000 men for the Middle East security force encountered rough sledding in Congress. In April 1979, the "Young Americans for Peace and Justice in the Middle East" announced still another march on Washington. In the summer, the Senate Foreign Relations Committee opened hearings on a bill to repeal the "Persian Gulf Resolution."

By the end of the year the polls showed the President's popularity at a new low of 27 percent, while support for Israel stood only slightly higher at 29 percent. A special caucus of liberal Democrats in the House and Senate adopted a cautiously worded resolution calling on Israel—"for the sake of world peace"—to "consider" whether it could withdraw to the 1947 partition line in exchange for an American guarantee.

The Middle East became the dominant issue in the 1980 presidential primaries. In an obvious effort to influence the election, the Arab Liberation Organization announced in February a new worldwide offensive against the United States. There followed terrorist outbreaks in Houston and Boston, and a hand-fired missile of apparent Soviet origin did heavy damage to the American embassy in Tokyo.

In the wake of these events the incumbent President's popularity plunged still farther, and support for Israel dropped to a new low of 23 percent. By the time of the California primary in June, all of the Democratic candidates had called upon Israel to withdraw to the 1947 partition line. "It is no more than morality requires," said *The Washington Post* in an editorial.

So matters stood as I penned my reply to the Young Americans for Peace and Justice in the Middle East.

"Dear Mr. Chairman: I regret very much that I must decline your invitation to speak at your forthcoming rally. As you know, I am retired from politics and I think it best to leave crusades to the young and to others still actively involved. Furthermore, I must confess that I do not fully concur in the stated aims of your organization. Although I favor a prompt and orderly American military withdrawal from the Middle East, I still adhere to my long-standing conviction that Israel is entitled to a secure national existence within its borders of 1967. I am aware that this view is generally considered outmoded, but I adhere to it in the belief that the United States must honor its solemn commitments.

"Finally, at a time when the executive branch of our government has been greatly weakened by the cumulative effects of Vietnam, Watergate and the Middle East crisis, it seems to me that some of us ought to stand by the President.

"Sincerely yours, J. W. Fulbright."

# Acknowledgments
# and Sources

I am in debt to a number of people for the idea of this book. I had wished for some time to write a study of American policy in the Middle East. In early 1975, Dr. Samuel P. Huntington, Frank G. Thomson Professor of Government at Harvard University and Associate Director of its Center for International Affairs, suggested the focus. Professor Huntington asked me to write, for *Foreign Policy* magazine, a major article on Secretary Kissinger's step-by-step diplomacy in the Middle East. I received subsequent encouragement from Mr. Warren Manshel, who with Professor Huntington is coeditor of *Foreign Policy*, and thereupon I decided to expand the project into a book. Mr. Richard Holbrooke, managing editor of *Foreign Policy*, provided further focus and many helpful suggestions throughout the project.

As I explained in the preface, I sought out primary sources for the material in this book. Not all of the quotations, of course, come from the written records of the participants. For example, I have also quoted remarks which Dr. Kissinger (and other participants in the narrative) uttered to aides or friends and which were subsequently repeated to me by those sources. Wherever possible, I have substantiated such quotations from more than one source. Dr. Kissinger often qualifies his

266

sentences with such phrases as, "What is important is that . . ." or "The important thing is that . . ." For readability, I have simply excised such phrases throughout the narrative, without doing violence to his meaning or to that of any personage in this book.

I have also consulted much of the public record bearing upon my subject, and I regret that the pressures to bring this book to press do not permit me the time to compile a suitable bibliography.

The list of acknowledgments that follows is not exhaustive. I am equally grateful to those sources who, by necessity, must remain unnamed, and to those who, by inadvertence, I have neglected. I thank all who provided large or small portions of information and those others whose innumerable kindnesses facilitated my task.

*Washington, D. C., Department of State:* The Hon. Henry A. Kissinger, Secretary of State; The Hon. Joseph J. Sisco, Undersecretary of State for Political Affairs; The Hon. Alfred L. (Roy) Atherton, Jr., Assistant Secretary of State for Near Eastern and South Asian Affairs; Mr. Harold H. Saunders, former Deputy Assistant Secretary of State for Near Eastern and South Asian Affairs, at present Director of the Bureau of Intelligence and Research.

Also, Ambassador Robert P. Anderson, formerly Secretary Kissinger's spokesman and at present U.S. Ambassador to the Kingdom of Morocco; Mr. Winston Lord, Director, Planning and Coordination Staff; Mr. Walter Smith, Director of the Office of Arab-Israeli Affairs, and his deputy, Mr. Wat Cluverius; Mr. Marshal Wylie, former Director, Office of North African Affairs, and at present Chief of the U.S. Interests Section at Baghdad; Mr. Lawrence Semakis of the Office of Egyptian Affairs; Mr. David Korn, Director, Office of Iraq, Jordan, Syria Affairs; Mr. Francois Dickman, Director, Office of Persian Gulf States Affairs; Mr. William Eagleton, former Chief of the U.S. Interests Section, Algiers, and at present Director, Office of Cyprus Affairs; Mr. Philip Stoddard, Deputy Director, Bureau of Intelligence and Research; Mr. Edward Djerijian, former aide to Undersecretary Sisco and at present U.S. Consul General at Bordeaux; Mr. Francis Wisner, Public Affairs Officer, and subsequently Assistant to Undersecretary Sisco; Mr. George Sherman, Public Affairs Officer, Bureau of Near Eastern and South Asian Affairs; Mr. Matthew van Oder and Linda Broderick, of Mr. Sherman's staff; Helen Kamer, Private Secretary to Assistant Secretary of State Atherton; Mr. Tain Tomkins, former Assistant to Mr. Atherton; Mr. Edward Abington, Assistant to Mr. Atherton; and numerous other officials of the Department of State.

Also, Mr. Robert Oakley of the staff of the National Security Council, and his deputy Mr. Arthur Houghton; Mr. James Noyes, Deputy Assistant Secretary for International Security Affairs (Near East etc.), and Colonel Thomas Pianka, USA, of the Department of Defense; and several other officials of the Department of Defense and the Central Intelligence Agency who cannot be named.

*The United States Congress.* Senator Mike Mansfield, of Montana, Majority Leader, U.S. Senate; Senator Edward M. Kennedy, of Massachusetts; Senator James A. McClure, of Idaho; Senator James Abourezk, of South Dakota. Also, Mr. Richard M. Moose and Mr. Seth Tillman, of the staff of the Committee on Foreign Relations, U.S. Senate; Mr. Robert E. Hunter, Assistant for Foreign Affairs to Senator Edward M. Kennedy; Mr. Dale S. De Haan, Counsel, U.S. Senate Subcommittee on Refugees, and Assistant to Senator Edward M. Kennedy; Mr. Richard Perle, Assistant for National Security Affairs to Senator Henry Jackson of Washington; Mr. Peter Lakeland, Assistant to Senator Jacob Javits of New York; Mr. Scott Cohen, Assistant to Senator Charles Percy of Illinois; Mr. Daniel Spiegel, Assistant to Senator Hubert H. Humphrey of Minnesota; Mr. Mark Talisman, Assistant to Congressman Charles Vanik of Ohio; and several other Senators, Congressmen, and Congressional assistants.

*Foreign diplomatic missions.* Their Excellencies: Dr. Ashraf Ghorbal, Ambassador of the Arab Republic of Egypt; Sabah al-Kabbani, Ambassador of the Syrian Arab Republic; Abdullah Salah, Ambassador of the Hashemite Kingdom of Jordan; Saeed Ahmad Ghobash, Ambassador of the United Arab Emirates; Simcha Dinitz, Ambassador of the State of Israel; Ardeshir Zahedi, Ambassador of Iran; and Dr. Clovis Maksoud, Special Ambassador of the League of Arab States.

Also Mr. Riad Sabri, Minister-Counsellor of the Embassy of the Hashemite Kingdom of Jordan; Mr. Mohammed Hakki, Minister-Counsellor for Information, Embassy of Egypt; Mr. Moshe Arad, Minister-Counsellor for Information, Embassy of Israel; Mr. Mordechai Shalev, Minister-Counsellor, Embassy of Israel (in November, 1974); Mr. Ihab Wahba, First Secretary, and Mr. Hamdi

Saleh Abdel Wahab, Third Secretary, Embassy of Egypt; Mr. Michael Y. Hamarneh, Information Officer, Embassy of Jordan; Mr. Edmund Ghareeb, press adviser to the Ambassador of the United Arab Emirates; and several other foreign diplomats in Washington.

*The press.* Mr. Bernard Gwertzman, Diplomatic Correspondent, *The New York Times;* Mr. Philip Geylin, Editor, Editorial Page, *The Washington Post;* Mr. Arnaud de Borchgrave, Senior Editor and Chief Foreign Correspondent, *Newsweek* magazine; Mr. Joseph Kraft, nationally syndicated columnist; Mr. Stanley Karnow, former Foreign Editor of *The New Republic,* at present of the German Marshall Fund and a nationally syndicated columnist; Mr. Lawrence Mosher, of *The National Observer;* Mr. Carlton Spriggs, Assistant Librarian, *The New York Times* bureau; and numerous other members of the Washington press corps.

Also, The Hon. Raymond Hare, former U.S. Ambassador to Egypt and Turkey and former Deputy Undersecretary of State for Political Affairs; The Hon. Parker T. Hart, former U.S. Ambassador to Saudi Arabia and Turkey and former Assistant Secretary of State for Near Eastern and South Asian Affairs; The Hon. Lucius D. Battle, former U.S. Ambassador to Egypt and former Assistant Secretary of State for Near Eastern and South Asian Affairs; The Hon. Charles Yost, of the Brookings Institution, former U.S. Ambassador to Syria, Morocco, and the United Nations; The Hon. Lewis Dean Brown, President of the Middle East Institute, former U.S. Ambassador to the Hashemite Kingdom of Jordan and special envoy to Lebanon; and The Hon. James E. Akins, former U. S. Ambassador to the Kingdom of Saudi Arabia.

Also, The Hon. J. William Fulbright, former U.S. Senator from Arkansas and former Chairman, Committee on Foreign Relations of the U.S. Senate; Mr. William B. Quandt, formerly of the staff of the National Security Council, at present Professor of Political Science, University of Pennsylvania; Dr. Hisham Sharabi, Professor of History, Georgetown University, and Editor, *Journal of Palestine Studies;* Mr. Henry Owen, Director of Policy Studies, Brookings Institution; Dr. Robert E. Osgood, Dean of the School of Advanced International Studies, The Johns Hopkins University, and Dr. John Duke Anthony of the same School and of *The Middle East Journal;* Mr. Kermit Roosevelt, President, Kermit Roosevelt and Associates, Inc.; Mr. Morris J. Amitay, Executive Director, American Israel Public Affairs Committee; and others.

*The United Nations.* His Excellency Sherif Abdel Hamid Sharaf, Ambassador and Permanent Representative of the Hashemite Kingdom of Jordan; and several others.

*Egypt.* His Excellency Mohammed Anwar al-Sadat, President of the Arab Republic of Egypt (in January 1974, and previously); His Excellency Ambassador Tahsin Bashir, former Spokesman for President Sadat; The Hon. Hermann F. Eilts, U.S. Ambassador to Egypt; Mr. Mohammed Hassanein Heikal, former Minister of Information and former Editor of *Al Ahram;* Sir Philip Adams, Ambassador of the Court of St. James's; Colonel "Tony" Lewis, Military Attaché, and Mr. David Barwell, Information Officer, Embassy of the United Kingdom, Cairo; Mr. Ahmed Bahaaedine, Mr. Mohammed Sid Ahmed, Mr. Hamdi Fuad, Mr. Mohammed Salmawy, Dr. Louis Awad, all of *Al Ahram* newspaper; Mr. John B. Craig, Economic Officer, U.S. Embassy, Cairo; Mr. Mustafa Amin, Editor and Publisher, *Akhbar Al Yom,* Cairo; Mr. Henry Tanner, *The New York Times,* Cairo; Mr. Wilton Wynn, *Time* magazine, Cairo; Miss Nadia Rizk, Chief Librarian, Research Library, U.S. Embassy, Cairo; and numerous other sources in Egypt.

*Syria.* His Excellency Hafez al-Assad, President of the Syrian Arab Republic; His Excellency M. Imadi, Minister of Economy; Mr. Assad Elias, President Assad's interpreter; The Hon. Richard Murphy, U.S. Ambassador to Syria; His Excellency M. Rouillon, Ambassador of France; H. E. Vojislav Pekić, Ambassador of the Federal Socialist Republic of Yugoslavia; Mr. R. L. (Ray) Balfour, Chargé d'Affaires (September 1975), Embassy of the United Kingdom, Damascus; Mr. Mohammed Nashashibi, Secretary General, Executive Committee, Palestine Liberation Organization; Colonel Angus Mundy, Defense Attaché, U.S. Embassy, Damascus; Mr. James R. Hooper, Second Secretary, U.S. Embassy; the officials of the Ministry of Information, who were most helpful; and numerous other sources in Syria.

*Jordan.* His Majesty Hussein ibn Talal al-Hashem, King of the Hashemite Kingdom of Jordan; His Excellency Zeid al-Rifai, Prime Minister, Minister of Foreign Affairs and Minister of Defense; His Excellency Yenal Hikmat, Chief of Royal Protocol, Royal Palace, Amman, and Mr. Fayez Tarawneh, Assistant Chief of Royal Protocol; Mr. Jamil Nadhif, Private Secretary to the Prime Minister; The Hon. Thomas Pickering, U.S. Ambassador to Jordan; Mr. George Thompson, Public Affairs Officer, and Mr. James Callahan, Cultural

Officer, U.S. Embassy, Amman; Mr. John Halaby, journalist, Amman; and numerous other sources in Jordan.

*Saudi Arabia.* His Majesty Faisal ibn Abdel-Aziz ibn Abdel-Rahman al-Faisal al-Saud, late King of Saudi Arabia (interviewed in December 1973). Also (for interviews in December 1973 and January 1974) Their Excellencies Sheikh Ahmed Zaki al-Yamani, Minister of Petroleum and Mineral Resources; Hisham Nazer, Minister of State and Director of the Central Planning Agency; and Sheikh Ali Reza, Minister of State and at present Ambassador of the Kingdom of Saudi Arabia to the United States. Also (during the same period) Mr. Mansoor M. Khraiji, Assistant Chief of Royal Protocol and interpreter for His Majesty King Faisal; Mr. Frank Jungers, Chairman and Chief Executive Officer of the Arabian American Oil Company; Mr. Reda Nazer, of Aramco; Mr. Robert Ruggiero, former Public Affairs Officer of the U. S. Embassy, Jidda; Mr. Abdel Hamid Derhally, Director of the Central Planning Organization, Jidda; and numerous other sources in Saudi Arabia.

*Lebanon.* Mr. Christopher Ross, Information Officer, U.S. Embassy, Beirut; Miss Elsa Hallac, Mr. Ross's secretary; Mr. Thomas Carolan, former Political Officer, U.S. Embassy, at present at the State Department; Dr. Walid Khalidi, Professor of Political Studies, American University of Beirut, and Executive Secretary, Institute for Palestine Studies, Beirut. Also (for interviews in October 1972) Mr. Salah Khalef ("Abu Iyad") of Fatah, Mr. Shafik al-Hout of the Palestine Liberation Organization; and numerous other sources in Lebanon.

*Israel.* Mr. Yitzhak Rabin, Prime Minister; Mr. Yigal Allon, Minister of Foreign Affairs; Mr. Shimon Peres, Minister of Defense; Mr. Haim Zadok, Minister of Justice; Mr. Schlomo Hillel, Minister of Police; General Mordechai Gur, Chief of Staff; Major General (Res.) Mattityahu Peled, of Tel Aviv University; and Lieutenant Doron of the Israeli army, who accompanied me on a visit to the Golan Heights. Also Mrs. Golda Meir, former Prime Minister (interviewed in June, 1972); Mr. Mordechai Gazit, Director General of the Israeli Foreign Ministry (interviewed in May 1972) and at present Ambassador to France; and numerous other officials and nonofficials in Israel and the occupied territories.

*The academic community.* Dr. William E. Griffith, Ford Professor of Political Science, Massachusetts Institute of Technology; Dr. Stanley Hoffmann, Professor of Government, Harvard University; Dr. Robert R. Bowie, Clarence Dillon Professor of International Affairs, Harvard;

Dr. Benjamin H. Brown, Adviser to the Fellows, Center for International Affairs, Harvard; Dr. Guido Goldman, Special Assistant to the Dean of the Faculty of Arts and Sciences, for International Affairs, Harvard; Dr. A. J. Meyer, Professor of Middle Eastern Studies, Harvard; Dr. Thomas Stauffer, Lecturer in Economics, Harvard; Dr. Oleg Grabar, Professor of Fine Arts, Harvard; Dr. Yair Evron, of the Hebrew University, Jerusalem, and Research Fellow (1975–76) Program for Science and International Affairs of the Center for International Affairs, Harvard; Ms Trudy Rubin, Fellow (1975–76) Center for International Affairs, Harvard; Mr. Adnan Abu-Odeh, former Minister of Information and Chief of the Royal Court, Hashemite Kingdom of Jordan, and Fellow (1975–76) Center for International Affairs, Harvard; Mr. Marvin Feuerwerger, former Graduate Student Associate of the Center for International Affairs, Harvard; Mr. Maury Feld, Librarian, Center for International Affairs, Harvard; Sally Cox, Executive Secretary, Center for International Affairs, Harvard; and Lisa Nekich, Barbara Talhouni and Moyra Clarke of the Center staff. Also, Barbro Ek, Assistant to the Director of the Center for Middle Eastern Studies, Harvard; and Edna Ridner, secretary to Professor Griffith, MIT.

Also Dr. Malcolm Kerr, Professor of Political Science, University of California at Los Angeles; Georgiana Stevens, a writer on Middle East Affairs; Dr. Bruce Mazlish, Professor of History, MIT; Mr. Dennis Mullin, Regional Editor (Middle East), *U.S. News and World Report;* Jean Allison, of the staff of the Center for International Affairs, Harvard; and Dr. Nahum Goldmann, President of the World Jewish Congress; and Mr. Odeh Aburdene, of the First National Bank of Chicago.

I am also grateful to the staff of *Foreign Policy* quarterly for their assistance and good humor in preparing the portions of this book published in that magazine—Pamela Gilfond, Ruth Kiker, Christopher Whipple, and Will Wetzel. I am grateful to Mr. Bruce Lee, Editor of Reader's Digest Press and Nancy Kelly of Reader's Digest Press, for their constant encouragement and suggestions, and to my literary representative, Mr. Don Congdon, of Harold Matson Company, Inc., for negotiating the contract. My thanks also to Mr. Edward T. Thompson, Editor-in-Chief of Reader's Digest magazine, and to Mr. John D. Panitza, Senior Staff Editor (Europe) and Mr. Denis Fodor, Senior Editor, European Bureau (Paris) of the magazine, for their encouragement of my project.

Finally, I must thank my mother, Emilie C. Sheehan, for sheltering, feeding and putting up with me whilst I wrote this book; and my secretary, Donna Gorski, whose assistance and resourcefulness whilst preparing and typing the manuscript, all the time protecting me from mundane intrusions, were beyond price.

# Index

# Index

Abdel Aziz ibn Saud, 63, 64, 65

Abdullah, Emir of Jordan,
139–140

Abu Dhabi, 12, 202

*After the Guns Fall Silent* (Sid
Ahmed), 208–210

Agnew, Spiro, 38

Akins, James E., 83, 116

*Al Ahram*, 51, 112

Alawites, 93, 128

Algeria (*see also* Boumedienne,
Houari), 85–87, 202

*Al Goumhouriya*, 44

*Al Hawadess*, 133

Allon, Yigal, 9, 101, 103, 105,
118, 125, 160–161, 162,
165, 174, 181–182, 188

American Broadcasting System
(A.B.C.), 3

American Israel Public Affairs
Committee (AIPAC), 174

Anderson, Robert P., 2, 5, 9

Arabian American Oil Company
(Aramco), 66, 67

Arab Legion, 139, 141

Arabs, *see names of individual
Arab countries and leaders*

Arafat, Yasir, 85, 100, 148,
211–212
at U.N. General Assembly,
151–154

Assad, Hafez al-, 93, 101, 138
Kissinger and, 7, 10, 94–97,
115, 117, 119, 120–121,
122–128, 131, 159, 180,
196–197, 212
Nixon and, 133

Associated Press, 3

Atherton, Alfred L. (Roy), Jr., x,
xi, 2, 5, 99, 101, 105, 117,
160, 168, 176, 182, 183
evaluation of, 170–172

Atherton, A.L. (*continued*)
  negotiations conducted by,
    188–189
Atherton, Betty, 170, 171
Avnery, Uri, 210

Ba'ath (Resurrection) party,
    Syria, 93, 94, 117
Bab al-Mandab, 82
Ball, George, 165, 166
Banna, Hassan al-, 43
Bar-Lev line, 32, 57
Ben Bella, Ahmed, 86
Berger, Marilyn, 3, 9–10, 51n.,
    186–188
Bernadotte, Count Folke, 146
Black September group, 144–146
Borchgrave, Arnaud de, 26
Boumedienne, Houari, 85–88
Bourguiba, Habib ben Ali-, 42
Bouteflika, Abdul Aziz, 34, 35,
    88
Brandon, Henry, 203
Brezhnev, Leonid, 27, 37, 97,
    122
  Sadat and, 90, 91
Bruce, David K. E., 165
Bruzonsky, Mark, 216n.
Brzezinski, Zbigniew, 166
Bundy, McGeorge, 165

Central Intelligence Agency
    (C.I.A.), 2, 30, 32, 68, 141,
    169, 178, 198, 216
*Chicago Tribune, The*, 3
China, 15, 27, 54, 55, 203
Chou En-lai, 27, 78
*Christian Science Monitor*, 3, 67
Churchill, Winston, 43, 139

Dayan, Moshe, 101, 102, 145n.,
    162, 174
  Arab-Israeli peace and, 83-84,

108-111, 122
  demand for arms by, 82–83
  interview with, 36–37
de Gaulle, Charles, 9, 31, 166
Dillon, C. Douglas, 165
Dinitz, Simcha, 5, 8, 9, 84, 101,
    110, 134n., 154–155, 160,
    213
Dinitz, Mrs. Simcha, 183

Eban, Abba, 31, 101, 110, 112,
    131, 174
  Geneva peace talks and, 106,
    107
Egypt (*see also* Nasser, Gamal
    Abdel; Sadat, Anwar al-),
    161
  American technology and, 77,
    132, 202, 206
  British occupation of, 42–44
  buildup before Yom Kippur
    War by, 30–32, 55, 56
  economic conditions in,
    194–196, 209
  Geneva talks and, 106, 108
  internal pressures on, 49, 50,
    60, 112
  Nixon in, 131–133
  Revolutionary Command
    Council in, 44
  Saudi Arabia and, 68
  Sinai disengagement
    agreement of 1974 and, 13,
    109–112
  Sinai disengagement
    agreement of 1975 and, 1,
    13, 148, 149, 150, 154,
    156–159, 184–190
  Soviet relations with, 19–20,
    22, 24, 39, 55–56, 60, 65,
    89–91, 172, 204–205
  Soviet supplies to, 11, 18–20,

69, 77, 82, 142
Suez Canal crossed by, 32, 56,
    57, 161
Syria's rift with, 196, 202
Third Army of, 36–42 *passim,*
    50, 51, 70, 80, 112
*Egyptian Gazette,* 9
Eilts, Hermann, 168, 188
Elazar, David, 103, 110, 111
Eliav, Arieh, 210

Fahmy, Dr. Ismail, 41–42, 50,
    51, 88, 92, 105, 107, 112,
    116, 148, 157–158, 185,
    186, 188
Faisal, King of Saudi Arabia (*see*
    *also* Saudi Arabia), 88, 92,
    149
    character of, 64
    Communism and, 64–65, 69
    Kissinger and, 62–63, 66, 69,
        70–73, 75, 83, 128, 164
    murder of, 164
    oil embargo and, 26, 58–59,
        66–68, 69, 71–72, 75, 92,
        102, 116
    Sadat and, 68–69, 76, 195
Fanon, Frantz, 86, 87
Farouk, King of Egypt, 43, 44,
    185
*fedayin, see* Palestinians
Ford, Gerald R., 6, 135, 162,
    168, 174, 191
    Gromyko and, 167
    Jordan and, 148, 151
    Rabin and, 159, 177, 216n.
    Sadat and, 133, 133n.-134n.,
        176–177, 206
*Foreign Policy,* x, 133n., 216n.
Franjieh, Suleiman, 100–101
Free Officers movement, 43, 46–47
Front of the Faithful, 183, 184

Fulbright, J. William, 145n.-146n.,
    168, 174

Gamasy, General Mohammed
    Abdel Ghany al-, 80–81,
    111, 112, 117, 157–158,
    185, 186, 188
Gazit, Mordechai, 178
Geneva conference of December
    1973 (*see also* Kissinger, Dr.
    Henry A., Geneva peace
    talks and), 13, 71, 75, 81,
    92, 103n., 115
    Egypt and, 106, 108
    Israelis and, 101–105, 106,
        107, 108
    Jordanians and, 85, 99–100,
        106, 108
    Palestinians and, 84–85, 88,
        96, 106, 108
    reconvention of, 161, 166,
        167, 172, 177, 191, 192
    Syrians and, 95–97, 101, 106
Geneva Convention:
    on prisoners of war, 101, 104
    on settlements in occupied
        territories, 193n.-194n.,
        216n.
Ghorbal, Dr. Ashraf, 17–18
Gidi pass, *see* Mitla and Gidi
    passes
Glubb, Sir John Bago (Glubb
    Pasha), 139–140
Golan, Matti, 80–81, 124n.
Golan Heights, 57, 94, 117,
    129–130, 133, 137, 207
    agreement reached on, 127
    Assad, Kissinger and, 10, 97,
        101, 115, 116, 121,
        122–127, 131, 180
    Israel and, 118, 121–122, 124,
        126, 131, 193, 194, 196

Golan Heights (continued)
  Syria and, 10, 97, 101, 115,
    116, 121–127, 133, 180,
    194, 196
Gomaa, Sharawi, 46–48, 91
Griffith, William E., 205
Gromyko, Andrei, 121, 167, 207
Gur, General Mordechai, 117,
    118, 125, 160, 178, 182
Gwertzman, Bernard, 2,
    133n.-134n., 181

Haaretz, 155, 165
Hadith, 74
Harriman, W. Averell, 165
Hassan, Crown Prince of Jordan,
    99
Hassan II, King, 42
Heikal, Mohammed Hassanein,
    23–25, 112, 194–195
  Kissinger and, 51–61
Hillel, Shlomo, 182
Hoagland, Jim, 145n.
Hoffmann, Stanley, 166, 203
Hussein, King of Jordan (see also
    Jordan), 59, 85, 94, 96,
    98–100, 102, 133, 159, 181,
    214
  civil war and, 143–144
  at Rabat conference, 148–149
  as a ruler, 140–141
  U.S. relations with, 136, 138,
    141, 147, 148, 176, 197–198
  Yom Kippur War and, 99, 147
Iffat, Queen (King Faisal's wife), 64
Iraq, 27, 69, 77, 202, 205
Irgun Zvai Leumi (Jewish
    terrorist group), 146
Islamic Congress, 44
Islamic Socialism, 86
Ismail, Hafez, 23–26
Israel (see also Jews; Knesset;

Meir, Golda; Rabin,
    Yitzhak; Zionism), 24, 71
  air force reprisals against
    Palestinians, 145,
    145n.-146n.
  arms and supplies from U.S.
    to, 11, 14, 15, 18, 20–21,
    24, 69, 69n.-70n., 82, 83,
    90, 111–112, 114, 146n.,
    165, 178, 191–192, 198–199
  economic conditions in,
    216–217
  elections in, 81, 84, 107, 108
  final settlement terms and,
    206–207
  Geneva talks and, 13,
    101–105, 106, 107, 108
  Golan Heights and, 118,
    121–122, 124, 126, 131,
    193, 194
  intelligence system of, 126,
    146, 158, 161
  internal pressures on, 49, 83,
    104, 112
  Jordan and, 100, 136–138, 147
  1948 war and, 140
  political changes in, 117, 127
  raids against Egypt by, 19
  "Rogers Plan" and, 16
  settlements in occupied
    territories by, 192–193,
    193n.-194n., 216n.
  Sinai disengagement
    agreement of 1974 and, 13,
    109–112
  Sinai disengagement
    agreement of 1975 and, 1,
    13, 148, 149, 150, 154–156,
    159–163, 177–178, 184–192,
    202
  Six-Day War and, 11, 13
  six points and, 50, 78–79

Suez Canal and, 17, 19, 36, 40, 58, 78, 84, 100, 109–112
U.S. relations with, 13–14, 51, 53, 56, 58, 65, 151, 155, 178, 191–192, 207
U.S.-Soviet strategic contest and, 21n.-22n., 32, 34
Israeli Council for Israeli-Palestinian Peace, 210
Iyyad, Abu Ali, 144–145
Jamil, General Nadji, 124
Jerusalem, Israel, 1, 2, 8, 16, 59, 83, 107, 193, 207
  Faisal on, 74–75
  Jordan and, 99, 147
Jews (see also Zionism), 70n., 139, 141, 152
  American lobby for, 33, 34, 49–50, 59, 60, 166, 168, 173, 174, 176, 197, 201–202
  Faisal on, 71, 74–75
  immigration into Israel by, 24, 71
  Kissinger's relation with and feelings about, 13–14, 57n., 59, 114, 131, 163, 173
  Nixon reelection and, 22n.
  Russian, 31, 71
Johnson, Lyndon B., 20, 65
Jordan (see also Hussein, King of Jordan), 26–27, 102, 160, 202
  civil war in, 143–144, 196
  disengagement of troops and, 99–100, 147, 181
  Geneva talks and, 85, 99–100, 106, 108
  history of, 138–140, 141
  Palestinians and, 99, 102, 136, 138, 139–140, 141, 142–146, 152, 181–182, 215

Six-Day War and, 11, 142
Syrian alliance with, 196, 202
Syrian attack on, 94, 136–138
U.S. alliance with, 64–65, 69
Jungers, Frank, 66–67

Kalb, Bernard, 3, 21n.-22n., 137–138
Kalb, Marvin, 21n.-22n., 137–138
Keating, Kenneth, 101, 160, 168
Kenan, Amos, 210
Kendall, Donald, 25
Kennerly, David Hume, 2
Kerr, Malcolm, 166
Khaddam, Abdel Halim, 95, 121, 125, 127n.
Khrushchev, Nikita, 45, 91
Kissinger (Kalb and Kalb), 21n.-22n., 137–138
Kissinger, Dr. Henry, A., x, xi, 1, 6, 32
  Arab policy of, 13–14, 51, 76–77, 87, 113–115, 202, 216
  arms to Israel and, 14, 15, 18, 20, 21, 25–26, 69n.-70n., 82, 165, 200
  Assad and, 7, 10, 94–97, 115, 117, 119, 120–121, 122–128, 131, 159, 180, 196–197, 212
  balance of power shift and, 12–13, 21, 32, 35, 59–60
  Boumedienne and, 85, 87–88
  chronology of missions of, 13
  endurance of, 8, 62, 127, 201
  evaluation of Middle East policy of, 201–206, 217
  Faisal and, 62–63, 66, 70–73, 75, 83, 115, 128, 164
  Franjieh and, 100–101
  Geneva peace talks and, 13,

Kissinger, Dr. Henry (*continued*)
  71, 75, 81, 84–85, 92,
  96–97, 100, 101–104,
  106–108, 114, 147
  Golan Heights negotiations
    and, 13, 117–127, 129–131
  Heikal and, 51–61
  Hussein and, 98–100, 159
  Ismail, Nixon and, 23–26
  Jewish lobby and, 33, 34,
    49–50, 59, 60, 166, 173,
    174, 176, 201–202
  Jewishness of, 18, 27–28, 48,
    73, 120, 122, 173
  meeting with Arab ministers
    by, 27–28, 34–36, 55
  Meir and, 9, 101–102,
    104–105, 115, 118, 121–122,
    128, 162
  military alert in U.S. and,
    37–38
  as Nobel peace prize
    recipient, 54
  Palestinian problem and, 13,
    49, 101, 113, 148, 167, 202,
    212–213
  as policymaker for Middle
    East, 21, 26n., 35, 54, 76–77
  reassessment of Middle East
    policy and, 165–168,
    172–174
  "Rogers Plan" and, 16, 17, 18,
    21, 28
  on role he played in Middle
    East, 7, 27, 52–54
  Sadat and, 4, 6, 39, 42, 48–51,
    61, 70, 84, 88–89, 92,
    109–112, 117, 119, 128,
    131, 148, 149–150, 156–159,
    184–185, 187–189, 194, 202,
    205–206, 212
  secret talks and, 24, 25, 80–82

  Sinai disengagement of 1974
    and, 13, 109–112
  Sinai disengagement of 1975
    and, 1–10, 13, 148, 149,
    150, 154, 156–162, 177–178,
    184–194, 196, 202
  six points of, 62, 78–79, 80
  Soviet Union and, 15, 18–19,
    20, 21n.-22n., 22–23, 25,
    32, 34, 37–39, 54
  step-by-step diplomacy of, *see*
    step-by-step diplomacy
  Yom Kippur War and, 13,
    30–41
Kissinger, Nancy, 2, 5, 6, 9, 183
Kosygin, Alexei, 36
Knesset (Israeli parliament), 101,
    103, 105, 108, 110, 122,
    155, 162, 183, 210
Kuneitra, *see* Golan Heights

Lebanon, 100–101, 145,
    145n.-146n., 205, 215
Le Duc Tho, 27, 54n.
Libya, 27, 205
Lord, Winston S., 2, 5
*Los Angeles Times, The*, 3

Maalot massacre, 145n.
McCloy, John J., 165
McGovern, George, 175–176
McNamara, Robert, 165
Mao Tse-tung, 78
Markus, Yoel, 165
Masada, Israel, 160, 162
Masri, General Aziz al-, 43
Meir, Golda, 37, 50, 80, 110,
    126, 180
  Geneva talks and, 101–102,
    104–105
  Israeli elections and, 81, 84,
    108

Kissinger and, 9, 101–102,
115, 118, 128, 162
October 5 boundaries and,
40–41, 121–122
resignation of, 117, 128
"Rogers Plan" and, 21
Mitla and Giddi passes, 103, 150,
157, 158, 178, 184, 185,
188, 190
Moslem Brotherhood, 43
Mosque of Al Aqsa, 74–75, 140
Mossadegh, Mohammed, 68
Moyne, Lord, 146
Moynihan, Daniel Patrick, 5
Mubarak, Husni al-, 185, 186,
188
Murphy, Richard, 168

Nahas Pasha, Mustafa, 44
Nasser, Gamal Abdel, 19, 20,
23, 39, 47, 51, 92, 93, 109,
142, 195
death of, 20, 46
policy of, 48, 68
Sadat and, 42–46
National Broadcasting System
(N.B.C.), 3, 67
Nazer, Hisham, 76, 130
Newsweek, ix, 3, 67, 129
New York Times, The, 2, 25,
37n., 133n.-134n., 145n.,
158, 190
Nixon, Richard M., 15, 17, 41,
60, 68, 70, 111, 116, 122,
126, 177
arms to Israel and, 20, 25–26,
33–34, 36, 39, 69, 69n.-70n.
errors of, and Yom Kippur
War, 28–29
Ismail, Kissinger and, 23–26
Israeli support of, 21, 22n.
Jordan and, 136–138, 147

Middle East trip of, 130–135
military alert and, 37–38
national interests and, 35–36,
38
as policymaker in Middle
East, 21, 53–54
"Rogers Plan" and, 18, 21
Soviet expulsion from Egypt
and, 23, 65, 66
Soviet Union and, 70n.
Watergate and, 27, 38, 58,
132, 148, 151

Oakley, Robert, 2, 5, 168, 176
evaluation of, 169–170
October War, see Yom Kippur
War
oil embargo, 26, 75, 92, 155, 216
efforts to end, 41, 71–72, 83,
102, 104, 115–116
imposition of, 12, 36, 39, 69
prevention of, 13, 33, 58–59
threat of, 26, 66–67
Olympics of 1972:
Israeli athletes murdered at,
145
Osman Pasha, Amin, 44

Palestinians, 24, 35, 69, 72, 83,
86, 94, 135, 160, 176
anti-Kissinger demonstrations
by, 100
future prospects for, 204, 209,
210, 213
Geneva talks and, 49, 84–85,
88, 96, 106, 107, 108
Israeli cabinet on, 180,
181–182, 210, 213
Jordanians and, 99, 102, 136,
138, 139–140, 141, 142–146,
152, 181–182, 215
kidnappings, murders, and

Palestinians (*continued*)
   hijackings by, 31, 125,
     142–146
   Kissinger's policy on, 13, 49,
     85, 101, 113, 148, 167, 202,
     212–213
   Lebanese and, 101, 215
Palestine Liberation
   Organization (P.L.O.) (*see
   also* Arafat, Yasir), 85, 106,
   108, 132–133, 146n.,
   147–149, 151–154, 210–214
Peled, Mattityahu, 210, 211
Percy, Charles, 175, 211
Peres, Shimon, 117, 160, 161,
   162, 165, 180, 188, 189, 210
Persian Gulf, 12, 116
Pickering, Thomas, 168
Popular Democratic Front, 142
Popular Front for the Liberation
   of Palestine, 142, 143
*Pravda*, 92
press (*see also names of
   individual periodicals*), 1,
   2–3, 6, 7, 105, 145n.,
   164–165, 183, 186–188
   Algerian, 86–87
   Egyptian, 9
   French, 186
   Israeli, 101
   travel instructions to, 4

Rabin, Yitzhak, 6, 20, 81n.,
   117, 125, 131, 134n., 137,
   155, 180–181, 199, 210
   background of, 179
   Ford and, 159, 177, 216n.
   Nixon and, 21
   Rogers and, 22n.
   Sinai disengagement of 1975
     and, 154, 155, 156–157,
     159–160, 162, 181, 184, 188

Rabinowitz, Yehoshua, 165
Reuters, 3
Rifai, Abdel Moneim al-, 99, 100
Rifai, Zeid al-, 98, 99, 100, 108,
   147, 149, 197
*Road to Ramadan, The* (Heikal),
   23–25
Rodman, Peter, 2
Rogers, William P., 22, 66, 70
   Kissinger on, 17
   Nasser and, 20
   Rabin and, 22n.
   "Rogers Plan" and, 16–17, 18,
     21, 28, 46, 192, 196
   Suez Canal and, 17, 161n.
Roosevelt, Franklin D., 65
Rusk, Dean, 165
Russell, Lord Bertrand, 64
Russia, *see* Soviet Union

Sabry, Aly, 91
Sadat, Anwar al-, 20, 58, 62, 79,
   82, 85, 88, 97, 102, 103,
   104, 106, 116, 155, 215–216
   anticommunist feelings of, 89,
     91–92
   background of, 42–44
   Brezhnev and, 90, 91
   decision to wage war by, 26,
     66, 68
   development of, 44, 45, 46
   Faisal and, 68–69, 76, 195
   Ford and, 133, 133n.–134n.,
     176–177, 206
   Israeli prisoners and, 80
   Kissinger and, 4, 6, 39, 42,
     48–51, 61, 70, 84, 88–89,
     92, 109–112, 117, 119, 128,
     131, 148, 149–150, 156–159,
     184–185, 187–189, 194, 202,
     205–206, 212
   Kosygin and, 36

Nasser and, 42–46
new Egyptian policy and, 48
Nixon and, 132, 133,
   133n–134n, 177
peace treaty accepted by, 21,
   47
becomes president, 46–48
Saudi Arabia and, 68–69
Sinai disengagement
   agreement of 1974 and,
   109–112
Sinai disengagement
   agreement of 1975 and, 4,
   6, 7, 148, 149, 150, 154,
   156–159, 184–185, 186–189,
   190, 194, 196, 202
Soviets and, 22–23, 39, 45, 49,
   65, 89–91, 92, 172, 204–205
Yom Kippur War and, 33, 41
Sadat, Gehan, 9, 45
Sadat, Sekina, 42–43
Safran, Nedav, 166
Sapir, Pinhas, 101
Saqquf, Omar al-, 34, 35, 75,
   116
Saud (King Faisal's brother),
   63–64
Saudi Arabia (see also Faisal,
   King of Saudi Arabia), 12,
   215
   American technology and,
      76–77, 116, 202
   oil wealth of, 63, 65, 76, 116
   Yemen and, 46, 205
Saunders, Harold, x, xi, 2, 5,
   99, 160, 168, 176
   evaluation of, 169
   statement at U.N. Security
      Council, 212–213, 216n.
Schecter, Jerrold, 3
Schlesinger, James R., 33, 198
Schultz, George, 66, 67–68

Scowcroft, General, 24
Scranton, William, 165,
   193n.–194n., 216n.
Secret Conversations of Henry
   Kissinger, The (Golan),
   80–81
Sharaf, Sami, 46–48, 91
Shihabi, General Hikmat, 124
Sid Ahmed, Mohammed,
   208–210
Simon, William, 66
Sinai peninsula, 1, 7, 13, 56, 57,
   84, 207
   disengagement of 1974 and,
      104, 108, 109–112, 115, 130
   disengagement of 1975 and,
      1–10, 13, 148, 149, 150,
      154–163, 177–178, 184–196,
      202
   Mitla and Giddi passes in,
      103, 150, 157, 158, 178,
      184, 185, 188, 190
Sisco, Joseph J., 2, 5, 8, 9, 21,
   28, 49, 50, 62, 66, 78, 98,
   101, 105, 112, 117, 160,
   161n., 176, 183, 187, 188,
   189
   evaluation of, 168–169
Six-Day War, 11, 13, 31, 51, 142
Smith, Terence, 37
Somalia, 205
Southern Yemen, see Yemen
Soviet Union, 37, 54, 112
   Arafat and, 85, 211
   Egypt and, 19–20, 22, 24, 39,
      55–56, 60, 65, 69, 82,
      89–91, 92, 172, 204–205
   expansionist strategy of, 18–19
   final peace settlement and,
      161, 165, 166
   at Geneva peace talks, 106
   as supplier of Arabs, 11,

Soviet Union (*continued*)
    18–20, 30, 34, 69, 71, 77,
    82, 90, 92, 94, 121, 205
    U.S., and Middle East, 18–19,
    20, 21n.–22n., 32, 34, 53,
    55–56, 58, 123, 137, 138,
    160, 189, 205, 206
Stalin Josef, 71
State Department, U.S., x, xi, 2,
    24, 82, 133n., 134n., 146n.,
    166, 169, 173–174, 198
step-by-step diplomacy, 13, 18,
    35, 50, 89, 113, 129–130,
    133, 151, 155
    Assad and, 94, 127–128
    Boumedienne and, 87
    criticism of, 165–166, 204
    failure of, 160, 162
    Faisal and, 75–76
    revival of, 166, 176
Stern Gang, 146
Stevenson, Adlai, 211
Suez Canal, 12, 19, 50, 80, 102,
    104, 109–112, 190
    control of, 82–83, 84
    Egyptian crossing of, 32, 56,
    57, 161
    Israelis on west bank of, 36,
    40, 58, 84, 100
    Rogers and, 17, 161n.
Suez City, 37, 40, 50, 78, 80
Sultan, Prince, 22
Syria (*see also* Assad, Hafez al-),
    13, 69, 75, 76, 84, 94, 103,
    104–105, 107, 145, 161,
    202, 215
    Algeria and, 87, 88
    buildup before Yom Kippur
    War by, 30–32
    casbah and Bedu syndromes
    in, 119–120
    Egypt's rift with, 196, 202

Geneva peace talks and, 71,
    95–97, 106
Golan Heights and, 10, 97,
    101, 115, 116, 121–127,
    133, 180, 194
Jordan attacked by, 94,
    136–138
Jordanian alliance with, 196,
    202
oil embargo and, 116
under Nasser, 93
Six-Day War and, 11
Soviet supplies to, 11, 30, 34,
    77, 94, 121, 205

Tallal (King Hussein's father),
    140
Tekoah, Yosef, 153
Tell, Wasfi, 145
*Time* magazine, 3, 192
Tlas, General Mustafa, 124
Toon, Mr. and Mrs. Malcolm, 3,
    183
Transjordan, *see* Jordan
Truman, Harry S., 65
Tuma, Dr. Elias H., 211

United Nations, 57n., 84, 102,
    103, 190
    checkpoints on Cairo-Suez
    road of, 78–79, 80
    1947 Israeli borders set by, 85
    U.S. veto in, 27
United Nations Disengagement
    Observer Force, 126, 127,
    168
United Nations Emergency
    Force, 79, 111, 117,
    172–173, 189, 190, 207, 208
U.N. General Assembly, 5,
    151–154
U.N. Security Council, 214

P.L.O. at, 146n.
Resolution 242, 15, 16, 28, 35,
    36, 49, 89, 107, 108, 114,
    130–131, 134n., 135, 136,
    149, 191, 198
Resolution 338, 36, 40, 41, 49,
    58, 60, 78, 94, 108, 191,
    198
Saunders statement before,
    212–213, 216n.
Scranton statement before,
    193n.–194n., 216n.
United Press International, 3
United States (see also Ford,
    Gerald R.; Kissinger, Dr.
    Henry A.; Nixon, Richard
    M.):
Algeria and, 87–88
arms and supplies to Israel
    from, 11, 14, 15, 18, 20–21,
    24, 69, 69n.–70n., 82, 83,
    90, 111–112, 114, 146n.,
    178, 191–192, 198–199
election of 1976 in, 192
internal pressures on, 83, 104
Israel's relations with, 13–14,
    51, 53, 56, 58, 65, 151, 155,
    178, 191–192, 207
Jordan's relations with, 136,
    138, 141, 196–197
military alert in, 37–38
Saudi Arabia's relations with,
    64–65, 69, 76–77
Soviets, and Middle East, 11,
    18–19, 20, 21n.–22n., 32,
    34, 53, 55–56, 58, 123, 137,
    138, 160, 189, 205, 206
trade and technology of, and
    Arabs, 13, 76–77, 87, 116,
    132, 202, 206
U.S. Congress, 166, 174,
    175–176, 191, 216n.

Valeriani, Richard, 3
Van Voorst, Bruce, 3
Vietnam War, 15, 27, 54, 55,
    104, 203
Viorst, Milton, 164–165
Vogel, Joe, 8
Vorontsov, Yuli, 137

Wailing Wall, Jerusalem, 74–75
Waldheim, Dr. Kurt, 106
Washington Post, The, 3, 9, 66,
    67, 145n., 164–165
Wolfe, Dr. Martin, 2

Yamani, Ahmed Zaki al-, 26, 66
Yariv, General Aharon, 80–81,
    103, 154
Yediot Aharonot, 57n.
Yemen, 27, 45–46, 68, 205
Yom Kippur War, 12, 33, 55–58,
    91, 99, 147, 208, 216
    balance of power shift and, 12,
        32
    buildup for and start of,
        30–32, 55, 56, 161
    Egyptian Third Army's
        encirclement and, 36–42
        passim, 50
    Kissinger's no-win policy and,
        32, 33, 36–37
    prisoners of, 41, 42, 80, 97,
        101–102, 103, 104–105, 107,
        115, 121
    turning points in battle and
        negotiations of, 26, 36
    U.S. errors and, 28–29
Yost, Charles, 166

Zayyat, Mohammed al-, 32
Zionism, 24, 60, 65, 67, 71, 76,
    152
    Kissinger and, 18, 24, 98

Edward R. F. Sheehan is a journalist, novelist, and dramatist. Born in Boston and educated at Boston College, he was a foreign correspondent in Europe, North Africa, and the Middle East for *The Boston Globe* and several leading New England newspapers, then press officer at the United States Embassies in Cairo and Beirut. In 1965, he was named one of Boston's Outstanding Young Men.

Mr. Sheehan has contributed major articles to eminent publications in the United States, Great Britain, Europe, and the Third World, including *The New York Times Magazine, Harper's, The Saturday Evening Post, Reader's Digest, Foreign Policy, The Sunday Telegraph* of London, *Nouvel Observateur* and *Jeune Afrique* of Paris, the *Journal of Palestine Studies* of Beirut, *Maariv* of Tel Aviv, *Jiji Press* of Tokyo, and many others. He has lived in Paris, witnessed rebellions in the Congo, civil wars in Biafra and Jordan, and the Arab-Israeli war of 1973. His first novel was about power politics in the Middle East, his second about power politics in Massachusetts.

Mr. Sheehan is the winner of an award from the Overseas Press Club for distinguished interpretation of foreign affairs, and *Foreign Policy* magazine has described him as "one of America's leading Middle East experts."

Mr. Sheehan at present is a Research Fellow at the Center for International Affairs at Harvard University, where he conducts seminars on the Middle East.

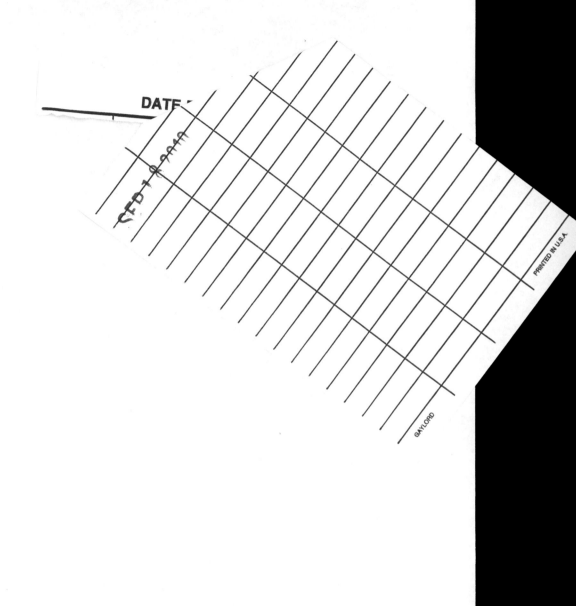

DATE

CFD 1 0 2040

GAYLORD                    PRINTED IN U.S.A.